In this beautiful book, K.J. Ramsey teaches us what it means to transform, rather than transmit, the pain in our lives. She chooses what is familiar, the Twenty-Third Psalm, to offer us the greatest possible form of hospitality in sharing the stories that make up her life. With warmth and wisdom, Ramsey chooses vulnerability over comfort in an effort to connect with all of us in ways that are both manageable and meaningful. This book is inviting and accessible, and a must-read for all who are trying to move forward with less anger and more grace, with less fear and more hope, and with fewer regrets and greater understanding. On every page, while demonstrating an abundance of faith, she shows us the path toward transformation.

—SUZANNE STABILE, author, *The Path between Us*
and *The Journey toward Wholeness*

The message those who suffer hear most often is self-heal, self-love, and self-help, which only adds shame, guilt, and a suffocating sense of powerlessness. When we are desperate, we need not advice to act on but a promise from God that he will be with us no matter what. If you have ever felt like darkness is your only companion, you won't find yourself blamed in this book. You'll find yourself pursued and embraced by the patient and compassionate love of a God who meets you in your pain. God does not command, "Heal thyself!" but declares, "You will be healed!"

—JUSTIN S. HOLCOMB, minister; seminary professor; author,
God with Us: 365 Devotions on the Person and Work of Christ

I trust people who have suffered to speak the deepest wisdom. K.J. Ramsey is such a person. In *The Lord Is My Courage*, Ramsey comes to us as a therapist with acute pastoral sensibilities who does not mince words about the destruction self-centered, power-hungry undershepherds unleash on individual parishioners and the wider church. But she does not stop there. She gently leads us through Psalm 23 and showcases God's love for and delight in us—our belovedness—as revealed throughout the psalm. As we wind our way through Psalm 23, Ramsey offers us grace and direction as we seek to become whole, especially when we are dealing with pain and shame related to abusive shepherds and churches. Ramsey deftly demonstrates that God is our good and beautiful shepherd seeking our flourishing, and not some tyrant feigning godliness who merely uses and abuses people for personal gain. Listen to her.

—MARLENA GRAVES, author, *The Way Up Is Down: Becoming Yourself by Forgetting Yourself*

K.J.'s helpful and hopeful words will lift some of the weight of the world off your weary shoulders. This book is a compassionate guide back to the communion for which our souls long.

—KATHERINE WOLF, survivor; advocate; author, *Hope Heals* and *Suffer Strong*

The Lord Is My Courage is a love letter to all of us. With gentle and compassionate words, K.J. Ramsey reintroduces us to God as a true protector, an empathetic redeemer, and a powerful presence who offers hope without fear. For doubters, believers, and those of us in between, this book is like balm for the soul.

—MATTHEW PAUL TURNER, *New York Times* bestselling author

K.J. Ramsey invites us to take an inward journey "to listen to the syllables of our senses," as she so beautifully describes in her new book, *The Lord Is My Courage*. With a powerful exploration of both Psalm 23 and the human body, Ramsey walks us through the depths of the human experience so that we may encounter the Good Shepherd, who holds us in our brokenness. This book is a pathway toward our healing.

—KAT ARMAS, author, *Abuelita Faith*; host, *The Protagonistas* podcast

K.J. has given the world a generous and desperately needed gift. She has given us not trite answers or pious platitudes but the kind of wisdom, compassion, and tender faith often borne out of suffering. I needed this book when I was in the immediate aftermath of church trauma, and I continue to need it now. I am thankful that *The Lord Is My Courage* is a book I can wholeheartedly recommend to suffering people with the confidence that K.J.'s words will comfort, guide, and point to Jesus.

—KAITLYN SCHIESS, author, *The Liturgy of Politics*

Tender, fierce, and committed to the unvarnished truth, *The Lord Is My Courage* holds our hand at whatever cliff's edge we find ourselves and reminds us we're not alone. Combining honest storytelling, incisive leadership, and therapeutic credentials, Ramsey shines a light on what it means to be more fully, freely human, through the courage of Christ. This one is for all of us who are struggling to trust our way through the dark.

—SHANNAN MARTIN, author, *The Ministry of Ordinary Places* and *Falling Free*

Ramsey writes as one who has both torn back the roof and been lowered through it. A prophetic voice, born of pain, she draws the brutalized back to their belovedness again. She fearlessly fords the sorrow-sodden swampland of spiritual abuse that shreds the soul of sojourners, and with crippled hands knits us together again.

—LORI ANNE THOMPSON, RKin, MA CHAD; survivor; storyteller; student

K.J. Ramsey's unique and incisive approach is both prophetic and poetic, providing a beautiful and compelling model for confronting hypocrisy and injustice as well as for healing the pain of betrayal and rejection, especially within the church. With clarity and grace, this book offers us a stunning invitation to care for the broken parts of ourselves with compassion and to be agents of healing and hope to the wounded along our path.

—RUTH MALHOTRA, whistleblower and advocate

THE LORD IS MY COURAGE

ALSO BY K.J. RAMSEY

This Too Shall Last: Finding Grace When Suffering Lingers

THE LORD IS MY COURAGE

STEPPING THROUGH THE SHADOWS OF FEAR TOWARD THE VOICE OF LOVE

K.J. RAMSEY

ZONDERVAN
REFLECTIVE

ZONDERVAN REFLECTIVE

The Lord Is My Courage
Copyright © 2022 by Katie Jo Ramsey

Requests for information should be addressed to:
Zondervan, 3900 Sparks Dr. SE, Grand Rapids, Michigan 49546

Zondervan titles may be purchased in bulk for educational, business, fundraising, or sales promotional use. For information, please email SpecialMarkets@Zondervan.com.

ISBN 978-0-310-12416-0 (softcover)
ISBN 978-0-310-12418-4 (audio)
ISBN 978-0-310-12417-7 (ebook)

Cover design and illustration: © *Conrad Garner*
Interior design: Sara Colley

Printed in the United States of America

22 23 24 25 26 27 28 29 30 /TRM/ 12 11 10 9 8 7 6 5 4 3 2 1

To Josh and Rachel,
two of the most courageous people
I will ever know

CONTENTS

PART 2: BROKEN

PART 3: GIVEN

FOREWORD

I MET KJ RAMSEY at a conference in Colorado in 2015. It began with a conversation, which led to a brief but meaningful time of prayer together. At that time, our author was early in her training in and exposure to the intersection of psychology, neuroscience, and spiritual formation. Little did I realize the degree to which hers was a life that was being drawn out of the deep waters of suffering—drawn to be further poured out as an offering of grace, wisdom, and courage, so much of which you will bear witness to in this book.

Between our first meeting and now, she not only has grown in the mastery of her craft as a psychotherapist, she also has emerged as an effective translator of the deep realities of the life of the mind—with all of its interpersonal, neurobiological, and spiritual complexities—for those of us who desperately need to comprehend what has happened to us, each in our own way. For indeed, in a world that is so pervasively broken, in which we often ask, "What is wrong with me?" our guide implicitly asks the more important question, "What happened to me?" And this question must be asked because so much *has* happened to so many of us, and happened to us in the places we would least expect it—our families and churches.

With *The Lord Is My Courage*, KJ brings her experience and her compassion to the text of Psalm 23. As you approach the book, do not for a moment assume that she is merely walking you through her personal valley that is or has been shadowed in death. This is not yet one more self-help expert's take on a text that is so familiar that it runs the risk of becoming banal. Nor does she simply provide the reader with a roadmap for how to traverse the minefield of spiritual abuse. Rather, she invites you into the soul of her heart. And in so doing, she creates the space for you to peer into your own with more courage than you know you have. All the while, you will be ingesting teaching and tactics that you will invariably want to digest and metabolize for the foreseeable future. In turning the pages you now hold in your hands, you will be awakened to the beauty that emerges from the pathos of every story to which God is permitted to gain access.

It is with confidence and comfort that I offer and commend to you this work. Confidence not only in its content but in its source, who will give you herself in vulnerability and humility. And comfort, because she knows so well the painstakingly hard work that must be done by each of us as we come to sit at the table that our good and beautiful Shepherd has prepared for us in the presence of all of our traumatic enemies.

Read this book slowly. Read this book repeatedly. But most certainly, read this book and come to know as you perhaps do not what it means for goodness and love to follow you as you practice dwelling in the house of the Lord forever.

—Curt Thompson, MD, author,
The Soul of Desire and *The Soul of Shame*

INVITATION

THIS IS A BOOK FOR THE BROKEN. It's for when you fear there's no path forward, when the shattered pieces of your story or self whisper *there's no way you are brave.*

If you are holding this book, you have also held hurt.

Calamity has been your houseguest. Chaos has clamored for your attention. Loud voices have made you feel small. You've been told you're too much. Or you've been labeled too loud. Maybe you've raised red flags only to be thrust to the ground. You've been shouted at or silenced. You've stood at the edge of all you dreamed of and watched it turn to mist in a moment. Without naming it, you've felt a curse clinging to your bones.

Psalm 23 has been part of my life as long as I can remember. It lingers somewhere in the minds of most people in our culture—religious or not—like an earworm to ease the pain of being a person. These are the words we speak over the dirt of graves and amid the horror of hospitals. Written by an ancient shepherd boy turned king, David, with only fifty-five words in Hebrew, making up six verses in our English Bibles, these few lines hold a large place in the consciousness of our souls. These are the words we wrap around our wounds when we feel most cursed and crushed.

The thing is, these words can heal or harm. One of my favorite singer-songwriters, Brandi Carlile, shares how hearing these words for the first time while at her grandfather's funeral stirred something deeply unhealthy in her soul. She writes, "It was the first time I heard the phrase *The Lord is my shepherd; I shall not want*. It stuck with me. That collection of words fed something in me that shouldn't have been sustained."[1]

Later, she encountered the writing of Brennan Manning and saw her own rugged faith reflected in his words, learning a different translation of the phrase "I shall not want" as "I lack nothing." The difference pierced her with possibility. Brandi says, "This subtle difference is night and day to a self-punishing person."[2]

Carlile's experience of Psalm 23 parallels what so many of us experience not just of the psalm but also of shepherds. We come to experience the Lord as a Shepherd who is far less than good and kind because we often experience shepherding figures as shaming, emotionally unavailable, demanding, and unkind. The story we experience as most true about our significance to and safety with God is formed by our experience of shepherding figures. Our capacity to experience the presence and abundance described in Psalm 23 as an extension of peace rather than a prompt for perfectionism is shaped by how people—from pastors to parents and caregivers to coaches—have shown up in our lives.

Within the coming pages, I'll lead you down the path of Psalm 23 while sharing some of my story of being cursed by those who were supposed to bless. I've broken Psalm 23 into thirty-five short words and phrases to help us slow down to hear the parts of ourselves that have been silenced, with insights from theology and neuroscience tucked in to help us better listen and see. I want to be honest with you; though I am a licensed therapist, I'm essentially allergic to the self-help genre, even if that's what's marked on the

---

1. Brandi Carlile, *Broken Horses: A Memoir* (New York: Crown, 2021), 27.
2. Ibid., 149.

back of this book. If you are looking for simple steps, this book will probably frustrate you. But if you are willing to go on a walk together, I think you'll find a path full of possibility.

While your story might not mirror mine, I am praying that these words will help you acknowledge your own places of pain. I pray that my honesty about what happened to me and my husband in a faith community can give you courage to be honest about the harm in your life. I pray this book can be a balm over the bruised parts of your faith, your family, your friendships, and your hope for the future. And as you name your own pain, I hope the insights and stories in this book give you space to imagine ways to practically experience the Good Shepherd's presence with you there.

And if Harm hasn't laid his hands on your life, I hope these words build compassion and courage in you to be a healing presence for those who bear invisible bruises and scars. The whole church needs to hear the cries of the crushed for wholeness and love to be our truest song.

This book is my marauder's map[3] of hidden passages and places respectable Christians like to keep folded away in locked cabinets. I'm unlocking the cabinet, and I'm throwing away the key. It's up to you whether you will follow me.

These stories won't be easy, and the path won't be smooth. But the destination is stunning, as the people we'll become will prove. I'll guide you over sharp stones of spiritual harm and suffering. I'll say things that might make you squirm, because sometimes love stings before it soothes. I promise to guide you gently through narrow places of pain. And I'll light a candle through dark valleys of shame.

I want to go first with my story of being a sheep without a

---

3. Don't even try to tell me the Harry Potter books aren't full of gospel truths. If you're *that* uptight, you might as well just *wingardium leviosa* my book straight to someone else's shelf now.

shepherd, so you can see your story of being forgotten or devoured or left behind in the stark relief that only shadows give.

Whether they meant to or not, shepherds cursed me and my family. And in the breaking, I came to see:

There is a Good Shepherd who is always with me.

I have seen the blessing that comes in our breaking. I have savored the wine that overflows from chipped cups. I have stepped through shadows. I have learned I am loved. I have realized I am courageous because I am always connected to someone who was not only blessed but also broken, who gave himself as bread for the life of the world.

So to all that has been cursed in you, let there come compassion. To all that feels not brave, may you find you belong.

BLESSED

*To have courage for whatever comes
in life—everything lies in that.*
—Teresa of Avila

*I believed that there was a God because I was told
it by my grandmother and later by other adults.
But when I found that I knew not only that
there was a God but that I was a child of God,
when I understood that, when I comprehended
that, more than that, when I internalized
that, ingested that, I became courageous.*
—Maya Angelou

1. THE LORD

WE BEGIN WITH A BLESSING.

Before you built a family, before you earned a diploma, before you made a career, before any hope or heartbreak or heroism, you were loved into existence.

Before Jesus made water into wine, before he raised the dead or healed the beggar born blind, before the obedience that would become our sign, he was named *Beloved*.

The Lord, our Good Shepherd, began his public ministry on the banks of the Jordan River not by preaching a stunning sermon or performing a great sign but by getting into the river and letting his cousin, John the Baptist, dunk his body in a baptism of repentance. Jesus—God incarnate, fully human and fully perfect—chose to begin his entire ministry with an act of repentance that one would assume he didn't need. Everything Jesus lived and did, he did to fully embody our humanness as an offering of trust and gratitude to the Father.

Jesus plunged backward in John's hands into the cold water, letting his body fall in trust for that moment and the greater submersion of the years to come. And as his head rose out of the river, "the heavens were opened to him, and he saw the Spirit of God descending like a dove and coming to rest on him; and behold, a voice from heaven said, 'This is my Beloved Son, with whom I am well pleased.'"[1]

On the muddy banks of the Jordan River, Jesus heard the words we so struggle to hear on our own: *You are my Beloved. With you I am well pleased.*

These are the words we all most long to hear. (And if the language of beloved doesn't resonate with you, substitute it with this: You are seen and secure.)

Most of us struggle to rise into our lives with courage and hear that we are beloved because we've all been baptized in different water—the stream of scarcity. Most of us learn early in life to stay by scarcity's stream of striving and strength, where the only way we are given the name Beloved is if we earn it every single day.

There's only so much room in a stream, so we usually become bullies or beggars—either pushing our way to have a place by the water or hanging back in case someone else elbows us out of the way or says we don't belong. So many of us live stuck in self-protection, pushing for a place at the stream, guarding it in case someone tries to shove us out of the way, hoarding whatever water we can get.

Most of us haven't been shown the way to better waters, where God bends low and says—regardless of your striving, strength, or success—Beloved is the name you carry with you everywhere you go.

Courage is standing in the mud of our ordinary lives and turning toward Christ, who still hears the words we most strain to hear on our own, who stands ready to help us hear Beloved in every mundane and even miserable moment we ever will encounter.[2]

---

1. Matt. 3:16–17 ESV. Capitalization of Beloved added.

2. These words echo what I wrote in *This Too Shall Last*: "On the banks of the Jordan River, turning toward his Father with trust, Jesus heard the words we cannot hear on our own: 'You are my beloved.' Standing in the mud of our ordinary lives, Jesus still hears what we strain to believe and trains us to hear *beloved* in every mundane and even miserable

I was baptized at two weeks old on Christmas Eve in 1988. My parents stood at the front of the church in their finest—my construction-worker dad in the suit he wore only for funerals, weddings, and baptisms, and my mom in a long black velvet dress, complete with puffy sleeves. I imagine them beaming, holding their bundle of a baby girl in a tiny frilly white dress, the glow on their faces matched by the crimson poinsettias covering the chancel.

They claimed God's promises as mine with the words "we do" and promised to bring me up to know it. The people gathered there promised too, because baptism is not a ceremony to watch; it is a story to share. Then my parents handed me to Pastor Bob, who dipped a hand into consecrated water and blessed me, body and soul, as baptized in the name of the Father, and of the Son, and of the Holy Spirit.

Pastor Bob's cheeks shined like jolly Saint Nick's as he held me up before the congregation, all dressed in their Christmas clothes. And with my head nestled in his hand and my body held strong in his arms, Pastor Bob swayed and led the congregation in song. "He's got the whole world in his hands. He's got the whole world in his hands. He's got itty-bitty Katie in his hands.[3] He's got the whole world in his hands." I can imagine it just like this because I spent the next seventeen years singing it to every baptized baby in that church, with promises on my own lips.

I was born wearing the shackles of generational trauma, abuse, and the American Dream. But that day, I was also baptized into a

moment we encounter." K.J. Ramsey, *This Too Shall Last: Finding Grace When Suffering Lingers* (Grand Rapids, MI: Zondervan, 2020), 9.

3. In case you are wondering, *you* can call me KJ.

story where the whole world was held in God's hands. I was named into those hands.

That day, I was given a small wooden cross to hang in my room, inscribed "Matthew 19:14." In that story, the crowds who were following Jesus brought their children to him to be blessed. The disciples pushed them away, perhaps thinking their leader was too important for kids. Religious folks often seem to think their leaders are too important for those at the bottom. But Jesus told them the words that are referenced on my cross: "Let the little children come to me, and do not hinder them, for the kingdom of heaven belongs to such as these."

He brings the blessing down to the ones who cannot even ask for it themselves.

The day I was baptized, I was blessed into that story. I became one to whom the kingdom of God belongs.

I was held, cherished, and given the same name and affection given to Jesus when the light of the Spirit shined down on him in the Jordan. As the waters of baptism pass over us, we are washed into a world of love where the words spoken over Jesus resound as ours as well.[4] Beloved.

Beloved is the name that brings a whole new world into existence.

Beloved is the story that unwrites every line of scarcity's plot to push you down.

Beloved is your birthright.

That cross is sitting on my desk next to me as I write, and I know, the God who took the time to bless the children who couldn't even ask for it themselves will always come to bless me.

---

4. Julie Canlis writes, "When we are baptized, we pass through the waters (which signify death) into this relationship—and into this declaration of divine love, spoken for us as well." Julie Canlis, *A Theology of the Ordinary* (Wenatchee, WA: Godspeed, 2017), 34.

But I didn't believe my blessedness.

I spent the first nineteen years of my life trying to earn a name I had already been given. I stuffed a bank account full of the cash of compliance and certainty. I became the good daughter my parents needed. I found my place on the map of meritocracy and extended my borders through the constant pursuit of exceptionalism. I was lovable, I thought, because I was especially good and especially diligent.

Midway through my junior year of college, my body wouldn't let me be good or work hard anymore. Instead, there was silence. No more dean's lists to make. No more As at the top of papers. Just the silent screams of a body suddenly disabled by pain. The borders of my life became small. And I wondered, who was I without applause?

One day I sat in silence, slumped onto pillows propped against my cold dorm-room wall, and tried but failed to find comfort in the Word of God. Inflammation had all but mutated my hands into lobster claws. The cover of the Bible on my lap might as well have weighed one hundred pounds, because there was no way my claws could pinch it open. It sat there taunting me with its worn spine held together by teal duct tape, reinforcing just how stuck and tattered I was.

God spoke into the silence.

I love you—not for anything you can do for me but for existing.

God called me Beloved.

When I couldn't come to God, God came to me.

In a body too sick to open a Bible, bankrupt of all my striving, I started to hear the words I would spend the rest of my life learning to receive as true.

You are my Beloved. With you I am well pleased.

Who is this Jesus whom the Father first called Beloved? Who is the Lord who calls himself our Good Shepherd?[5]

Look around you. Notice the pages of this book in your hands. Look at the coffee cup on your side table. See the sun streaming through your window. Jesus is the one by whom all of this was made.[6]

Everything you see is matter, spoken into existence by God in Christ. Let's take a moment to let our eighth-grade science memories come together with our adult spirituality. All matter is made up of protons, neutrons, and electrons, bound together as atoms. And Jesus is the one who holds it all together.[7] Matter is energy, held together by Christ.[8] The one whom the Father called Beloved is holding together everything you see and every part of who you are. *Love* is the energy that holds the universe together.

But there is energy beyond what you can even see. One of the most surprising scientific discoveries of the twentieth century is that ordinary matter composes only 5 percent of the mass of the universe.[9] Scientists believe the rest is made up of dark matter and dark energy, which have revealed that the universe is expanding rather than shrinking. Decades earlier, Albert Einstein theorized that a "cosmological constant" is what keeps the universe from

---

5. John 10:11.

6. Col. 1:16.

7. Col. 1:17.

8. In his book of teachings on Psalm 23, the late Dallas Willard wrote about energy being "the basic reality." He says, "You have energy at your disposal, and in this respect, you are like God. *You* are *like* God. God has made you so you have energy at your disposal, and that energy comes in the form of your thoughts and your feelings. By these you are able to exercise your will." Dallas Willard, *Life without Lack: Living in the Fullness of Psalm 23* (Nashville: Thomas Nelson, 2018), 11.

9. National Geographic, "Dark Matter and Dark Energy," www.nationalgeographic .com/science/space/dark-matter/.

collapsing in on itself. When his theory was debunked, he called it his biggest blunder, but scientists today see dark matter as the cosmological glue holding the universe up.[10] While dark energy is expanding the universe, dark matter is holding it together. Invisible Love is sustaining the universe every moment of every day.

We were made because of the overflowing energy of Divine Love in the Trinity. We were made not because God needed us but because God *wanted us.*

Invisible Love wants your company and delights in the fact that you exist.

Everything about your existence is a participation in God's energy of joy. *You* are energy. Your emotions are energy. Your breath is energy. Your sight is energy. And though your energy is limited—as you acutely realize when picking up a running habit or caring for an infant—you were made by one whose energy and power are limitless.

This fact can sting when we consider all the ways we think God could have used divine power to protect us—from cancer, autoimmune disease, divorce, debt, depression, doubt. Yet the one whom the Father called Beloved is also the one who cried out, "My God, my God, why have you forsaken me?"[11] Jesus felt the same sting as us. Even this is energy—energy that can bring us into honest intimacy with God. So bring your sting with you.

Jesus' energy expands the scarcity we see into abundance. He traveled all around Israel speaking and showing life to crowds of people society and religious folks deemed suspect or insignificant. One day while trying to find some peace and quiet in the wilderness outside of the towns, Jesus saw that tons of people were still

---

10. Christopher Wanjek, "Dark Matter Appears to Be a Smooth Operator," Astronomical Society of the Pacific, https://astrosociety.org/news-publications/mercury-online/mercury-online.html/article/2020/12/10/dark-matter-appears-to-be-a-smooth-operator.

11. Mark 15:34.

following him, and they were hungry. Because he saw that "they were like sheep without a shepherd,"[12] Jesus was moved with compassion for them to meet both their physical and spiritual hunger.

So the one who spoke the world into existence, whose energy formed the very dirt he walked on toward them, took five loaves and two fish from the crowd and made it more. He made enough matter to feed the entire crowd, which scholars think was upward of fifteen thousand people.[13] And there was food left over. Jesus' energy takes the little we have and makes it more than enough.

This is the Lord through whose baptism we are blessed, broken, and given access to a new energy, a new story, and a new kingdom right now.

In Christ, every part of your life has been made a passage into God's kingdom. Every day of your life can be lived as part of the story where Jesus is present making ordinary matter into more than enough.

The light that shined on Jesus as he came up out of the muddy waters of the Jordan River is the light that can illuminate our whole lives. No darkness is thick enough to evade this light. No fear is fierce enough to extinguish this fire. Nothing can separate you from the courage available to you in your union with Christ. Courage is choosing to spend the rest of your life listening for and receiving these words as true:

You are my Beloved. With you I am well pleased.

12. Matt. 9:36; Mark 6:34.
13. E. Ray Clendenen and Jeremy Royal Howard, eds., *The Holman Illustrated Bible Commentary* (Nashville: Broadman and Holman, 2015), 1028.

2. IS MY SHEPHERD,

THEY SAY I WAS ALMOST BORN IN THE CHURCH PARKING LOT. While my mom cried out with contractions at home, my dad was at church finishing up his shift acting as Joseph in our church's annual, multiple-weekend outdoor Christmas pageant, which was very originally named the Jesus Walk.

While Mom panted, Dad stood in full costume in the cold, hammering birdhouses to give to the crowd—gotta sell that Joseph was a carpenter!—while passionately reciting his lines about how the angel of the Lord convinced him not to divorce Mary. (I bet Mom was hoping an angel would come with a divine message for Dad right about then.) I love the mental image of my very pregnant mom at home reaching for the telephone on the wall to call the church to get someone to let "Joseph" know his real baby was coming whether Jesus was or not.

Families huddled around each stand on the Jesus Walk, crowding together against the bitter mid-Michigan chill. When visitors rounded the corner from visiting Joseph and then Zechariah and Elizabeth, they saw a group of actors dressed as shepherds—complete with staffs—and a massive star perched to the east, hanging from one of my dad's cranes.

My dad was the owner of a small construction business, and it was his pride and joy to light up the sky with a signal of Christ's birth so bright you could see it for miles from the highway. Every year, the church, my parents and myself included, prayed the big, bright display of the true Christmas story would shine so brightly that visitors would come to accept Christ to shine in their hearts as well.

Some of my best childhood memories are of the Jesus Walk. The taste of hot chocolate and Christmas cookies on my tongue. The scratchy fabric of costumes over layers of coats and gloves. The warm feeling of pulling off something together that no one could do alone.

But after spending many of my adult years in a different church, one fixated on numbers and image, I can't help but notice the subtext to our Christian spectacles. So many Christians believe sharing Christ looks like emulating the star that heralded his birth, rather than the lowliness of being born as an infant. We think the larger and brighter we make our lights, the more people will come and believe.

We shine so brightly it hurts our eyes.

"The Lord is my shepherd" can sound trite if you've been trampled on by someone who calls themselves a shepherd but prefers to stand on a bright stage. Most of the people I know who have deconstructed their faith or find themselves questioning whether they still belong in God's flock (or even just the flock of evangelicalism) are disillusioned with shepherds who do not actually shepherd. People say we're tearing down the church. I think we're tearing down the stages.

There are many reasons Scripture speaks of those who are responsible for the care of souls as shepherds, especially because Scripture arises from ancient agrarian cultures. One reason I believe Scripture places the metaphor of shepherd at the center of the Christian story is that shepherds stand among the flock. It is a profession of dirt and grime, painstaking protection and commitment, long hours and long-suffering love.

A shepherd is not a spectacle.

And shepherding doesn't happen from a stage.

The opening phrase of Psalm 23 sits on the side tables of our souls like a warm mug of hot chocolate on a cold day—a pleasant thought. But when it comes to our pain, I believe so many of us don't really sense and experience that the Lord is *our* Shepherd because we have rarely been shepherded by people who stand with us in the dirt of our distress.

The Good Shepherd, Jesus Christ, never disregarded or circumvented human suffering. Right after the Father called him Beloved at his baptism, the Spirit drove Christ out into the wilderness, where Satan tempted him to shepherd without the suffering.

One of the most painful and important realities to grasp about the Christian life is that our belovedness doesn't guarantee our ease. Christ's baptism as beloved didn't wrap his life into a swaddle of security, and ours doesn't either.

The brutality and barriers in life do not cancel out the truth that we are beloved. They are the wilderness through which we must walk to trust that truth as ours no matter what.

The Spirit who shined down on Jesus at the Jordan River filled him and led him directly into the danger of the wilderness, where for forty days his belly swelled with hunger and his lips cracked from thirst while he was tempted by the devil.[1] Christ allowed his body and soul to be made as vulnerable as ours, to feel the ache of hunger and the pangs of thirst, and the accompanying disintegration of the mind that follows.

My husband's two favorite adjectives for the monster I morph

1. Luke 4:2.

into when I'm hungry or in pain are hangry and paingry. If I haven't eaten all day, I'm on a fast track to frustration. Pain acts like a meat-grinder in my mind, grinding my usual somewhat-sunny attitude into scowls and shortness. We tend to think of Jesus as all placid and sweet, but I like to imagine him as human as me—hangry and paingry before being tempted, choosing to trust the Spirit to empower him to transcend selfishness in a way I know I often don't. His humanness and trust recreate mine.[2]

With no pillow for his head at night, no blanket to keep himself warm, no companions to scare off wild animals, and no sunscreen or shade to cover his skin in the scorching heat of the day, Jesus faced Satan in the wilderness utterly unprotected. And that's what theo-logian and biblical scholar Kenneth Bailey describes as the meaning of the beginning line of Psalm 23, writing, "'The Lord is my shep-herd,' among other things, means 'I have no police protection.'"[3]

Bailey's words carry a weight we cannot ignore.[4] In the wilder-ness, my Good Shepherd positioned himself away from power and any semblance of protection to be where the vulnerable stand.

---

2. I reflected at length about the humanity of Christ and how his trust in the Father recreates our trust in *This Too Shall Last: Finding Grace When Suffering Lingers* (Grand Rapids, MI: Zondervan, 2020). See especially chapter 6.

3. Kenneth E. Bailey, *The Good Shepherd: A Thousand-Year Journey from Psalm 23 to the New Testament* (Downers Grove, IL: IVP Academic, 2014), 37.

4. A June 2020 article in *Forbes* states, "For the black community, law enforcement has long been experienced as 'harass and brutalize' rather than 'protect and serve.'"[1] A 2018 piece in the *New York Times* reminds us that contrary to common belief, the Supreme Court has repeatedly held that neither the Constitution nor state laws impose a general duty on police officers to protect individuals from harm. It came as a shock to me to learn that the police are only responsible to protect those who are in their custody.[2] When I read Psalm 23, I hear the collective voice of the unprotected. I hear, "I can't breathe." I pray, for more than just myself, "I will fear no evil." I long for the day Love has the final word.

[1] Monica Melton, "Why the ACLU, Black Lives Matter and Others Want to 'Defund the Police' While This Weapons Supplier Disagrees," *Forbes*, June 8, 2020, www.forbes.com/sites/monicamelton/2020/06/08/why-the-aclu-black-lives-matter-and-others-want-to-defund-the-police-while-this-weapons-supplier-disagrees/?sh=75e28fb82f92.

[2] Adeel Hassan, "Officers Had No Duty to Protect Students in Parkland Massacre, Judge Rules," *New York Times*, December 18, 2018, www.nytimes.com/2018/12/18/us/parkland-shooting-lawsuit-ruling-police.html?referringSource=articleShare.

"The Lord is my shepherd" evokes a cry of the vulnerable and a commitment to God as the source of security in a place where there is none or where there has not been nearly enough. "The Lord is my shepherd" means there is no one here but God to protect us.

Because I am an American with a disease and a disability that have made me vulnerable to harm and discrimination, Christ's courage in the wilderness shows me that God stands in solidarity with me. Psalm 23 is a song of the wilderness, of a man who knew what it was to be hunted, hungry, and hurting. Christ stood in the psalmist David's sandals when he was tempted in the wilderness, with only the Spirit to protect him. Jesus placed the vulnerable at the center of the story of resisting evil and trusting God.

Whether you have been made vulnerable by disease, discrimination, or hard things you aren't even ready to call trauma or abuse yet, your experience of lacking protection places you in the center of Christ's story. You are not on the outside here. In Christ's Spirit-driven walk into the wilderness, our experience of defenselessness can become part of the story of courage overcoming the world.

Jesus' baptism as beloved drove him straight into the wilderness, where that identity was attacked. And ours does too.

When Jesus walked into the wilderness, Satan tempted him to prove his identity as the Father's Beloved Son by bypassing the slowness of seeing that the Father's relationship with him was secure, even in suffering. Satan's three temptations of Christ are ours too, taunting us to turn away from the pain and possibility of relationality:

Have more. Hurt less. Rule faster.

These are the temptations of every shepherd and every soul.

Evil is always tempting us to reach for a faster way to bypass the potential pain of feeling rejected. But relationality is the foundation of what it means to be both a sheep in God's fold and a shepherd of others in God's care.

With each temptation, Jesus didn't respond with the anxiety of needing to prove who he already was—beloved by the Father. Instead, he resisted Satan by placing himself inside the slow story of God's covenant love toward Israel. When tempted, the Good Shepherd chose relationship every time.

Let's look more closely.

Jesus was out in the heat, with no shelter or food, probably hungrier than either of us has ever been in our lives. Christ's physical weakness and need, his hunger, were what Satan first attacked. He pointed down at some stones and taunted him, saying that if he was really "the Son of God," he should just tell those stones to become bread.[5] And Jesus could have done it. Instead of proving his power by reaching out to turn the stones into something that could satiate his hunger, Jesus spoke from the Scriptures: "Man shall not live on bread alone, but on every word that comes from the mouth of God."

Jesus let being hungry and dependent on his Father be part of his identity as one who is still beloved. The words he spoke were from Deuteronomy 8:3. By speaking them, Jesus placed his present moment into the people of God's past, a people who also hungered in the wilderness and had to learn to receive their bread from God alone. God sent the people manna, which in Hebrew means "what is it?"[6] In relationship with this wild God of the wilderness, nour-

---

5. Quotes from the interaction between Satan and Jesus are taken from Matt. 4:1–11.

6. Walter Brueggemann writes, "God's love comes trickling down in the form of bread. They say, '*Manhue?*'—Hebrew for 'What is it?'—and the word *manna* is born." Walter Brueggemann, *Deep Memory, Exuberant Hope: Contested Truth in a Post-Christian World* (Minneapolis: Fortress, 2000), 71.

ishment and provision often come in forms we struggle to define. And as theologian Walter Brueggemann points out, the Israelites had "never before received bread as a free gift they could not control, predict, plan for, or own."[7]

In the wilderness, God humbles us by reminding us of our need for nourishment. And then God feeds us *personally*. Placed in the story of God's people along with Christ, our hunger can become a prompt to see God provide in strange and stunning ways with bread we could never bake ourselves.

Christ rejected Satan's proposal to feed himself with bread baked by the means of his own control. Christ rejected Satan's temptation to circumvent trusting the Father to provide for his needs.

Satan then walked Jesus to Jerusalem and climbed to the highest point of the temple, where he jeered at Jesus. Pointing to the ground, Satan used Scripture to dare Jesus to just throw himself off the ledge of the temple, because if he was really God's Son, he could command the angels to guard his body from breaking on the stones below. Instead of getting pissed as hell and just pushing Satan off the ledge, like I probably would, Jesus fought Satan's sneers with more Scripture, answering, "It is also written: 'Do not put the Lord your God to the test.'"

Jesus is weaving the story of Israel's testing God at Massah into this story with these words, drawn from Deuteronomy 6:16. They too had been wandering in the wilderness, parched in the desert sun. There, they grumbled and questioned the goodness of God's salvation. "Why did you bring us up out of Egypt to make us and our children and livestock die of thirst?"[8] they asked.

I know I've asked similar questions. Like the Israelites, I strain to see salvation in the deserts of my discouragement. I've echoed their exasperation. We expect salvation to mean God will pluck

---

7. Ibid.
8. Exod. 17:3.

us out of difficulty and plop us down into prosperity. When we're thirsty and tired or experiencing trauma, the Israelites' question is the one beneath ours: "Is the Lord among us or not?"[9]

We forget that the places touched by death are the places Christ chose to go. We forget that Jesus said that whoever wants to be his disciple must deny themselves, take up their cross daily, and follow him.[10] The answer to our question is that Christ has already chosen to go to the places where we feel abandoned, angry, and afraid.

Following Christ means following him into every place he regarded worthy of his hands, heart, and time—all the way to the cross. Following Christ means following him into places of hunger and thirst, to tend to the lepers of our day on the edges of town, to receive water from women labeled too promiscuous to belong, to cast out demons from those deemed too disordered or dirty to sit in our pews. Following Christ means choosing to speak words that will get you questioned and maligned by religious folks. Following Jesus means walking the wilderness way, trusting along with him that *God is among us* and will quench our thirst.

Christ rejected Satan's proposal to bypass death and all the people and places touched by death that he would bless on his way to the cross. Christ rejected how Satan *used* Scripture, twisting it away from God's intention, something religious folks do to bar the vulnerable from belonging or to dismiss their cries of injustice. Jesus deemed the least and the lost worthy of his attention and life. Jesus took the long route to our ultimate rescue, determined to defeat death and to gather up all who have been shamed into God's glorious embrace.[11]

Finally, Satan took Jesus to a high mountain with a panoramic view of all the kingdoms of the world and their splendor. "All this

9. Exod. 17:7.
10. Luke 9:23.
11. Isaiah 50:7 describes the Messiah setting "[his] face like flint," confident he would not be put to shame.

I will give you," Satan enticed Jesus, "if you will bow down and worship me."

Jesus wouldn't trade his allegiance and adoration for a quicker path to power. Once again, he rebuked Satan with Scripture, speaking the truth that God alone is worthy of worship. And yet again, Jesus met temptation with truth, saturating his present moment in the story of the people of Israel, who were meant to find their truest identity—their wholeness—in the worship of God alone.[12]

God had promised the Israelites that through Abraham they would be a great nation with a great name, blessed by God to become a blessing for all the people of the whole earth.[13] But when the blessing felt bleak and far away, the people of Israel kept giving their attention and adoration to other gods who promised shortcuts to waiting on God.

Like the people of God throughout the ages, we trade worship for ease. We spend the sacred currency of our attention and adoration on the screens, pastors, and politicians who give us the fastest route to feeling blessed and great again. But where we succumb again and again to temptation, Christ was faithful to worship God alone.

Jesus rejected Satan's proposal to trade his sacred attention for a faster route to reigning over the world. With Christ, we must reject Satan's temptation to circumvent waiting as part of worship, as the well where God will fill us and this world with the blessing of wholeness.

Have more. Hurt less. Rule faster.

Satan's three temptations of Christ in the wilderness touch on our possessions, pain, and power. They are underneath the

---

12. Deut. 6:13.
13. Gen. 12:3.

temptations we face every day as we seek security, belonging, and joy. The joy and well-being we long for are found only in relationships that shift our nervous systems toward connection—a process called regulation.

Every temptation is about reaching for the benefits of regulation without the risk of relationship.

By tempting us to accumulate more possessions, Satan tries to convince us we can feel secure without being seen. By tempting us to focus our attention on constantly reducing or avoiding pain, Satan convinces us to silence the good signals of our souls that protect us from harm, lead us into safety, and remind us we need to change and grow. By tempting us to amass and hoard power, Satan convinces us we can protect ourselves apart from knowing and being known.

There is no lasting regulation without the vulnerability of relationships.

Because Jesus, the Good Shepherd, relied on the reality of his relationship with God when tempted, as part of his flock, we can risk receiving this as ours:

We have nothing to possess, for we already belong with and to God.

We have nothing to protect, for we are already in Christ's protection.

We have nothing to prove, for he already proved we are worth the cost of his life.

3. I LACK

WHEN A VIRUS INVADES THE HUMAN BODY, the body is initially blind to the fact that her borders have been breached. But security guards, called T cells, are always patrolling our hallways, ready to pounce on any pathogen. It doesn't take long for the guards to trip an alarm, like an internal security system, alerting cytotoxic T cells, natural killer cells, and antibodies to annihilate the invader inside.

When I was twenty years old, my body decided the invader was me.

Year after year, vials of blood and x-ray after x-ray told a story I couldn't accept: I shouldn't have been as sick as I was. We all were starting to blame . . . me. When doctor after doctor couldn't find evidence of the silent civil war happening within me, they started to treat me and my vulnerability like a virus. I was not so subtly blamed and shamed. *Maybe you just have a low pain tolerance. Maybe it's psychosomatic. It's all in your head. It's not your body that is breaking; it's your mind.*

When my pain could not be explained, I became a problem. My lack of evidence for what ailed me was treated like a threat to my doctors' competence. Each time a test came back negative, I noticed a pattern in most of my doctors. The attentiveness and compassion they had shown in their initial visit was replaced by dismissal. Their tone became impersonal. The conversation brusque. Eye contact minimal. The appointment over faster than I had waited for it to begin.

I felt like an algebra problem missing a variable. But instead of trying to find it, I was treated like I just didn't add up. Doctor after doctor seemed to reject the reality that the variables of my vulnerability and pain belonged in this equation at all.

My lack of proof made me a liability.

They were protecting their precious schedules and maybe their standing with insurance companies, and I was too sick to stop fighting to be believed. The scarcity of proof for what was causing my body to treat my hands and spine like a virus made me live on the precipice of survival and shutdown. For the first four years of being sick, I lived screaming to be heard and sinking into despair every time I wasn't.

Scarcity—of proof, answers, health, and help—was my story, and the story was even scarier than the pain itself. It taunted me: *Unless you make yourself better or less needy, you will always feel alone.*

Though my illness was turning up the sounds of scarcity like a loudspeaker, scarcity is always speaking into all of our relationships, writing chapters of chaos in our lives through the sentences of stress in our bodies. Scarcity shouts through our pounding chests. It growls through our tight shoulders. It yelps in our pain. It screams through our upset stomachs. It frowns through our numbness. It taunts us in the distracted or dismissing faces of others. *Maybe I don't matter. Maybe I'm not good enough.* And what we feel within ourselves and from each other, we sense with God too.

Scarcity lives in the shadows of our stories like an unacknowledged narrator, always manipulating the plot of our lives to keep us proving our worth, striving to rid ourselves of a constant sense of shame, never quite feeling like we belong.

The *Cambridge Dictionary* defines scarcity as "a situation in which something is not easy to find or get" and "a lack of something."[1] But when it comes to how our bodies experience life, scarcity is not just an occasional situation of lack but an ongoing internal story of feeling unsafe, unseen, and unheard.

When I started out as a therapist, I focused hard on catching everything my clients said. But there was often a mismatch between what they said and what they experienced. Over time, I realized I needed to listen to what their bodies were saying underneath their words.

Often, our bodies are speaking what our minds are afraid to say, stories most of us have never had space to tell. The tales our bodies tell through our sensations reveal our deepest wounds, truths, and hopes. So as we consider the embodied storyline of scarcity, I want you to listen to the syllables of your senses.

One area of science that has helped me practice this more than any other is polyvagal theory, which therapist and author Deb Dana calls "the science of safety—the science of feeling safe enough to fall in love with life and take the risks of living."[2] Scarcity is an embodied storyline about our safety that is always shaping us all. And polyvagal theory shows us how to feel safe enough to live in our own skin in a story where we are loved right now.

Sometimes our mouths say, "The Lord is my shepherd," while our bodies hear only a limerick of lack. Your daily experience of feeling seen by God and secure with God has more to do with your

1. *Cambridge Dictionary*, s.v. "scarcity," https://dictionary.cambridge.org/us/dictionary/english/scarcity.
2. Deb Dana, *The Polyvagal Theory in Therapy: Engaging the Rhythm of Regulation*, Norton Series on Interpersonal Neurobiology (New York: Norton, 2018), xvii.

body's sense of scarcity around safety than any confession of faith you've made or prayer you've prayed. You were wired for safety—built through attentive relationship—to be the foundation of a faith where you know you are always wanted.

If you want to experience that story as truer than anything scarcity says, it's time to befriend your body, starting with getting to know your nervous system.

Your brain's first concern and chief job is to keep you alive, and your autonomic nervous system works like a stealth surveillance system toward that end.[3] It is constantly scanning within you and outside of you for cues about how safe you are. This surveillance process is what the founder of polyvagal theory, neuroscientist Stephen Porges, calls *neuroception*.[4]

Without your even being aware of what it is doing, your autonomic nervous system is constantly engaged in the process of neuroception. Your body is always looking for *cues of danger* and *cues of safety* so that it can prepare you to protect yourself from harm or allow you to connect. *Cues of danger* are signals of misattunement, apathy, judgment, or threat from others, as well as perceived hazards in your environment—like seeing a snake slither across the sidewalk ahead of you or cars slamming on their brakes in front of you. (Or seeing a doctor throw up his hands in resignation or not make eye contact with you.) *Cues of safety* are signals of kindness, resonance, or peacefulness from others as well as your environment—like the

---

3. And those of us with trauma histories usually have highly sensitive surveillance systems. Our alarms get tripped easily and often.

4. Stephen W. Porges, "The Polyvagal Theory: New Insights into Adaptive Reactions of the Autonomic Nervous System," *Cleveland Clinic Journal of Medicine* 76, Suppl 2 (April 2009): S86–90, https://doi.org/10.3949/ccjm.76.s2.17.

smile of a passerby, the sound of a babbling brook, or the smell of dinner coming from the kitchen.[5]

Our nervous systems are always communicating with each other underneath the surface of our awareness. And the signals we send out—the cues of safety or danger conveyed by our faces, tone, body language, and words—are received by others' nervous systems to either invite connection or initiate self-protection. Your presence matters a lot more than you might realize or want to own!

When our internal surveillance system picks up on more cues of danger than safety, we sink into states of stress.

Stress is the physiological and neurological shift that starts in our bodies when we encounter more cues of danger than safety.[6] We'll talk more about what our stress states look and feel like in later chapters.

I lived mostly stuck in states of stress all those years, not because I wasn't trying to trust God with my life but because there were so many cues of danger drowning me every single day. Back then, the only way I knew how to deal with stress was to sermonize or shame it away. And let's just say that didn't work.

You get stressed and afraid not because you are bad at remembering Romans 8:28 or don't have enough faith over fear but because your body does not feel adequately safe. It is the neuroception of a scarcity of safety that keeps us sinking into states of stress to self-protect. All our "negative" emotions are really about a perceived lack of safety.

---

5. There are so many more cues of danger and safety than these examples, and many of these cues are highly personalized, based on your story. What is a major cue of danger for me might not be for you! And vice versa. What matters is that our bodies *do* respond significantly to too many cues of danger (i.e., not enough safety). Appreciating that reality can help us see our stress responses and coping habits as attempts to seek and reestablish safety.

6. Emily Nagoski and Amelia Nagoski, *Burnout: The Secret to Unlocking the Stress Cycle* (New York: Ballantine, 2019), 5.

Both the self-proclaimed healing gurus on Instagram and their Bible-teacher counterparts—who, coincidentally, both seem to have a corner on the market for perfect beach-wave hair and minimansions—are going to keep telling you, "Change your thoughts. Change your life." But changing your thoughts will last only as long as their perfect hair does in the rain.

You can't change your thoughts to change your life because stress will keep shouting throughout your body until you help your body move through it back to safety. When we are in states of stress, our nervous systems become disintegrated and disconnected, unable to activate the grounding resources of the parts of the brain that help you feel like you, the social engagement system and prefrontal cortex. This experience is called *dysregulation.*[7]

When we are dysregulated, we struggle to connect with others or keep perspective because our bodies are overwhelmed by simply trying to survive. We struggle to believe we're loved, seen, and ultimately safe when we're in states of stress because our bodies are physiologically disconnected from the parts of us that enable us to feel and remember all of those things.[8]

This is because, as Deb Dana says, "Story follows state."[9] The story you tell yourself about God, yourself, your life, and your relationships is always forming from the way your body is shifting between stressed and social autonomic states.

---

7. Theodore P. Beauchaine, Lisa Gatzke-Kopp, and Hilary K. Mead, "Polyvagal Theory and Developmental Psychopathology: Emotion Dysregulation and Conduct Problems from Preschool to Adolescence," *Biological Psychology* 74, no. 2 (February 2007): 174–84, https://doi.org/10.1016/j.biopsycho.2005.08.008.

8. And because our nervous systems are incredibly interconnected, dysregulation tends to be contagious. (I'm sure that my going into fight mode when in stress didn't exactly help my doctors stay grounded. And vice versa.)

9. Dana, *Polyvagal Theory*, 6.

The story you believe about the Good Shepherd and your place in his flock emerges from the shifts happening in your nervous system.

Scarcity sinks us into physiological states of stress that can keep us stuck living out stories of self-protection and striving instead of kindness and joy.

Maybe if we had more possessions, we'd feel like we belong.

Maybe if we had more power, we'd feel safe.

Maybe if we could prove our worth, we'd finally be loved.

You can't will your way out of the wounds of scarcity that speak into your story every day. You can't preach your way to the peace you need. Scarcity will keep being a scary, self-fulfilling prophecy that can never be satisfied by reaching for possessions, power, and perfect faith—*until* we acknowledge its presence in our physiology, reach for its roots, and tend to its shoots.

The truth is that scarcity is a story that lives in your body. And if you don't reckon with scarcity, it will rule you.

4. NOTHING.

OUR CAPACITY TO SAY "I lack nothing" is formed by the presence of the shepherds with whom we have belonged. It's the shepherds in your life—people in roles of caregiving, leadership, and authority—whose presence has primed your nervous system toward tightfisted fear or openhanded joy. Your past experiences of safety and connection with others—or the lack thereof—have shaped your nervous system's capacity for connection and calm.

The proper nouns of people and places and communities have written the language of love in your life. The adjectives of their presence—like reassuring and accepting or rigid and angry—have set the storyline for how you experience yourself, others, and God as characters in your life.

Psychiatrist Curt Thompson says that we're all born "looking for someone looking for us."[1] From the moment we can open our tiny eyes, we are looking for eyes looking back at us with love.

Our search for significance and safety is innate and sacred. Even God felt the need for this gaze. The God of the universe chose to be born into this world as an infant just like you and like me. The one whose death and resurrection save us first was a baby

---

1. Curt Thompson, *The Soul of Shame* (Downers Grove, IL: InterVarsity, 2015), 138.

who looked up at his mother in total dependence, looking for love, needing to see that he was safe and that she was responsive.

This is called *co-regulation*, and it lays the foundation for a lifetime of being able to regulate with resilience. *Regulation* is the process of returning our bodies to a state of connection and calm.[2] We first absorb the rhythm of regulation wrapped in our parents' arms, found and fed and held no matter how many times we cry. Love isn't just a verb; it's the songwriter setting down the physiological chords and chorus in your nervous system of your whole life's song.

Life in a broken world leaves us singing a song of scarcity. I have never encountered a pair of eyes that have been met with as much love as they needed. I have never met a person whose nervous system hasn't been shaped by some scarcity of connection. None of us receives all the love we need. And we carry that lack of love as distress in our nervous systems. Lack of co-regulation early in life forms neural pathways that sink into stress and shutdown easily and often.

The shepherds in our lives shape the song of our souls into abundance or scarcity. But we can learn to help our bodies sing a better song. We can start to wander the paths of peace. We can walk with a Shepherd whose presence changes everything.

Place a hand behind your head, right where your neck meets your head. The spot you are holding is where your vagus nerve begins. Now take that same hand and place it over your heart. Then lower your hand all the way down to the bottom of your belly. You have just traced the path of the vagus nerve, the longest cranial nerve

---

2. Stephen W. Porges, "The Polyvagal Perspective," *Biological Psychology* 74, no. 2 (February 2007): 116–43, https://doi.org/10.1016/j.biopsycho.2006.06.009.

in your body. *Vagus* means "wanderer," and this wandering pathway is the internal highway of your body where traffic is constantly shifting to protect you from harm and prepare you to be known.[3] This pathway can pull your body toward self-protection or peace, contention or connection.

In a moment, I want you to set down your book and cup your face with your hands. Then come back to this page. Really. Go ahead and do it right now.

In addition to moving down to your belly, the vagus nerve also reaches upward through your face in roughly the same place your hands just were. When your nervous system feels adequately safe and secure, the social engagement system of your brain is switched on, activating nerves that allow you to hear, see, smile, speak, and sing.[4] The opposite is true too. When we sense a scarcity of safety, we will struggle to connect.

Like the brakes on a car or a bike that slow us down when engaged, our vagus nerve regulates the flow of energy in our bodies through something called the vagal brake. The vagal brake varies the rhythm and pace of our hearts and lungs to meet the demands of life. When our system is overwhelmed by a sense of too much danger, the vagal brake releases, activating the sympathetic nervous system to keep us safe. In micromoments, our hearts pound, our blood pressure rises, and our breathing becomes rapid and shallow, charging the body with energy to fight or flee. When that energy becomes too much for the sympathetic system to handle, we sink

---

3. I draw heavily from polyvagal theory in my work as a therapist. I first learned how to explain the anatomy of the vagus nerve through therapist Deb Dana, a polyvagal expert. Her guidance on this podcast interview, in particular, has informed my instructions here: "Deb Dana: Befriending Your Nervous System," *Sounds True: Insights at the Edge*, hosted by Tami Simon, https://podcasts.apple.com/us/podcast/deb-dana-befriending-your-nervous-system /id307934313?i=1000478267382.

4. Stephen W. Porges, "Cardiac Vagal Tone: A Neurophysiological Mechanism That Evolved in Mammals to Dampen Threat Reactions and Promote Sociality," *World Psychiatry* 20, no. 2 (2021): 296–98.

into shutdown, which serves like a shield to protect us from extreme threats.

Your capacity for connection with others is an expression of your nervous system's sense of safety, and it is regulated by the neural pathways you just traced with your hands.

The year I got sick with my autoimmune disease, I got engaged to Ryan. Though I was elated to be marrying my best friend, I was flooded with self-contempt for my suffering. I felt shame about being a constant inconvenience, always canceling plans. While other brides worry about their dresses or their caterers, I worried I wouldn't be well enough to even walk down the aisle when our wedding day came. I mentally whipped myself for being weak, ashamed of the anxiety attacks I was starting to have in the car or on dates. If my faith couldn't heal my sickness, at least I should be able to have enough strength to rejoice in all things. Wasn't my faith supposed to help me rise?

The spring before we got married, we went to premarital counseling with our pastor, who, though he remains a dear friend of ours, gave us some dangerous advice. If I am a stormy sea, Ryan is a still pond. Faced with my whirling waves of emotion, Ryan felt lost. Our pastor's solution: leave me alone. But it wasn't just that. He made sequestering me alone with my shame a moral imperative.

While our pastor's exact words elude my memory, he said something like this: "When KJ's in the pit of shame, don't go in with her. If you go in, she'll never learn to find her way out on her own. She must learn on her own that Christ already died for her, so she doesn't need to punish herself. She needs to preach the gospel to herself."

Partial truths can cause great pain. In the early months of our marriage, when I spiraled with stress or sickness into a pit of shame,

Ryan gave me space to try to get out of the pit alone. Behind the slammed door of our bedroom—mind you, I was the one doing the door-slamming—I curled into a fetal position, disgusted with myself and terrified that my brand-new husband would eventually just decide to leave for good.

Story emerges from our autonomic state, and my state was often shutdown. The story I started to believe—that *both* of us started to believe—was that I was bad for getting so stressed. I prayed that maybe someday I'd be as good at trusting God as Ryan. Little did we know, I had a whole different roadmap for regulation than my husband because of enduring complex childhood trauma. I didn't have access to the same paths of peace as him. Asking me to get out of the pit of shame alone was like reenacting the worst traumas of my childhood. Every time Ryan left me alone with my shame, we were both just pouring asphalt over the path of self-soothing through self-rejection and striving to be more perfect.

For many of us, our vagal pathways have been paved into paths of condemnation by a scarcity of co-regulating love. In times we've been mired by stress, instead of being shepherded, we've been scolded and shamed. Instead of support, we're given a sermon. In many Christian churches, families, and friendships, it's as though we believe the resurrection of Jesus Christ means we should just be able to look at the cross and instantaneously rise out of any stress, discouragement, or depression.

We've cut both our physiology and relationality out of participating in Christ's love. The resurrection happened in a human body. It doesn't cancel our humanness; it compels us to go with Christ into the depths of disconnection and death in our bodies, trusting the Spirit will always help us rise.

When a sheep is lost or hurt, a shepherd doesn't wait for them to find their way back to the flock. A good shepherd seeks their lost sheep. A good shepherd knows their sheep's worth and goodness is not contingent upon their capacity to find their own way back home.

Somehow, we've decided shepherding means expecting sheep to be self-sufficient. Somehow, we've erased "seeking" from the job description and replaced it with more preaching. And when preaching is the main form of pastoring we've encountered, it's no wonder that "preach to yourself" is the main way we know how to relate to our pain. Like sheep stuck in thick brush, our bodies were not made to preach our own way out of emotional pain. It's no wonder that when stress is shouting in bodies, we end up sinking in pits of shame.

The vagus nerve can show us a better way through the lack of safety and love we experience in our nervous systems. In later chapters, I will share more about how we can walk this pathway with Christ and one another to shift out of states of stress. For now, all you need to know is that your body works like a road. Just as I can't teleport from Denver to see my dear friends in Chattanooga, you can't teleport yourself from stress to safety.

You were never meant to crawl your way out of the pit of stress and shame alone. We were created to walk the path of regulation together to guide our bodies back home from stress and shutdown to feeling safe and social again.

We experience lack.

It's a fact of life.

It's how we respond to our lack—ours and each other's—that leads us into lives where we'll be able to say with authenticity:

In Christ, I lack nothing.

5. HE MAKES ME LIE DOWN

WE OFTEN EXPECT GOD TO BE A PARENT who scolds us rather than a shepherd who soothes us. We come to God in the pages of Scripture and the hard parts of our stories carrying apprehension of judgment rather than the anticipation of kindness.

In the early months of getting sick, I spent most of my time in bed. I was a junior in college whose landscape for living had suddenly shrunk to the size of one dorm room. I felt like God had forced me to lie down, as though my ambition and busyness were sins for which I needed punishment and discipline. The traditional English translation of Psalm 23:2 is "he makes me lie down," which certainly sounds akin to putting a toddler in timeout.

I was plied with others' platitudes and crushed by a theology of cause and effect; if I was sick, surely it had to be some hidden sin in my heart that needed punishment. So I prayed and prayed, begging God to let me get out of bed.

My prayers were a loop of longing and loss. *God, heal me. Tell me what I need to repent of, and I will. God, help me find out what's wrong with my body. God, give me answers. God, do you even hear me? Father, heal me.* Eventually, I would run out of words and stare out the window instead, peering over the edge of Lookout Mountain and its forests and boulders, pining for the day I could climb out of bed and climb its stone face again instead.

It was on one of those lengthy days of longing that I realized I was waiting for the wrong thing.

Suffering was silencing me. I needed words to wrap around my wounds. I needed speech to break the silence of the violence of the autoimmune civil war raging inside my body.[1]

I found my voice again in the words of the psalms.

The day my longing found lament, my prayers for healing became prayers to see God.

I had opened my Bible to Psalm 27, where I encountered a saint as hard up as me. David, who wrote both Psalm 27 and Psalm 23, knew what it was like to have an enemy, knew how it felt to be afraid, and knew how much it hurt to wonder if you are heard. Yet in his haunting fears, he told himself to trust. "The Lord is the stronghold of my life," he prayed. "Of whom shall I be afraid?"[2]

By the time I got to the end of the psalm, I was stunned into a better story.

> Wait for the Lord;
>> be strong, and let your heart take courage;
>> wait for the Lord![3]

All those days looking out the window, I had been waiting on God to heal me. But the psalm showed me that what I was really waiting for *was God.*

1. Walter Brueggemann, *Deep Memory, Exuberant Hope: Contested Truth in a Post-Christian World* (Minneapolis: Fortress, 2000), 7. Brueggemann writes, "We of all people have the textual resources authorizing and legitimating and modeling *speech that breaks the silence* of violence and the violence of silence."

2. Ps. 27:1 ESV.

3. Ps. 27:14 ESV.

I was being led through one of the darkest valleys of my life, facing more suffering than I imagined I could endure. I thought I was waiting to be rescued. God was waiting for me to see that he was already with me. Hearing my cries. Moved by my pain. Ready to meet me with mercy for the season ahead.

The interpretation of "he makes me lie down" in Psalm 23 can lead us into a story of either punishment or peace. And the translation history of this passage tells a different story than the common English translation leads us to expect. The Greek translation of the Old Testament uses the word *kataskenoo* in this passage, which can be translated as "rest" or "settle down."[4] The Arabic text in the *London Polygot* (1657) similarly translates this as *ahallani*, which means "he settles me down."[5] As such, scholars like Kenneth Bailey prefer to translate this line of Psalm 23 as "he settles me down," noting that the more forceful language of most English translations creates unnecessary problems.[6]

I thought God was a shepherd who made me lie down. I needed to encounter God as a shepherd who settled me down.

That day, I started realizing that to be strong and let my heart take courage, I needed to wait on the Lord not as the one who was punishing me with pain and expecting me to be stoic about it but as the Shepherd coming to care for me. I needed to encounter my emotions not as signs of failure but as cries for connection.

I needed to change the goal of my waiting. I had to shift the aim of my anticipation.

4. H. G. Liddell, Robert Scott, and H. S. Jones, *A Greek-English Lexicon*, rev. J. S. Jones (Oxford: Clarendon, 1966), 912.

5. Cited in Kenneth E. Bailey, *The Good Shepherd: A Thousand-Year Journey from Psalm 23 to the New Testament* (Downers Grove, IL: IVP Academic, 2014), 33.

6. Ibid., 40.

The heart of life is learning to anticipate the presence of a Shepherd who wants to respond to our stress. Emotion is the energy and substance that guides us there.

If you grew up in the American evangelical church, there's a good chance you might instinctively believe your emotions are bad distractions that make you lack faith. While there is neither time nor space here to fully show you why your emotions belong in your faith, take a risk and consider what I have to share.[7] Demonizing and dismissing our emotions is what most keeps us from experiencing God's love.

Many people think our emotions are our reactions to the world around us. But emotions are more like constantly renovated edifices, built by our brains from the construction site of context. As neuroscientist and psychologist Lisa Feldman Barrett writes, "An emotion is your brain's creation of what your bodily sensations mean, in relation to what is going on around you in the world."[8]

Your brain is an architect of anticipation, continuously adjusting blueprints of hypotheses of what to expect and how to be. Emotion is built from the timber of your past experiences and the nails of your present physical sensations and stimuli around you to make a world of meaning, whether that world is delightful or devastating.

"Trauma is not what happens to us," doctor and addiction expert Gabor Maté writes, "but what we hold inside in the absence of an empathetic witness."[9] Our past experiences of our stress being ignored, shamed, or silenced can build us into people who expect to be alone with our pain. Like rooms without windows, we carry

7. I have an entire chapter in my first book, *This Too Shall Last*, on the goodness of our emotions. See chapter 4, "Emotion." I also discussed Christ's emotions at length. For that discussion, see chapter 6, "Fully Human."
8. Lisa Feldman Barrett, *How Emotions Are Made: The Secret Life of the Brain* (New York: Houghton Mifflin Harcourt, 2017), 30.
9. Gabor Maté, foreword to *In an Unspoken Voice: How the Body Releases Trauma and Restores Goodness*, by Peter A. Levine (Berkeley, CA: North Atlantic Books, 2010), xii.

that dark anticipation within our bodies in our sensations and the meaning we reflexively ascribe to them through emotion.

Your past shapes your present and projects your future.

But your *present* experience can change the way you sense the past and hold hope for the future.

There is a Shepherd who stands with scars still on his hands, who is always reaching toward you in every moment of your stress, because he has been where you are and knows the way home.

As we pay attention to ourselves as people Jesus already loves and is already seeking, we will experience our stress differently. Our sensations don't have to tell the same old story. We can practice anticipating the Shepherd's presence—even when we fear we have been left alone.

Courage isn't the opposite of fear. *Courage is the practice of risking to trust that we have a Good Shepherd who is with us always—no matter what.*

And the beautiful thing about a practice is you do not have to do it perfectly. You can begin right where you are. In your fear. In your overwhelm. In your stress. You can stumble and struggle while building trust that you are being strengthened. You will become what you build, day by day rearranging the energy of your life into a home where Love resides.

Emotion is energy that can build your life into a home where you always belong. Your stress can become a place to practice being settled down by the Shepherd. Practicing courage through intentional rhythms, rituals, and relationships can renovate your life.

Just as shepherds in Palestine and the western United States guide their flocks summer after summer into distant mountain ranges, we will travel the same paths year after year of our lives, where our stress continually presents us with choices to solidify a story of scarcity or be reshaped by sacred communion into joy.[10] Psalm 23 is a song written in a circular, repetitive form called a "ring composition."[11] David presents a series of ideas in the form of a story that comes to a climax, and then he repeats his ideas backward in a slightly different way, creating "a literary ring."[12]

Within a ring composition, matching cameos form a pair that inform a mutual meaning. "He makes me lie down" (v. 2) pairs with "you prepare a table before me" (v. 5). Within the context of its matching cameo, "he makes me lie down" shows us God is always preparing a feast for us even in the middle of our fear. Courage is not a one-sided practice but a continuous and reciprocal participation in being present and expectant.

The circular literary structure of Psalm 23 reinforces the reality that we must return again and again to the same rocky ground where our trust in the Shepherd was first forged. Psalm 23 gently corrects our one-and-done expectations for faith, showing us that the practice of presence is the only way the provision expressed in Psalm 23 becomes our felt reality.

Just as Psalm 23 forms a circle, courage is a circle. Every time we find ourselves in another dark valley of discouragement or surrounded by enemies and stressed out of our minds, rather than being defeated or ashamed, we can trust that we are precisely where we are supposed to be to encounter the Shepherd again. Courage is a circle of communion, in which we choose—again and again—to risk trusting that the Good Shepherd *will* be with us.

I love that Psalm 23 forms a circle, not just because my mind is like a canvas on which I'm always painting the world into concentric

10. W. Phillip Keller, *A Shepherd Looks at Psalm 23* (Grand Rapids, MI: Zondervan, 2015), 68.

11. Kenneth E. Bailey, *The Good Shepherd: A Thousand-Year Journey from Psalm 23 to the New Testament* (Downers Grove, IL: IVP Academic, 2014), 24.

12. Ibid., 24, 34.

circles of connectedness or because the ring composition of Psalm 23 basically gives me literary permission to be more repetitive in this book than picky reviewers would prefer. I *love* that the structure of the psalm mirrors the reality of our lives and the way our nervous systems were created for repetition to rewire us into resilience.

Our neural pathways are paved by our habits and choices. Neurons are connected by dendrites, and the more we repeat a habit or behavior, the more dendrites connect those neurons.[13] It's as though our choices can bushwhack a path into the wilderness of a new way of being, and the repetition of those choices and habits clears the land into a trail. Eventually, repetition of practices and habits paves the path, so that we can walk down it even when our feet hurt or there's heavy fog blocking the way. Every day, we are learning to trust we know our way back home.

With repetition over months and years and a lifetime, habits of choosing connection, love, and joy can become nearly automatic. Courage is choosing the communion you were made for, trusting that your innate need to travel this circle will always lead you into more life.

We'll travel down the road of stress every day of our lives, sometimes getting stuck in ditches of despair. But ours is a Shepherd who does not punish our symptoms of stress. False shepherds will always make us lie down in submission, but true shepherds settle us down into safety.

Our Good Shepherd doesn't make us lie down, grounding us for getting lost or stuck in the first place. *He settles us down.* He makes space for our stress to be settled and soothed through compassion in action. God meets us within our stress—even through the compassion we offer ourselves (self-regulation) and receive from

13. Julie Hani has an easy to read article on our neuroplasticity: Julie Hani, "The Neuroscience of Behavior Change," StartUp Health, August 8, 2017, https://health transformer.co/the-neuroscience-of-behavior-change-bcb567fa83c1?gi=bc7ed3d2b115.

others (co-regulation)—suffering with and alongside us to soothe us into safety at the pace our bodies most need.

We begin to expect the Shepherd's kind presence when we practice letting God settle our souls. This means that noticing and acknowledging our stress are both essential and sacred parts of becoming whole. With every pounding heartbeat or searing loss, we can practice placing the energy of our emotions into the context of a story where there is a Good Shepherd who always wants to respond to us with love.

6. IN GREEN PASTURES,

EVERY SHEEP'S CAPACITY to be led by the Good Shepherd to lie down in green pastures is directly connected to the condition of their community.

As former shepherd Phillip Keller said in *A Shepherd Looks at Psalm 23*, sheep can't lie down in green pastures unless four stipulations of safety are met: they need to be free from hunger, friction with other sheep, pests and parasites, and fear.[1] Similarly, our human bodies require that our needs for sustenance, shelter, and safety are met before we can connect deeply or do creative work.[2] Like sheep, we can't lie down in God's green pastures unless we are assured we are safe to belong there.

We can't rest in God's grace unless we are freed from fighting with other sheep and striving to be significant. Our fears about provision for possessions, pain, and power find solace in the attention and awareness of a Shepherd who cares.[3]

One of the most striking features of the early church was its

---

1. W. Phillip Keller, *A Shepherd Looks at Psalm 23* (Grand Rapids, MI: Zondervan, 2015), 41–42.

2. See, for example, Maslow's hierarchy of needs: www.simplypsychology.org/maslow.html#gsc.tab=0.

3. Kenneth E. Bailey, *The Good Shepherd: A Thousand-Year Journey from Psalm 23 to the New Testament* (Downers Grove, IL: IVP Academic, 2014), 40.

reversal and rejection of the reigning dominance structures of the day. When the Galatian Christians tried to place Jewish Christians and their customs above the Greeks in their midst, Paul reminded them that their baptism as beloved in Christ had canceled every racial and gendered pecking order they had previously known. "If you have been baptized into Christ, you've been clothed with Christ and are all one—equals in importance and position," Paul says in Galatians 3:26–29.[4]

We still don't hear him.

One of the most common dynamics that keeps sheep from lying down in green pastures is what Keller calls "the butting order."[5] Domineering, older sheep maintain their position as leaders by butting other, often younger, sheep from the best grazing ground. The other sheep mimic what they see, shoving around those below them in the butting order.

So many of our church and family systems are just like flocks of sheep, stuck in a spiritual butting order, confusing dominance with godly authority, subconsciously so afraid we'll lose our spot in God's heart and world that we shove each other out of the way.

When applying the shepherding metaphor to humans, remember: shepherds are just sheep who have been given authority. Like everyone, their nervous systems have been shaped by scarcity's story that there is not enough space, time, or love for us all. Even pastors can preach great words about the gospel without being holistically rooted in the security that they are loved no matter what. Pastors, parents, and leaders of all kinds shepherd from a posture of scarcity when we don't practice the trust that we are loved regardless of results.

In the church, we might *say* we're a family, but our pursuit of dominance and control reveals a different truth about how we see

---

4. My paraphrase.
5. Keller, *Shepherd Looks at Psalm 23*, 27.

each other. Neurotheologian Jim Wilder describes this dynamic as living in "enemy mode," which is simply another way to describe what our bodies experience and enact to survive when we are stuck in states of stress.[6] Naming the reality of *enemy mode* in our bodies can help us see and shift out of living like we must shove or be shoved around.

As we've discussed in earlier chapters, when we are flooded by the sense of too much danger—small or large cues that make us feel unsafe, unseen, and unwanted—the relational capacities of the vagus nerve and social engagement system reach their limits. The subcortical region of the amygdala springs into action, activating the self-protective functions of the body to fight, flight, freeze, or fawn to keep us from harm. This is the start of being in enemy mode.[7]

Whether the cue of danger is big or small, it can elicit a stress response of going into enemy mode. A pastor might see fewer people in the pews and fear their church plant is going to fail. At staff meeting the next day, their stress comes out sideways, snapping at their staff. When facing fewer tithes, an elder or a leadership team might make decisions that are more about anxiety about the bottom line and the church's mortgage than about caring for the people inside the building. You might see someone at the grocery store who was rude to you in a small group last year, and instead of saying hello, you are curt to the cashier. The worship leaders at your new church might start singing a song you sang all the time at the church where you were harmed, and suddenly you wish you could run outside.

When we go into *simple enemy mode*, our social engagement system (or as Wilder calls it, our relational circuits) is shut down. We

6. E. James Wilder, *The Pandora Problem: Facing Narcissism in Leaders and Ourselves* (Carmel, IN: Deeper Walk International, 2018), 189.

7. Ibid.

want to flee from people and our problems. We struggle to listen, become argumentative, and quick to criticize and judge.[8]

In *predatory enemy mode*, we use our relational energy to prey on weakness. Wilder and his coauthor, Michel Hendricks, write that in this mode, "We attune to others, not to show compassion but to exploit their weakness. We track the emotions of others in order to pounce."[9]

Enemy mode can happen everywhere, not just in church-related relationships. Every time we don't feel adequately safe inside our skin, we tend toward self-protection to survive. We might say we're one in Christ and that every person is made in the image of God, but if we're subconsciously living in enemy mode, we will experience and treat people as potential threats or problems to fix. Our nervous systems will always be scanning every relational encounter ready to shove others out of the way of the significance and safety we've worked so hard to cultivate.

I used to live in enemy mode. I grew up learning life was a battle to be the best. Stress was my fuel. Striving was my sword. And shutdown was my safe haven. In the absence of attunement, my ambition to know the right answers in Sunday school or get the highest grades taught me that if I mostly stayed unemotional and compliant and sought certainty, I could be wanted and maybe even known.

It's no surprise that I ended up being attracted to a community that traded real relationship for ungodly ambition and shepherding for shame and control.

My husband, after years of working menial jobs to be my

---

8. Jim Wilder and Michel Hendricks, *The Other Half of Church: Christian Community, Brain Science, and Overcoming Spiritual Stagnation* (Chicago: Moody, 2020), 173.

9. Ibid.

caregiver during seasons of severe illness and to get through seminary at the same time, ended up getting his first paid church job. We were thrilled to be chosen to serve in a way we had longed to for years.

Being wanted can be dangerous when you don't yet have the discernment and courage to see there is one with whom you already fully belong.

At work, Ryan quickly noticed how often his boss got angry at his coworkers, but we just accepted everyone's lines about why: "That's just how he is, but no pastor is perfect." "He's working on it." His standards were exacting, but we called it valuing excellence. Only the shiniest people were allowed to stand on the stage. Only the best worship leaders and preachers were allowed to lead in ways that were seen. The pastor wasn't friendly or accessible for much conversation, but we called it "being focused on building the kingdom." In sermons, he'd cast a vision as though we were the only faithful "gospel-centered" church around. Behind the scenes, he'd put other pastors down.

Sure, there were things our pastor said that hurt us and ways he led that concerned us, but we were sheep and he was the shepherd. We felt like we should just be grateful we had been chosen to be part of the greatest church in town.

Jesus said that the kingdom of God comes in the smallness of a seed,[10] but we found ourselves in a system with a clear butting order, serving under domineering shepherds whose values and choices made it clear they believed the kingdom was advanced through more. They wanted more butts in seats to "make more disciples" across our city, and they expected more and more of everyone's energy and unquestioning loyalty to make that mission happen.

Of course, it would be years before we let ourselves see all of

10. Matt. 13:31–32.

this. A community like that can look so positive from a pew or the place where your passion is being appealed to. You often can see the problems only in proximity to the people who hold power.

At first we lauded the church's vision, wanting more people in our city to know Christ, wanting to express the gospel in a way that was relevant to our culture. So many people in the church had caught the vision too, and it felt *good* to be part of a group of people who had the "right" way to be relevant, the right answers to our city's needs, the right approach to Scripture, the right way to be both in the world and not of it. All of the stress that swirled around the staff and all of the pastor's outbursts or snide comments were just speedbumps on the road to advancing the kingdom of God. The ends were good, so we figured we needed to put up with some not-so-fun means to get there.

But with every passing year, Ryan's shepherding responsibilities piled higher while the goal line of expectations to be affirmed in the authority of his vocation only moved farther back. We thought if we served harder and longer and showed enough loyalty, Ryan would eventually secure the pastor and elders' rubber stamp of approval to move from director to pastor. With every passing year, Ryan kept being derided for his focus on spiritual formation and his desire for the pastors to spend more of their energy shepherding. But our sense of scarcity about being able to find a job at any other church served as a powerful numbing agent for the pain inside us telling us that something was wrong.

We weren't lying down in green pastures, because we were too busy proving we were worth keeping around.

When the enemy mode within ourselves isn't soothed into safety by empathy, our flocks end up focused on striving and shoving, silencing anyone who is no longer willing to put up with it. Like the bullies in elementary school, when we don't tend to our pain, anxiety, and stress, we end up protecting it by projecting it onto others and shoving them around.

It's sheep shoving other sheep that most often makes us feel like there isn't a Shepherd with whom we belong. We can't lie down in green pastures when we're constantly trying to guard our spot on the ground.

Every flock has sheep that try to shove others around. Make no mistake: Scripture says God *will* judge between us. And Scripture makes it clear: God sides with those who have been shoved around. In Ezekiel 34, God declares, "Because you shove with flank and shoulder, butting all the weak sheep with your horns until you have driven them away, I will save my flock, and they will no longer be plundered. I will judge between one sheep and another."[11]

In the same passage, God denounces shepherds who devour their sheep's gifts instead of caring for their needs. We need to listen soberly to God's words in Ezekiel 34. Leaders who rule harshly will be held accountable for their presence. "Building the kingdom of God" is no excuse for bullying.

Our anxiety about doing great things for God ends up keeping us from seeing that God is for us and with us. When our attention is occupied by looking at the Good Shepherd, we don't have to spend it on guarding our turf, enlarging our territory, controlling others, or constantly protecting ourselves from harm.

When he worked as a shepherd, Phillip Keller noticed that when his sheep became aware of his presence, the infighting in his flock would stop. He writes, "Whenever I came into view and my presence attracted their attention, the sheep quickly forgot their foolish rivalries and stopped their fighting. The shepherd's presence made

---

11. Ezek. 34:21–22.

all the difference in their behavior."[12] When we see that we have a Good Shepherd, we don't have to shove our way to significance.

In Jesus' flock, you do not have to be shiny to be seen.

He seeks out the struggling, not the strong.

This is a flock where you do not have to fight to be found.

Jesus put himself in the place of battered lambs. He was judged, critiqued, and spit on by the shepherds of his day—all the way to the cross. They feared losing their precious power to his uncommon presence too. Jesus let them shove him all the way out—out of life itself—so that we shoved-around sheep might see:

> There is no imperfection in you
> that can keep you from being included in
> Christ's flock.
> There is no brokenness in your story
> that can revoke your belonging.
> There is no bruise on your body
> that is not seen by our Shepherd.
> Because he chose to be rejected, you always
> belong.

> No one can steal your belovedness
> as a sheep bought by Christ's own blood.
> No fear can take away your place.
> No one can shove you out of the Good
> Shepherd's sight.

> Only in the light of his face can you see the
> grace of your place.
> This green ground is where you already belong.

---

12. Keller, *Shepherd Looks at Psalm 23*, 47.

7. HE LEADS ME

METAPHORS PROMPT US TO PAY ATTENTION. While the words of Psalm 23 can feel as comfortable as slipping on our favorite pair of jeans, if we let our minds slow down and stand in front of the mirror wearing these words, we might see some strange and stunning things about the person staring back at us.

Psalm 23 is describing you and me like sheep—common farm animals that are incredibly dependent on their shepherd to survive. The man who wrote this song became the king of Israel and you might be an executive or have an advanced degree, and yet Scripture is saying you and I are like something we'd normally see as insignificant.

In every sermon I've ever heard that included the sheep-shepherd metaphor, the preacher pointed out how "stupid" sheep are. In a blog post reflecting on Psalm 23, popular Christian blogger Tim Challies writes that "the first reason sheep need a shepherd" is "because sheep are *dumb*."[1] Sheep have become Christianity's pet metaphor for submission, a convenient comparison that tends to reinforce a power dynamic that elevates a pastor and their wisdom over parishioners and their sin.

---

1. Tim Challies, "Dumb, Directionless, Defenseless," *Challies* (blog), August 26, 2013, www.challies.com/christian-living/dumb-directionless-defenseless/.

If sheep aren't smart and Scripture says we're like them, how can we trust our sense of wisdom about what's good and true and right?

Most of us live like following the Shepherd means leaving part of ourselves behind.

And if you grew up in church, chances are good that at some point you've believed your emotions are the part of you that keep you from following. I can't tell you how many times I've seen Christians posting quotes on social media saying things like "Feelings aren't facts" or "Your feelings are lying to you. Trust God." Common Christian wisdom seems to lead us to think that our big feelings are what lead us far from God, like stupid sheep wandering away from the flock.

Spoiler alert: sheep are much smarter than a lot of pastors and political pundits give them credit for.[2] This whole sheep-shepherd metaphor might mean more than we've been told.

Most of us don't believe we belong because we believe we are too much.

Too might be the word I most internalized from my childhood. In third grade my classmates at my new school told me I was a weirdo for wearing dresses with frog prints. *Hello! Why not wear your favorite animal on your clothes?* (I wasn't a dog lover yet.) I was the misfit kid who didn't get invited to birthday parties, but because I was so immersed in friendship with my books, it took me a while to notice.

The other day a friend and I stopped at a mall. A boy and his dad strolled past us with their noses in books, held just low enough

---

2. Mark Townsend, "Sheep Might Be Dumb, but They're Not Stupid," *Guardian*, March 6, 2005, www.theguardian.com/uk/2005/mar/06/science.animalwelfare.

not to trip. I nudged my friend. "Mish, if you've ever wondered what I was like as a little girl—there's your picture."

Books gave me what I didn't have. When the fighting in my family was too much—which was often—books were almost enough to shelter me. Just pages away were places where I could be safe. Alongside the kind voices of Anne of Green Gables and Marilla or Lucy Pevensie and Aslan, the shouting in my family would lull to a distant drone. Because of books, I could live with the hope of another world.

Books had already survived their stories. They had sturdy spines to withstand stress and hands to hold them up from falling to the ground.

I could almost hide myself between the pages like a partial invisibility cloak to block myself from being bullied. To this day, like most complex trauma survivors, I don't remember large portions of my childhood.[3] Some of us dissociate into temporary oblivion. I dissociated into books. Books were my safest place.

I needed a place to hide from a world that felt like too much, and somewhere along the way I started believing that I was too much. As a kid, my mom made it clear I was too sensitive and my classmates made it obvious that I was too strange to be worth knowing. As I've gotten older, I've often experienced being too nerdy for normal conversation and too passionate to fit into other peoples' expectations of what a woman should be.

---

3. When we hear the word *trauma*, we often think of single incidents. Complex trauma describes the effect of long-term exposure to multiple traumatic events. This can include both pervasive abuse *and* the absence of attunement from caregivers. Trauma is not just the bad that happens to us; it is also all the good that was supposed to happen and didn't. This kind of trauma has a profound effect on the way we form attachments throughout life, how we see our own worth, and, underneath it all, the extent to which we feel safe and secure in our own bodies as we move through the world each day. Complex trauma is often a severe attachment injury that has profound effects on how our nervous systems function. The damage can be healed, but first it must be acknowledged.

It seems a perennial part of being human is simultaneously feeling like too much and not enough.

I felt too much, too deeply, too often to be convenient for others to know. The stress of feeling so astonished by the world while also never quite fitting into it chained me to shame. Quizzical looks and mean jabs do take a toll, and I clearly got way more overwhelmed than most people. The logical conclusion was: something must be wrong with me.

My husband and I concluded that I had a "stress problem," so when I was twenty-six I found myself back in therapy on a plush grey couch next to a fluffy blanket facing a kind-eyed blonde woman with a few framed diplomas behind her chair.

For probably twenty minutes straight, I listed off a litany of facts about how life had been hard but I was too stressed. Lauren nodded, tracking along with my wild story of how I came to be this weird. When I finally had drained my mouth of words and emptied my cup of wild orange blossom tea, a scary silence filled the room.

And then even scarier words.

"Have you ever heard the term *highly sensitive person?*" Lauren asked.

Her question pressed a tiny button on a detonator in my nervous system. *Shit. She thinks I'm too sensitive too.*

I heard the ticking of a miniature bomb in my heart, but just as I started to sink into a self-protective shell of shame, I noticed that Lauren was smiling at me, like she respected me.

"Highly sensitive people process just about everything more deeply than the rest of the population," she shared. It was like her soft tone was expertly dismantling the wires of my internal bomb. "From sensations like hearing noises and feeling temperature, to feeling emotions deeply—both positive and negative—to thinking critically, HSPs are wired in a way that makes them constantly process stimulation deeply," she explained. "We get overstimulated easily."

We. She said *we.*

I no longer heard any bomb ticking or any voices judging. For the first time in my life, I was hearing someone in a position of authority say *she was just like me.*

I instantly unclenched my jaw and sighed. It was like I had just opened the cover of a book into a story where it was finally safe to be me.

All my life, I had learned I had to make my sensitivity small, and here was Lauren, looking at me like I should sit tall. She introduced me to the research of Dr. Elaine Aron, who has theorized that about 15 to 20 percent of the population are born with nervous systems that are genetically wired to be more sensitive to subtleties in their environment, are more capable of deep inner reflection, and are, accordingly, more easily overwhelmed by the world.[4]

Within minutes, my new therapist had nailed all of the quirks I'd been hiding from the world in case they noticed I was too weird. She saw the one part of myself it had seemed that everyone— including myself—had labeled as too broken. And she blessed it instead.

In the months after that session, I practiced honoring the part of myself that gets too stressed as the part of me that sees the world in striking colors while many just see shadows. I started responding to my nervous system as a wise friend who deserves attention. By being gentle with my own need for breaks from loud places or intense conversations, I found I was no longer "too stressed" most of the time. Instead of locking away part of myself in a closet, I started to let my sensitivity have a seat at the table.

The more I stopped shaming myself for being different, the

---

4. Elaine N. Aron, *The Highly Sensitive Person in Love: Understanding and Managing Relationships When the World Overwhelms You* (New York: Broadway, 2000), 3.

more I experienced my sensitivity as a special kind of sight. I could pick up on subtle shifts in others' emotions. I could make connections between conversations and the systems that shaped them. I realized there is a spring of empathy inside me that can quench others' thirst—if I am willing to treat it as a well instead of a pit.

The part of me that had been most shamed and silenced was the part of me that was wisest. I came to realize that the sensitive parts of our bodies and souls—whether or not you fall into the 20 percent of the population that inherited "high sensitivity" like me—are the parts through which God most consistently speaks to lead us into life.

"Remember, the body is a major, not minor prophet," Geri and Pete Scazzero of Emotionally Healthy Discipleship often say.[5] But if the body is a prophet, religion had taught me to treat mine like Israel's prophets of old—with silence, shame, and scorn. For years, I had been shoving down my sense that something was sick in our church and her leaders. I thought being gracious meant burying my flesh and her feelings.

Years before, I had to practice courage to keep listening to my body when she shouted with pain, even when doctors, based on my blood work, dismissed my pain as impossible and exaggerated. To be whole and well, *I had to keep believing myself.* I had to keep listening to the loud, inconvenient truth that a twenty-year-old shouldn't hurt as much as I did.

Now I was finding myself learning to listen again. Over time, as I learned to honor my sensitivity, I started hearing the sounds

---

5. Pete Scazzero, "Your Body Is a Major, Not Minor Prophet," Emotionally Healthy Discipleship, February 14, 2014, www.emotionallyhealthy.org/your-body-is-a-major-not -minor-prophet-2/.

of my stress as symptoms of a deeper sickness. There wasn't anything wrong with me. There was wrong happening *to me*. There was sickness present in the body of our church silencing my and others' souls.

In taking our stress seriously, Ryan and I started to pay closer attention to the patterns of stress and shaming among the church staff and key leaders. Just as I faced the excruciating pain of autoimmune disease—where my own body attacks itself—we were slowly realizing we were in a body of believers afflicted with an autoimmune disease of arrogance and anxiety.

We couldn't silence our senses any longer. The body's health was at stake, and so was our own.

It turns out, sheep aren't so dumb after all. Researchers at Cambridge discovered that the brains of sheep are remarkably similar to ours.[6] They can even recognize familiar human voices and faces, even from photographs.[7] Maybe the sheep-shepherd metaphor isn't meant to make us feel small. Maybe rather than stoking self-contempt and mistrust of ourselves, the strong flock-instinct of sheep is meant to humble us over how interdependent—and vulnerable to each other's sense of scarcity and unsoothed stress—we are. Maybe we're like sheep who need a shepherd because there are so many predators both outside and within the church who will devour our vulnerability—wool, weakness, wounds, and all.

6. "Counting On Sheep," University of Cambridge, June 10, 2015, www.cam.ac.uk/research/features/counting-on-sheep.

7. K. M. Kendrick, "Sheep Senses, Social Cognition and Capacity for Consciousness," in *The Welfare of Sheep*, vol. 6, *Animal Welfare*, ed. Cathy Dwyer (Dordrecht, Netherlands: Springer, 2008), https://link.springer.com/content/pdf/10.1007/978-1-4020-8553-6_4.pdf; University of Cambridge, "Sheep Are Able to Recognize Human Faces from Photographs," Science Daily, November 8, 2017, www.sciencedaily.com/releases/2017/11/171108124220.htm.

The Shepherd leads those who listen, and if we are not listening carefully to the inner world of our sensations and emotions, we will be vulnerable to being led to the slaughter by both religious and political false shepherds whose aim is their own utility and adoration rather than our common good.

Courage is practicing listening to Christ even from within the stress in your own body—especially when your body is telling you something is wrong. And then stepping toward the true Good Shepherd based on what you hear, even if that means confronting and leaving the shepherds and systems you've always been taught deserve your loyalty.

8. BESIDE QUIET WATERS,

ON THE DAYS WHEN I AM MOST STRUGGLING to shift out of stress, I like to visit the Denver Botanic Gardens. Often, I'll end up at the very back, in the rock alpine garden, where a stone bench sits hidden under a scrubby pine tree next to a stream. I cocoon myself on the bench outside of everyone's view and let the melody of the brook bathe away my burdens.

In Psalm 23, David sings of a shepherd who leads us to quiet waters where our stress can be soothed and our thirst can be quenched. His song lifts our eyes to the landscape of our thirst, where only the Shepherd knows the way to the water we need. As Phillip Keller writes, the shepherd knows where the best watering spots are for the flock, and it is the shepherd who—usually at great personal cost and effort—provides places to drink.[1]

On the night Jesus was betrayed, before he walked the road to the cross and his death, he gathered his disciples around a table to break bread together in remembrance of God's deliverance of his

---

1. W. Phillip Keller, *A Shepherd Looks at Psalm 23* (Grand Rapids, MI: Zondervan, 2015), 38, Kindle.

people from Egypt. Before they feasted, Jesus took their feet in his hands, bending low before each disciple at the basin to wash away the dirt of the day.

In a time and place before paved roads, Nike sneakers, and hot showers, in a climate hot enough for sandals to be the standard footwear, it was typical to have fairly grimy feet and for servants to do the work of washing them before meals. Purity and cleanliness was incredibly important in Jewish culture.

So as Jesus bent low, Simon Peter bellowed in confusion, "Lord, are you going to wash *my* feet?"

"You do not realize what I am doing, but later you will understand," Jesus replied.

But Peter protested. "No! *You* shall never wash my feet!"

I imagine Jesus looking up with both gentleness and strength as he answered him, "Unless I wash you, you have no part with me."[2]

Like Peter, we expect a Shepherd who stands above us. We protest being seen and touched by God down to the dirt of our darkest thoughts and worst defeats. We walk away from being washed, preferring to keep our weakness and sense of unworthiness hidden behind smiles and outward success.

I'm writing this on Maundy Thursday, the day Christians remember that the true Shepherd bends down to the basin. When I was a girl, we'd observe Maundy Thursday in a circle of chairs at church, kneeling to wash each other's feet. In the quiet of the sanctuary, we'd encircle ourselves in the story of a God who is not above getting on the ground and touching the dirtiest parts of us.

Friends would wash the feet of friends. Grown men would stoop to wash the feet of elderly widows. Church elders would bend

---

2. John 13:6–8, paraphrased with emphases added.

to wash the feet of teenage kids from youth group. No stinky feet disqualified someone from being worthy of care. No foot left that sanctuary unwashed.

I remember my pastor, the same pastor who baptized me, kneeling down in front of me, asking if he could wash my feet. *My feet. Just unimportant, little kid me.* He slowly prayed out loud over my future while washing my tiny feet in his big hands.

In early adulthood, in a church and with a pastor much different than that of my childhood, as the scales of self-contempt about my sensitivity were falling from my eyes, I started noticing that our pastor never bent low. He had staff and volunteers to do that. The spiritual imagination of my childhood had been buried under the bravado of the church of shiny shepherding.

We just got home today from a vacation where we walked miles upon miles, and I just sank into the couch to put up my tired feet. Right now, I can almost feel my feet arching in remembrance of what it feels like to be held in a story where I am one for whom God bends down to the ground.

Other shepherds may have squashed our spiritual imagination into the flatness of feeling special to be in some shiny person's orbit, but our real Good Shepherd doesn't stand apart on stages. Our true Good Shepherd holds dirty feet in his God-hands and asks us to let him love us down to the dirt under our toenails.

Faith comes in letting God lead us lower than we expect or wish to wash us where we most need. Faith is finding that God delights in loving every part of me.

Unless we let God wash every part of us, we have no part with him. Unless we let Jesus be a servant, we cannot experience being his friend. In an age of pastors with green rooms, Maundy Thursday reshapes our spiritual imagination with a Shepherd who bends down to the ground.

Many early Christians carried out Christ's example of foot washing as part of the baptismal liturgy and sometimes even as baptism itself.[3] In the practices of the early church, we see Christ's humility and our holiness linked in the water of the foot-washing basin. Both the waters of the basin and baptism soak us in the story that says you are never too dirty or undignified to be welcomed by God.

Your body is composed of about 60 percent water. Your heart alone is made up of about 73 percent water and your lungs are about 83 percent.[4] When we don't have access to water, we become weak and eventually die. The human body can survive only a few days without water.[5]

We begin to feel our need for water through the sensation of thirst, reminding us we need something from outside of ourselves to keep us alive.[6]

Both the waters of baptism and the water composing the majority of our bodies remind us that we exist and thrive only in relationship to someone and something beyond us. Baptism is the birthplace of a belonging we cannot earn and must not hoard.

---

3. Ralph P. Martin, "Following in the First Christians' Footsteps," *Christian History*, www.christianitytoday.com/history/issues/issue-37/following-in-first-christians -footsteps.html; Mark Galli, "Washing Souls by Washing Feet," *Christian History*, www .christianitytoday.com/history/issues/issue-37/washing-souls-by-washing-feet.html.

4. "The Water in You: Water and the Human Body," USGS, www.usgs.gov/special -topic/water-science-school/science/water-you-water-and-human-body?qt-science _center_objects=0#qt-science_center_objects.

5. Jon Johnson, "How Long You Can Live without Water," *Medical News Today*, May 14, 2019, www.medicalnewstoday.com/articles/325174#:~:text=The%20body%20 needs%20lots%20of,water%20for%20about%203%20days.

6. When I was writing this, I had forgotten to eat all day long, got all lightheaded, and was like, *Am I dying?* And then I realized, *Nope. I just forget I am a HUMAN BEING who has to eat food to live.* Kind of like that . . .

Jesus brought us to the water by bending low himself. He stooped down—by becoming human, by being baptized in a repentance he did not need, by giving his time and attention to those whom religious folks deemed as unworthy of belonging, by washing feet and blessing the meek. Then he climbed high, not onto a stage but to a cross, where he let his body descend to the lowest place, death itself. Our Shepherd leads us to living water at the greatest cost to himself.

If sheep are thirsty and are not led to clean, still water, they will "end up drinking from the polluted pot holes where they pick up such internal parasites as nematodes, liver flukes, or other disease germs."[7] Like sheep, our spiritual and emotional thirst for love and safety leads us to drink from water from wherever we can get it.

We've downed dismissal and called it faith. We've swung back communion cups of criticism for the very parts of us through which God chose to most reveal his love. In systems of scarcity, we learn to leave the most discouraged and doubting parts of ourselves outside our churches' and friendships' front doors. We aren't sure the Good Shepherd actually wants to be with us because we've barely experienced Christians in roles of authority welcoming any of our weaknesses and vulnerabilities.

Many of us in the American church barely know what it feels like to drink deep beside quiet waters, because we're too busy trying to keep up with our shepherds' and society's search for success. We've looked for love from people who prefer standing on stages to bending at basins. We so often hustle hard to "build the kingdom," when we're really just striving for a belonging that was already bestowed on us.

---

7. Keller, *Shepherd Looks at Psalm 23*, 38–39.

While religious people build barriers to belonging—demanding certainty where there is mystery and compliance where Scripture isn't black and white—baptism brings the bar for belonging remarkably low. Our belonging is less contingent on certainty of beliefs or conformity to religious norms than on being brought forward and blessed with water we couldn't obtain ourselves. Baptism brings us low, to waters that remind us we belong because we were born and we are loved because we exist.

Because Christ our Good Shepherd was willing to get into the rushing waters of death itself, his very presence is a pool in the raging river of our stress. His presence makes a place where we can bend down to drink without being drowned by our despair. We don't have to pretend away our pain or make ourselves more productive or perfect to belong.

Your anxiety and anger, fear and frustrations, and doubt and despair are signals to look to your Shepherd to quench your thirst. We don't have to drown our distress in spiritualized shame. Transformation into a person who experiences the Shepherd as near and kind happens by practicing a different posture toward the darkest parts of your self and story. Every anxious thought arises from a physiological need for safety. Every sorrow is a spot to be soothed.

It's only in bending down that we can drink. There is no place of danger or threat where Christ has not already gone before us, making a place to be refreshed and rise again. There is no mud of misery or loneliness or despair where Christ does not already stand, always guiding you into pristine, quiet streams of love.

We need to remember to let ourselves be led beside the quiet waters of our true and better baptism. In a world of judgment and self-protection, both the waters of baptism and the cost of the cross should be forming Christians into a posture of inclusion and kindness, starting with refusing to reject the hurting parts of our own selves. *Christians should be the people of belonging,* who so readily and repeatedly remember our baptism that we cannot forget we are loved. Love this abundant can't be hoarded.

Baptism births us into Jesus' story and its trajectory. In stress, we can remember with our whole, embodied selves that we have been placed inside a story where we matter, have a Father who is irrevocably pleased with us, and have been filled with a Spirit of courage and love.

Like Christ in his own baptism, death, and resurrection, we the baptized become people who bend low, because we have seen the miracle that nothing qualifies us to be loved and that it is sinking that makes a person rise. Baptism bathes us in humility and hope that even that which tries to drown us is but a motion in the movement of resurrection and that every time we dip into the darkness, there will be a Voice saying, *You are my Beloved.*[8] *You are mine.*

---

8. Alexander Schmemann similarly wrote, "A Christian of the past knew not only intellectually but with his entire being that through Baptism he was placed into a radically new relationship with all aspects of life and the 'world' itself . . . Baptism for him [gave] . . . a permanent sense of direction guiding him firmly throughout his entire existence." Alexander Schmemann, *Of Water and the Spirit: A Liturgical Study of Baptism* (Crestwood, NY: St. Vladimir's Seminary Press, 1974), 9.

9. HE REFRESHES MY SOUL.

IN THE BEGINNING, THERE WAS BREATH. The earth was empty. The darkness was deep. And One Wind pulsed over it all.

The Hebrew word for the Spirit of God or Breath of God that fluttered over the waters is *Ruach*. Let it linger on your lips: rooakh. Even saying it is participating in it, filling your lungs with breath.

This Wind, this Breath, is the same *Ruach* who has always whirled through the world to protect, strengthen, and shift God's people into life. This is the Wind who brought locusts on the land of Egypt,[1] carried quail from the sea to the Israelites in the wilderness,[2] filled Gideon with courage to rise up for Israel,[3] and departed from the self-serving shepherd King Saul.[4] The Breath protected Elijah from a wicked king and assured him with God's presence in the cave at Horeb when his heart felt torn in two.[5] This Wind has

---

1. Ex. 10:13.
2. Num. 11:31.
3. Judg. 6:34.
4. 1 Sam. 16:14.
5. 1 Kings 18:46; 19:11–12.

always been hovering over the hearts of God's people where we feel empty and void.[6]

Our life begins and ends with Breath. The word human is rooted in the Latin word *humus*, meaning earth or dirt. In the ancient Genesis story of our origins, we take shape as God stoops down to the dust of the earth to breathe us into being.[7] The first human became "a living being," a *nefesh*, when God's breath met dirt and soil and dust. We greet this world with breath and give it our last exhalation before we become dirt again.

When David sings that God refreshes his soul, he is evoking *this* primal image of God bent over his body with Breath. While the New International Version (NIV) that I have chosen to use for our chapter titles translates the beginning of Psalm 23:3 as "he refreshes my soul," Hebrew scholar Robert Alter translates it as "my life he brings back."[8] The NIV translates *nefesh* as "soul," but Alter says it more accurately means our "life breath."[9] Elsewhere, Alter stresses that the Hebrew Bible has no concept of a soul-body duality, urging us to resist reductionistic assumptions about what God is restoring.[10] The image of this verse, Alter says, "is of someone who has almost stopped breathing, and is revived, brought back to life."[11]

---

6. The Breath of God empowered the prophet Zechariah to speak hard words to God's people (2 Chron. 24:20), whispered truth to Job in his suffering (Job 4:15), and is the "new spirit" Ezekiel said God will place within us (Ezek. 11:19).

7. Gen. 2:7.

8. Robert Alter, *The Book of Psalms: A Translation with Commentary* (New York: Norton, 2007), 78.

9. Ibid.

10. Robert Alter, *The Hebrew Bible: A Translation with Commentary* (New York: Norton, 2019), xv.

11. Alter, *Book of Psalms*, 78.

The Shepherd doesn't just refresh your soul. The Shepherd seeks you where you are sinking—physiologically. The Hebrew word for refreshes in Psalm 23:3 is *shuv*. Translated literally, this phrase is "he brings me back."[12] *Shuv* means to return or even repent, and in the context of this verse, *the Shepherd is the one who repents* the lost or wounded sheep by seeking and returning them back to safety. This verse is asking us to expect to be sought by the Shepherd in our stress.

Learning about your stress states can help you see where the Shepherd wants to meet you. Deb Dana describes the autonomic nervous system as a ladder.[13] Take a second to picture the cobweb-covered giant ladder you've got stashed in your garage behind plastic bins of Christmas decorations and old clothes. Take it out and set it up in your mind. Your nervous system is like this ladder, with three main physiological states that you are continuously stepping up and down through. I love the ladder metaphor, because it gives us a practical picture of what climbing in courage with Christ can look like.

The top of the autonomic ladder roughly corresponds with the top of your body, where you are able to access the parts of you that make you most feel like yourself. When you are at the top of your autonomic ladder, you are able to access the regulating powers of your prefrontal cortex and are able to connect with yourself, others, and God through the capacity of your social engagement system.[14]

12. Kenneth E. Bailey, *The Good Shepherd: A Thousand-Year Journey from Psalm 23 to the New Testament* (Downers Grove, IL: IVP Academic, 2014), 44.

13. Deb Dana, *The Polyvagal Theory in Therapy: Engaging the Rhythm of Regulation*, Norton Series on Interpersonal Neurobiology (New York: Norton, 2018), 10. Dana's metaphor of a ladder is the best picture of the autonomic nervous system I can find. Many thanks to her for this incredible contribution to the field of therapy and process of regulation.

14. Remember when you held your hands on the sides of your face? That's the area of social engagement system, connecting your vagus nerve with your middle ear, the muscles of your smile, and your eyes.

This nervous system state is called the *ventral vagal state*, and with my clients and myself, I like to call this place *home*.

Imagine the last time you felt most like yourself. Picture the last moment you felt loved, seen, and satisfied. That is what it feels like to be in ventral vagal. This state is the home you were made to live in. Your ventral vagal state is the place you were made to return to at the end of each day, complete with a table for your soul, where each part of you has a place to eat, laugh, and be filled along with Christ.

But you were also made to leave the house, face hard things, go on adventures, and come back all in one piece. Imagine your autonomic ladder again. When your nervous system senses too many cues of danger, the vagal brake is released and you sink from the top of the ladder (ventral vagal) down a couple of rungs into a sympathetic nervous system state.

Now try to remember the last time you felt afraid, unsafe, or overwhelmed. Maybe it was when a car almost rear-ended you. Or perhaps it was while waiting for test results at your doctor's office. Maybe it was when you tried to share a painful part of your story with a church small group or friend. Recall how your body felt. Maybe your chest tightened and your heart raced. You might have felt breathless, and maybe your neck became tight and your shoulders crept up to your ears. This is a *sympathetic state*, and even recalling it is probably activating some similar sensations in your body right now. (Take a second to notice how that feels. And then feel free to take a deep breath with a long exhale too.) When we are in a sympathetic state, we feel anxiety or anger and the strong urge to protect ourselves from harm.

We slide down into a sympathetic state when something triggers our neuroception of danger, and while those triggers will be unique to you and your story, anything that brings up feelings of fear, distress, shame, or uncertainty can trigger the dysregulation of the sympathetic state. A neuroception of danger sinks us into sympathetic, alerting our adrenal glands to send out stress hormones like cortisol and adrenalin to mobilize us to fight or flee the danger we see. The heart beats in a blaze. Muscles brace themselves for impact. Senses become sharper. And our breath becomes rapid and shallow in an effort to quickly get oxygen-rich blood distributed to the body like an ambulance to an accident.

But when the danger feels too great, we drop. When our bodies feel flooded by the energy of being in a sympathetic state or when we instinctively sense extreme life-threat, the dorsal vagal nerve takes charge to shut many of our body's systems down in an effort to conserve energy to stay alive.[15] We sink to the bottom of the ladder, into the deep dysregulation of the *dorsal vagal state.* Similarly to how a possum plays dead when in danger, we collapse and freeze, numbing and disconnecting from the danger that seems like it could kill us.

When we feel trapped, as though we can't escape or withstand the danger or chaos coming our way, we're in dorsal. Like a turtle suddenly snapping its head into its shell until it's safe to be seen again, sometimes we shut down and shut everything and everyone else out to survive. In the presence of complex trauma, sometimes we also fawn.[16] At the bottom of the ladder, we often feel despair and dejection, as though we are unloved and unseen, cut off from love.

We go up and down the autonomic ladder to some extent every

---

15. Dana, *Polyvagal Theory,* 9.

16. Fawning involves shutting down our sense of our body's sensations to survive a chaotic and traumatizing relational environment. We essentially cut off our awareness of how overwhelmed we feel to keep the peace, which can lead to derealization and depersonalization symptoms of feeling like we are floating above our bodies or living in a fog. On the outside, we might seem like we are there, but inside we're split from ourselves. Fawning can also look like faking being fine without meaning to and focusing our energy so much on placating others' social cues that we become cut off from ourselves. Many of us sink into fawning without realizing it, and beginning to recognize our fawning behaviors can help us practice new ways of feeling safe without having to shut parts of ourselves down.

single day. The important thing to realize is that just like the ladder in your garage, the rungs of your autonomic ladder are there for a reason. You cannot jump from the bottom of the ladder to the top.

Sheep who get lost or wounded in the wilderness cannot rescue themselves. A sheep's only hope is that the Shepherd is coming to find it, bind up its wounds, and carry it home. "He (the good shepherd) *brings me back*," Bailey writes. "Unaided, the lost sheep cannot find its way home."[17]

The Shepherd doesn't expect you to suddenly not be a sheep. The Shepherd isn't asking you to pole-vault over your painful feelings so you can praise him faster. The same Shepherd who knit you together in your mother's womb and breathed the first human into being knows what your body needs to rise.

Two things bring us back home from the bottom of stress: breath and the attuned, compassionate presence of someone else.

The self-regulating power of our breath can gently activate the sympathetic state, helping our hearts and hands find the rungs of the ladder to rise. Likewise, the co-regulating presence of someone else who is grounded and gracious, whose nervous system is in ventral vagal, can serve like an arm reaching down the ladder to give us strength to find the rungs again. When we are at the very bottom of the ladder, our bodies *need* the co-regulating presence of another person to be able to rise.

When we relinquish a dualistic reading of Psalm 23:3, we begin to realize that the psalmist intuited what neuroscientists and therapists have been finding millennia later. We do not have—nor are we able—to jump from trauma to trust or from fear to faith. Rather,

---

17. Bailey, *Good Shepherd*, 45.

we have a Shepherd who finds us in our fear, breathes us back from breathlessness, and brings us back home.

Faith isn't jumping over our feelings and sensations. Faith is being found where we are sinking and choosing to climb with Christ back home.

We rise rung by rung.

In my many years of dealing with autoimmune disease that forces me to rest, I've become a bit more of a TV connoisseur than my younger and more pretentious self would have been proud of. A show I return to again and again is *The West Wing*. There's one scene I think about often, where a character named Josh is constantly feeling triggered at work after being shot in an assassination attempt on one of his coworkers. He's been hiding how hard it is, but eventually his boss, Leo, brings a trauma therapist in to help. When Josh comes out of his daylong session, Leo asks him how it went. After a long pause, Josh finally tells Leo about the darkness he's been experiencing. And instead of judging him, Leo tells Josh this story:

> This guy's walking down a street and he falls in a hole. The hole is so deep he can't get out. A doctor passes by and the guy shouts up, "Hey you! Can you help me out?" The doctor writes a prescription, throws it down in the hole, and moves on.
>
> Then a priest comes along and the guy shouts up, "Father, I'm down in this hole, can you help me out?" The priest writes out a prayer, throws it down in the hole, and moves on.
>
> Then a friend walks by: "Hey, Joe, it's me. Can you help me out?" And the friend jumps in the hole. And our guy says, "Are you stupid? Now we're both down here!" And the friend says, "Yeah, but I've been down here before and I know the way out."

When we descend to the dark regions of fear and despair in our nervous systems, we are descending to a place Christ has already gone. He comes all the way down to the bottom with us because he has already been down there and he knows how to rise.

When we were realizing just how stuck in stress we were in our church, when the lack of safety in our relationships was sinking us to the bottom of the ladder, we were still not outside the reach of Christ's staff. We were still on ground where Christ had already walked.

Your distress is an invitation to descend to the place where Christ has already gone through his baptism and death, ready to reanimate you with Breath.

There is a Shepherd coming to refresh your soul—to *repent* you (*shuv*), to find you and carry you home.

Repentance isn't something we reach for. Repentance is first a practice of descending with the Good Shepherd to seek and find the stressed, scared, and scorned parts of our souls.

Repentance begins in being found by Christ on the bottom of the ladder, in our darkest states of dysregulation, and it is his friendship that regulates us to rise. Day after day, descending with Jesus, we will begin to anticipate being able to climb.

Redemption is God's great gathering up of every distressed, dismissed, and despairing part of you to bring you safely home.

So don't be afraid to go low.

We rise from the bottom.

10. HE GUIDES ME

THE CLASSIC ARMENIAN TRANSLATION from the fifth century for this section of Psalm 23 reads, "He brings me back from the wrong path to the right path."[1] My experience is that when it comes to our souls, we often don't realize we are on the wrong path. We too often live anesthetized to the inner anguish that is trying to tell us we are stuck in states and systems of stress.

Last week my friend Sam told me about a book he recently read about the emergence of fascism in Germany titled *They Thought They Were Free*. Sam was struck by how the book demonstrated that average Germans—people just like us—became enslaved to Nazi ideals because those ideals assuaged the people's heightened sense of scarcity.[2]

In the wake of the First World War, fear of scarcity sat as a nightly guest at most dinner tables across Germany. Citizens faced skyrocketing unemployment rates, poverty, political unrest, and no clear way into a better future. The Nazi Party spoke to those fears and longings while exploiting them to win party loyalty.

---

1. Kenneth E. Bailey, *The Good Shepherd: A Thousand-Year Journey from Psalm 23 to the New Testament* (Downers Grove, IL: IVP Academic, 2014), 44.

2. Milton Mayer, *They Thought They Were Free: The Germans, 1933–45* (Chicago: Univ. of Chicago Press, 2017).

They didn't broadcast their more extreme goals of racial extinction at first. Instead, the Nazi Party soothed the people's sense of scarcity without promising any plan for delivering a better life for every German. They spotlighted the scarcity Germans were experiencing, while building a racialized myth of meritocracy. In *Caste*, Isabel Wilkerson says that perceived scarcity is what upholds our American system of racialized subjugation too.[3]

Perceived scarcity serves like the rungs of a different ladder where we have to keep climbing over others to get to the top. We attempt to self-regulate by striving and subjugating anyone and anything that gets in our way on the path to the top.

This is how evil gets us. Our sense of scarcity is spoken to and enlisted in the battle for a better life. Our discouragement gets deployed in the service of evil's schemes to keep humanity defeated. Our longings and loves get exploited in an army that annexes someone else's power and prestige. We keep believing that supporting this pastor or that politician or buying another product will finally give us the life of freedom and joy they all promised, but it never happens.

Our sense of scarcity is only getting addressed and anesthetized—and often amplified—rather than truly soothed. As such, we become stuck in cycles of stress, reflexively giving away the votes of our attention and affection to people, places, and things that give us a temporary hit of relief without ever truly soothing our souls.

Just as my therapist began helping me honor my sensitivity, Ryan and I started traveling to Southern California every four months for a soul care intensive with other pastors and spouses within the same

---

3. Isabel Wilkerson, *Caste: The Origins of Our Discontents* (New York: Random House, 2020), 183, 289.

church planting network. Two weathered old men guided us from the front of the room, perched on stools while talking slow and telling stories of the stormy, good path of being known by God. They led us in rhythms of relationship, giving us homework to practice spiritual disciplines like centering prayer and the examen.

Praying the examen alone, we each dared to ask questions that had felt easier to leave unasked. I knew deep inside that asking would require action. We probed the space between what we believed about our community and values and what we were actually experiencing.

We started to see how our scarcity in feeling unseen and underappreciated was dangled in front of us to keep us performing, always looking for the next pat on the back but never feeling fully loved. We formed words around the wounds of being diminished or hearing others be yelled at by our pastor or being demanded to do more. We felt the ache of how we were being made small.

Praying our aches awakened our ears to hear God calling us better names than we had heard in years. We were waking up to the wonder of being loved by God and wiping away the crust of sleep from our eyes to see that most of our staff and congregation were living lulled to sleep by pride.

In the stillness of centering prayer, we started unlearning our habits of hustling to be loved by God. Day by day in the quiet of our apartment, we held cups of coffee and started to feel held by a God who actually wants to know us and spend time with us. With the sun streaming through our windows, we started to soak in the gaze of the God who loves us not for how we can serve but for who we already are.

We were taking an exit ramp off the highway of hustling to sit still in the field of fellowship with God, and it changed our lives. God guides us from the wrong path to the right one by leading us *through* the wilderness within ourselves.

Instead of sheltering ourselves from it or silencing the noise out of fear, we were sensing the storm of scarcity inside us for what felt like the first time in our lives, and it was making us indignant and strong.

Back when I was still a dream in the space between my parents' hearts, some scientists dreamed up an experiment to re-create the optimal conditions of earth for space.[4] After years of research and planning, in 1986 they started constructing an elaborate biodome in the Sonoran Desert outside of Tucson, Arizona, in the hope of creating the technologies humans would need to survive in space if and when earth can't be made great again.

By the time that little dream of me was walking and talking, eight brave souls had pledged to live inside Biosphere 2 for at least two years to test the viability of the experiment.[5] Halfway through the first year, the experiment almost failed when the oxygen levels inside the biosphere dropped so low the humans inside required more to survive. In 1994, when they resumed the habitation experiment, it came to a crashing halt again after just six months when a combination of mismanagement and crew members sabotaging each other threatened safety.

One might call that a failure, but John Adams, a deputy director of Biosphere 2 saw it differently. Reflecting on those researchers, he remarked, "What they did learn, and in my opinion the single most important lesson, was just how little we truly understand Earth's

---

4. "About Biosphere 2," University of Arizona, https://biosphere2.org/about/about -biosphere-2.

5. Cole Mellino, "The World's Largest Earth Science Experiment: Biosphere 2," EcoWatch, October 16, 2015, www.ecowatch.com/the-worlds-largest-earth-science -experiment-biosphere-2-1882107636.html.

systems."[6] It's as true of the world all around us as it is of the world within ourselves.

One story that's been widely attributed to the Biosphere 2 experiment pertains to trees.[7] The biosphere was outfitted to reflect earth's biodiversity, with climates and landscapes ranging from desert to rainforest. With such pristine conditions, the trees inside the biosphere grew quickly. But they kept falling over before they reached reproductive age. From soil to sun, it seemed like the trees had everything they needed to grow strong. But the one condition that could not be recreated in the perfectly controlled environment of the biosphere was wind.

Without gentle breezes or strong storms, the trees could not develop deep roots. The wood within them was too soft, much softer than any species of tree would be in the wild. The trees grew fast, but the speed and lack of resistance ended up being their downfall.

As I write this, I'm facing a forest of subalpine fir and limber pine dotting a rolling hill in front of the Sangre de Cristo mountains. The woody scent of their resins is filling me with warmth. These pines are a picture of resilience. They tower because they have endured season upon season of storms.

How often in our communities and families and churches do we attempt to quickly create the perfect biosphere of the body of Christ? Like the biodome, we put up panes of high-performance glass and frame ourselves in with the strongest steel to build a life insulated from suffering and impervious to scarcity. Our churches

---

6. Ibid.

7. I came across this story in the Sources of Strength Training Manual, though it is told anecdotally on blogs all over the internet. Scott LoMurray, *Sources of Strength Training Manual* (Lakewood, CO: Sources of Strength, 2020), 68.

raise millions of dollars for stunning buildings while the building of our bodies burns out from overfunctioning to make God's name great. We order our lives around the image of perfection and progress, not realizing that wind and storms are what turn us from sapling to strong.

How do we reckon with the reality that the trees of our lives are falling over in our communities? In the 1950s, social psychologist Leon Festinger suggested the theory of cognitive dissonance to describe the discomfort we experience when we face a conflict between what we believe about who we are and what we actually do.[8] Cognitive dissonance is what we experience when our self-concept of being kind and wise is threatened by the fact that we have done something that hurt others or led to harm.

When our belief in our own health or goodness—or the goodness of the community of which we are a part—is endangered by the evidence of something contrary, the discomfort often leads us to dismiss the evidence,[9] defend the behavior, or dismantle our self-concept by shaming ourselves.

We have a neural bias to rationalize bad behavior to reduce discomfort,[10] which serves like an anesthetic against the pain of seeing ourselves or our communities as having less health than we believed. But like any narcotic, dampening pain does nothing to treat the disease causing it.

We also feel the discomfort of cognitive dissonance when we try to hold two opposing truths at the same time. Often, our beliefs about God stand in opposition to each other. How can God be

---

8. Leon Festinger, Henry W. Riecken, and Stanley Schachter, *When Prophecy Fails: A Social and Psychological Study of a Modern Group That Predicted the Destruction of the World* (New York: Harper and Row, 1956).

9. Which often looks like blaming or gaslighting the other party.

10. Johanna M. Jarcho, Elliot T. Berkman, and Matthew D. Lieberman, "The Neural Basis of Rationalization: Cognitive Dissonance Reduction during Decision-Making," *Social Cognitive and Affective Neuroscience* 6, no. 4 (September 2011): 460–67, https://doi.org/10.1093/scan/nsq054.

just *and* kind? Our drive to eliminate the discomfort of dissonance is strong. We end up spending the energy of our faith dismissing evidence that seems contrary to God's goodness or defending the goodness of the one who needs no defense.

Dodging dissonance keeps us from the hard and necessary task of becoming both tall *and* strong. Instead of sheltering ourselves from the storms of dissonance, we need to practice welcoming their fierce truth. What if we have been building a biosphere to protect our beliefs when what we needed was wind all along?

Wind, the *ruach* of God, is what welcomed this world into existence. "If we wish to understand the Old Testament word *ruach*, we must forget the word 'spirit' which belongs to Western culture," theologian Jürgen Moltmann writes. "If we talk in Hebrew about Yahweh's *ruach*, we are saying: God is a tempest, a storm, a force in body and soul, humanity and nature."[11] The same Wind who was present at the precipice of creation is still blowing through the wilderness of our lives, shaking us into strength.

A hummingbird just buzzed over my computer and hovered by my side, a visual reminder clothed in pink and purple that we can be disrupted into delight. In the distance, the pine trees are gently swaying in the wind, like a slow dance of recognition for the real pattern of resilience.

The harder the wind blows, the deeper our roots grow. Resistance is part of resilience.

Storms are what will make you strong. Storms are a symphony with a song: *Dare to be disturbed.*

Discomfort and dissonance can disrupt us into life. The Good

---

11. Jürgen Moltmann, *The Spirit of Life: A Universal Affirmation* (Minneapolis: Fortress, 2001), 40.

Shepherd guides us out of the places where predators costumed as shepherds prey on our goodness and, as the prophet Ezekiel wrote, make us into food to feed themselves.[12] If you don't feel free, if you don't feel joy, if you don't feel seen and heard and known, dare to be disturbed.

Let yourself be startled out of the narcotic narrative of having to do good things for God to be loved by God. Let the wind sweep away the story that you have to put up with hurt to be part of a community. There is a whisper in the Wind telling you that you are already loved and valuable and worthy of belonging just as you are. Do not silence the storm of sensing the wrongness of all the shepherds and systems that try to tell you otherwise.

God speaks in the storm of the internal signals of our souls that tell us something is off, unjust, and dissonant. God guides us in our anger. God leads us in our anguish. And sometimes God shatters our comfortable certainties with a storm to shake us out of being silenced and small. God is too kind to keep us from growing tall.

Witness grace in the gale. Let the storms of suffering and stress strip away your dead branches and move you into a new story. The Spirit still hovers and howls like wind over water, and what seems like chaos might be creation.

Welcome the wind.

---

12. Ezekiel 34.

11. ALONG THE
RIGHT PATHS

THE WILDERNESS IN ISRAEL is crisscrossed by faint tracks that flocks of sheep have made over centuries. Only the shepherd knows which paths lead to good grazing land or back home, rather than the edge of a cliff or some dangerous detour.[1] On a yearlong research trip in Israel observing shepherds and their flocks, theologian Timothy Laniak noticed the "curious behavior of sheep" that when "one picks a trail, the rest simply follow the *tail* in front of them without regard for their destination."[2]

How often do we follow another sheep who calls themselves a shepherd without pausing to consider whether we're on the right path?

Theologically, the "right paths" of Psalm 23:3 are the paths that reflect the righteousness of God.[3] God who is Father, Son, and Spirit exists in the continuous communion of relationship. The right paths will always reflect who God is. And God showed us

1. Kenneth E. Bailey, *The Good Shepherd: A Thousand-Year Journey from Psalm 23 to the New Testament* (Downers Grove, IL: IVP Academic, 2014), 46.

2. Timothy Laniak, *While Shepherds Watch Their Flocks: Forty Daily Reflections on Biblical Leadership* (Franklin, TN: Carpenter's Son Publishing, 2007), 201.

3. Bailey, *Good Shepherd*, 46.

the face of divinity in Jesus Christ, the Good Shepherd who took time to walk and talk with his disciples, blessed little children, bent before the sick to help them, and, finally, sacrificed his own life for his sheep. The righteous paths will be those that lead us in relationships that reflect Christ's kindness and courage.

Over that next summer, our church's elders solicited anonymous feedback from the staff about the lead pastor and his co-pastor. People started to get honest about how discouraged they were. Many felt overworked, bullied, and pushed down by the lead pastor. And in the freedom of an anonymous feedback form, they were daring to be honest about it and maybe even a little hopeful for change. (Instead of continuing to act like everything was fine.) After a whole year of quiet prayer and discernment, I remember my husband being so encouraged that the elders were finally getting an accurate picture of what it was like to work at the church.

After a couple of months, the elders eventually brought the pastors and staff together to debrief the results of the feedback. The lead pastor was given the floor.[4] "None of this would have become a problem if you all would have just been direct with me!" he blasted.

I ran my counseling practice upstairs in the church offices. I was in session during their staff meeting and could hear his voice booming below through the floor vent. My client looked at me quizzically, and I just shrugged my shoulders like it was no big deal. We were so used to minimizing his anger that the excuses came easily. "He just gets passionate sometimes." My body and my mouth both knew the party line by heart. I was used to hearing him yell in the office at least multiple times a month, but the subsequent silence downstairs told me something was going terribly wrong.

God guides us along the right paths for the glory of *God's* name—not the glory of the name of a pastor, church, politician, or powerful person—*God's* glory.

We were so disturbed by the way our pastor refused to hear the feedback on the ways he was hurting our staff. Their honesty was met with more harm, with the pastor shaming the staff as though they were responsible for his rage and controlling. Through the dissonance of how our pastor dodged feedback and repentance and then how the elders enabled his behavior, God was stirring up a storm in us to become strong. God was waking us up to the wind of our weariness to keep accepting the status quo. Like the trees in the biosphere, we wanted to grow fast and tall in the church's climb to be amazing. But the ways we were being subtly belittled, shamed, and mocked at church had made our roots shriveled and small.

Our good and our growth were clearly not as important as our pastor's thirst for glory.

When nothing changed after that elder feedback process ended in a tantrum, except that work became even more tense and stressful, we spent evening after evening processing with our friends Josh and Rachel how confused and concerned we felt. Josh worked alongside Ryan as the church's small groups director, and he felt just as crushed by our pastor's domineering personality and behavior as we did.

From our coworkers to people in the congregation to ourselves, too many people were being crushed by our pastor's ego. And in our shared lament, God was waking us up to the wonder of true belonging. Together, we decided we could no longer stay compliant and small.

Like most thirtysomething white ladies in America right now, I have an obsession with plants. I don't have a yard of my own, but I do have a garden of green in every corner of my apartment that's kissed by the sun. Last month I repotted all of my plants—a long overdue chore that I knew had to happen unless I wanted to confirm my husband's theory that I am actually a plant killer in disguise. I spread out my plants on our kitchen table beside a yellow bag of potting soil and a stack of new, larger terra-cotta pots for my semineglected plant babies.

It wasn't until the dirt got under every last fingernail that I realized:

What we call unruly and disruptive is often just a plant looking to be healthy, needing a bigger pot.

My husband, friends, and I were labeled disruptive for daring to be healthy. The more time we spent absorbing the kindness of God in contemplative prayer and each other's company, the more we all sensed that we needed more relational space and safety to thrive. Our roots were rotting in the relational soil of our church system. The path that church was on—of wanting to be a personality-centric megachurch—didn't lead to the destination of flourishing.

Josh was the first of us to be courageous enough with his calling to name that he had outgrown the small, stifling pot of our church. After years of being told *someday* and *maybe* and *once you're older*, Josh emailed the church's staff and elders to ask for prayer about his desire to explore planting a new church. His email was winsome and well within the scope of the DNA of the church and its network. (We were supposed to be churches that plant churches, after all!) But we soon learned that naming the desire to grow or seek health wasn't safe at all.

When you've been following the flock for so long, it can take a lot to get you to consider changing course. When your livelihood, community, and sense of self center on a particular Christian community, it feels like losing part of yourself to even consider that you might need to leave. Sometimes it takes seeing something so starkly wrong, you can't deny what you're sensing is wrong anymore.

Ours was a church of choreographed perfection. The worship band was tight. The announcements were short. And the sermons were meaty and long. Mistakes simply didn't happen. But the Sunday three days after Josh sent his email, they did.

As the band started to lead the congregation in song, the amps cut out. High-pitched noise scratched across the sanctuary like nails on chalkboard. Everyone was looking around in confusion—remember, we were not used to electronic feedback, or any imperfection in the worship service for that matter. The band finished most of their set acoustic, and when the amps finally powered back on, the congregation cheered.

I often struggle to sit still through a whole church service because of my arthritic joints, especially services of the frozen chosen variety.[5] My joints are like kids on a road trip begging their parents to know when all the sitting will be over. I had just slumped down on the floor behind rows of chairs to roll out my hands and ankles and shimmy my stiff spine when the pastor started to preach. He beamed while making a joke about how the mics were working now that it was time for *him* to preach the Word of God. He was barely a paragraph into his sermon before a sound like the screeching of a horde of furious mermaids filled the sanctuary again.

---

5. White Reformed folks aren't exactly comfortable moving the bodies God gave them. That's all I'm saying.

From my shoulders to my toes, I tensed at the sound, but also from something more than the sound. My whole body shifted forward in apprehension, like the eerie moments before a tornado touches the ground. It was a sermon about loving one another, supposedly an exposition of a passage in 1 Peter, but somehow the pastor had decided to center his entire sermon on people being envious of their leader's power. I knotted my face in confusion as he started to condemn anyone who confronts their leader or who want to serve in bigger, bolder ways, as though they were only out to take what was his. Then he compared himself to Jesus, like he was being persecuted.

At first I was stunned—shocked into immobility. I scanned the room to see if anyone else was disturbed or seemed to get what he was indicating. I tried to talk myself down from alarm. *No. Surely he's not talking about us and Josh? No way.* But the longer I listened, the more it stung; we were getting a spanking in the form of a sermon.

Months later, we had an abuse expert independently review the sermon, because when you hear things like this but no one else speaks up, you start to feel like you are crazy. After reviewing the sermon, the expert agreed with our sobering interpretation.

The moment after someone speaks up about experiencing any kind of harm or pain in our church communities reveals much about the path our whole flock is following.[6] Similarly, the way leaders and

---

6. As Scot McKnight and Laura Barringer write in *A Church Called Tov*, "When an allegation arises against a pastor, a leader, or a volunteer within a church, what the pastor or leadership does *first* will reveal the culture of the church—whether it is toxic or *tov*." Scot McKnight and Laura Barringer, *A Church Called Tov: Forming a Goodness Culture That Resists Abuses of Power and Promotes Healing* (Carol Stream, IL: Tyndale Momentum, 2020), 41.

pastors react or respond to someone's vocational longings reveals whether they are operating from a place of scarcity or stewardship.

A church might use righteous-sounding words to describe their mission while leading people down unrighteous paths that are rutted with a lack of relational integrity and safety. "We must not assume that our family, church, community, country, or organization is always right just because the people in it use the right words," psychologist Diane Langberg reminds us.[7]

There are no righteous ends that come by unrighteous means. Deception can be dazzling, and like Eugene Peterson warns, it is "nowhere more common than in religion. And the persons most easily and damningly deceived are the leaders."[8] Like Peterson says, the devil's typical strategy of deception doesn't look undoubtedly evil. Rather, the devil deceives with "an apparent good."[9] We might see the flash of a growing church, a great worship band, or a powerful preacher and assume we have found the place where God's kingdom is palpable.[10] But what is the path people in the church must walk to produce such shine?

The right paths of Psalm 23 will be rutted with a righteousness that looks like Christ's, who did not hoard his power or feel the need to defend it at all costs but gave it up freely for the good of all. The Good Shepherd is the shepherd whose calling card was being interruptible and welcoming of both hard questions and people

---

7. Diane Langberg, *Redeeming Power: Understanding Authority and Abuse in the Church* (Grand Rapids, MI: Brazos, 2020), 87.

8. Eugene Peterson, *Under the Unpredictable Plant: An Exploration in Vocational Holiness* (Grand Rapids, MI: Eerdmans, 1994), 14.

9. Peterson continues with a haunting warning: "The commonest forms of devil-inspired worship do not take place furtively at black masses with decapitated cats but flourish under the bright lights of acclaim and glory, in a swirl of organ music." Ibid., 15.

10. These aren't the only things that dazzle, and what dazzles will be a matter of personal preference. The dazzle of some churches might look simpler than these examples: Our own version of sound theology. Certain gender or sexuality stances. Being part of an aeons-long tradition. The list is long.

religious folks called questionable. Both his sermons and the blood that poured from his side overflowed to empower those with less power.

Whether or not the wounding and weariness in your life has come from a church, it is worth pausing to consider what path you have been following. Is it a path of hustle and hurry or quiet hope? Is it a path of crafting the right image or cultivating intimacy?

Like a sudden storm stops you in your tracks, for us that sermon served as a startling pause. Even though a hurricane had been brewing for some time, we were now standing in its eye.

12. FOR HIS
NAME'S SAKE.

WHAT IS THE CHIEF END OF MAN?" Pastor Jim asked.

I smiled proudly at the other eleven- and twelve-year-olds at my side before we all answered in unison, "Man's chief end is to glorify God, and to enjoy him forever."[1]

I grew up catechized by the Westminster Confession of Faith, and my whole life has been shaped and steered by that answer.

But somewhere along the way, I internalized an expectation that glorifying God meant glorifying those who preach about God as well as the local church who is God's body on earth. God's glory and my joy became bound to pleasing and esteeming my pastors and church.

When David sings that Yahweh is his shepherd who leads him along the right paths for his name's sake, he is finding hope and joy in this fact: a shepherd's good name is tied to their commitment to care for their sheep. God "is a *good* shepherd, and a good shepherd *does not* lose his sheep."[2]

---

1. Westminster Confession of Faith, Shorter Catechism, https://prts.edu/wp-content/uploads/2016/12/Shorter_Catechism.pdf.

2. Kenneth E. Bailey, *The Good Shepherd: A Thousand-Year Journey from Psalm 23 to the New Testament* (Downers Grove, IL: IVP Academic, 2014), 46.

I don't know your story, but my own story tells me that when a shepherding figure's reputation is at stake, all too many choose to keep their good name by leaving their hurt and wounded sheep behind.

After we finished our church duties on the Sunday we heard the Sermon from the Pit of Hell™, we walked out to the parking lot and got into our car, where we started getting really bitchy with each other.

After dishing out a few choice jabs, I paused.

"Wait. *Why* are we mad at each other?" I asked. "This doesn't make any sense."

My husband shook his head in agreement. (He's a man of few words.)

"Were you disturbed by what he just preached?"

"Completely," Ryan said. "I think he was talking about *all* of us. And I'm pretty sure he's about to hurt Josh."

We had no idea what that would look like—and the thought was jarring—but in our bodies, we knew something was coming. Pádraig Ó Tuama has spoken to this inner knowing, writing, "When we are in a moment of courage—whether we call that God's voice, or indigenous bravery—it is the body that tells us a deep truth; it is the body that speaks to us, and it is from the body that courage comes."[3]

Only a few seconds of silent shock elapsed before Ryan's courage welled up and he reached for his phone to warn Josh.

"Josh, did you hear the sermon today?" Ryan asked. From the other end, I could hear Josh saying he had been outside volunteering

---

3. Pádraig Ó Tuama, *In the Shelter: Finding a Home in the World* (London: Hodder and Stoughton, 2016), 51.

FOR HIS NAME'S SAKE.

at the welcoming table during the sermon, so he didn't hear it. "I don't know what he is going to do. Maybe yell at you? Maybe fire you? But that sermon felt like a threat to both me and KJ. *Be careful.*"

We felt crazy for warning Josh like that, for even considering that *our pastor* was about to intentionally hurt our friend. But we knew what we had heard. We loved Josh too much to dismiss how disturbed we felt.

While Josh was drinking his coffee the next morning, he got a text from our pastor asking to meet up. In a coffee shop just down the street from the church offices, while people sipped their lattes and laughed at tables nearby, our pastor laid into Josh. Later, Josh told us that as the pastor started to talk, his neck became swollen, with veins visibly popping out of his skin, and the longer he talked, his eyes began twitching. He ended up cussing at Josh with words my publisher would never let me put in this book.

For wanting to explore planting a church. For continuing to address the pastor's bullying, angry, domineering behavior, even though the elders and most of the other staff had just let it go. For wanting shepherding to be more than exercising power over people.

I'll never be more proud of Josh than I am for what he did next.

Josh stood up, told the pastor he was not allowed to speak to him that way, got on his bike, and rode away.

Boundaries often piss off people who benefit from you having none.

We do not know what happened behind the scenes after Josh notified the elders of how he was wronged, whether they tried to get the pastor to deeply repent, apologize, and do the work of repairing the relationship. But we know what they decided. By the next day, even though Josh was the one who was cussed out, the elder board demanded that he "reconcile" with the pastor or pack up his things and be out of the office for good by the end of the week.

While Josh would have explored reconciliation had our pastor owned what he did and attempted a profound and slow relational repair, the burden of reconciliation was placed on the person whose trust and safety were ruptured by someone with extensively more power. No one in a shepherding role went after the sheep who was bloodied.

Josh went home to his wife, Rachel, and their six-month-old baby girl and never stepped foot in that church again.

It's strange how a system can demand "reconciliation" from someone who has been harmed, yet demand no restitution from the person doing the harming. In the wake of a profound relational wound, instead of courage we often see collapse and more complicity in our leaders and bystanders.

There is no reconciliation without repentance. There is no peace without justice. Christian leaders might like the word reconciliation, but few tend to own the work that it involves. It is an abomination that reconciliation has become a weapon in the hands of leaders who would rather guard an institution's power than their most vulnerable people.

Sometimes faith is a shelter, and sometimes it becomes a storm.[4] The stories we tell about our storms and stress reveal what we most wish to keep in the shadows.

When the pressure of our shame, fear, and anger do not find safe harbor in connection, they must find a place to go. Pain cannot

---

4. These are an echo of Pádraig Ó Tuama's beautiful words: "Faith shelters some, and it shadows others. It loosens some, and it binds others." Ó Tuama, *In the Shelter*, 11.

stay stuck inside. Stress is a cycle that needs completion. And when it does not find it, it becomes a cyclone.

A cyclone grows into a hurricane as the emptiness at the center of the storm gets amplified. That emptiness acts like fuel that feeds more energy into the storm. Bands of rain spiral around the eye of the storm as the moisture from warm water gets converted into heat. Air gets sucked into the eye, where, in rapid succession, it rises, condenses, cools, and then releases more heat into the atmosphere. All of the energy around a storm system gets gathered up to feed the emptiness at the center of the cyclone. This is how a hurricane forms.[5]

The cyclone of our needs for love and belonging and safety—when unmet—can create an emptiness at the center of our relationships that grasps the energy of everyone else's goodness and insecurity to fill the void inside. When we live in the enemy mode of the sympathetic nervous system state, we make the lives around us a silent storm. The cyclone of our unsoothed cries to be loved can end up becoming a hurricane of hustling and then hiding any evidence that we're part of a system that leaves destruction in our wake.[6]

In hindsight, I can see that the hurricane that tore through our lives in that season was the brewing storm of hidden and unhealed pain in both our pastor and community. Priest and beloved author Henri Nouwen put it like this: "When the members of a community of faith cannot truly know and love their shepherd, shepherding

5. Ocean Tides, "Barometric Pressure and Hurricanes," Sciencing, May 14, 2018, https://sciencing.com/barometric-pressure-hurricanes-22734.html.

6. Family systems theory shows us that most people prefer to maintain homeostasis in their relationships, even if the homeostasis is hurting people. The anxiety of having to address harm often feels too distressing for the nervous systems of those in the system. It is much more calming in the short run to engage in amnesia, trying to move on and forget the harm that just happened. In the long run, our amnesia ends up enabling cycles of harm to continue. Sharie Stines, "Abuse Amnesia: Why We Stay with Our Abusive Partners," *Good Therapy*, October 3, 2017. www.goodtherapy.org/blog/abuse-amnesia-why-we-stay-with-our-abusive-partners-1003175#:~:text=Once%20the%20chaotic%20encounter%20between,at%20a%20state%20of%20equilibrium.&text=Thus%2C%20a%20person%20who%20is,on%E2%80%9D%20and%20feel%20good%20again.

quickly becomes a subtle way of exercising power over others and begins to show authoritarian and dictatorial traits."[7] In the expanding energy of that emptiness, ours and the elders' unmet longings for love were sucked into the center of our church system's storm.

I do not hate our former pastor. I hate how he demeaned us. I hate how his volatility created an environment where our nervous systems learned to live in fear and constant stress. I hate how he demanded perfection out of people who were doing their best. I hate how burnt out and beleaguered so many volunteers became in his orbit. I hate how he subtly used the pulpit as punishment. I hate how he mocked his co-pastor around the office and to his face. I hate how he shamed those who didn't agree with his ideas or theology. I hate how so many people, myself included, got sucked into a system that said it was about making Jesus' name great but actually made us more anxious about our own greatness and belonging. I hate that he gave us a picture of a pastor, a shepherd of God's people, that reinforced an image of God as punitive, demanding, detached, and unkind.

I hate that the good desires of shepherds and sheep to "build God's kingdom" can get sucked into the storm of insecurities, unresolved shame and trauma, and constant stress so much so that what we end up building isn't God's kingdom at all.

I hate that people who call themselves shepherds like Jesus can have so much hiding in the shadows of their souls and our church systems that their fear of losing the image of goodness they've so meticulously crafted prompts them to leave God's beloved sheep behind.

I do not hate our former pastor. My heart breaks for him. Because now I know, the only wounds that become weapons are the wounds that are not tended with care.

---

7. Henri Nouwen, *In the Name of Jesus: Reflections on Christian Leadership* (New York: Crossroad, 1994), 44.

Interestingly, the good shepherd doesn't defend his reputation by exiling the lost sheep or shaming it but *by finding it*.[8] Biblical Aramaic translator and scholar George Lamsa, who grew up living on the land that is the backdrop of both Psalm 23 and Jesus' life, describes the shepherd of Psalm 23 as exceedingly loving. He writes, "The shepherd is very careful about the paths, because he loves the sheep, and for his own name's sake *he would do anything to prevent accidents and attacks by animals.* He has to keep his reputation as a good shepherd."[9]

The Good Shepherd's good name is inextricable from his willingness to lay down his life for his sheep.[10] It turns out there is no glory for the Shepherd apart from caring for you and finding you. No matter what.

God is not a storm that gathers up all of your energy to fill the emptiness in himself.

God is a Shepherd whose glory is bound up with your good.

---

8. See Luke 15:1–7.

9. George Lamsa, *The Shepherd of All: The Twenty-Third Psalm* (Amazon Direct Publishing, 2014), 36, Kindle. Emphasis added.

10. John 10:11.

BROKEN

It takes outrageous courage to face outrageous loss.
This is precisely what we are being called to do.
Any loss, whether deeply personal or one of those
that swirl around us in the wider world, calls us to
full-heartedness, for that is the meaning of courage.
—Francis Weller

Why is it so powerful to say that God was
on the cross in Jesus Christ? Just what is the
power of the cross? It's not about valorizing
trauma, which the church has too often done,
but actually about exposing trauma.
—Serene Jones

13. EVEN THOUGH

IT'S NOT MY GOAL IN THIS BOOK to share everything that unfolded in that season of our lives, all the conversations we had and ways we were crushed—there's a lot more goodness to share with you than *that*. But I want to affirm the cost of courage. I want to attest that even though courage may cost you everything, it will ultimately give you more.

Courage is choosing to let your life match your worth. And to God, your worth is infinite. Belovedness is your birthright. Wholeness is the aim of a person who is practicing the willingness to let every part of their body, story, and life align with the truth of how beloved they are.

The man who wrote Psalm 23 knew the cost of courage. David was pushed out of his place in the community of Israel by a king who feared losing authority and admiration so much he became violent. David had to flee to the wilderness for years to protect his own well-being and life, and often, we do too.

You might be looking at your life and wondering what shadowed valleys of darkness might be ahead: the relationships you might lose, the loneliness you might have to bear, the boundaries that will be searing to set, or the suffering that never seems to quit. The promise of Psalm 23 is that even though you will walk this wilderness way, there is one walking with you who is more committed to your wholeness than even you are. All God asks is that we follow.

In the months after Josh's resignation, we refused to pretend that what had happened to our friends hadn't happened. We dared to stay disturbed, even though we knew we were risking being treated the same way. We chose to speak the truth about what had happened to Josh instead of dismissing it into something smaller than it was. We didn't "badmouth" our pastor to the congregation, but we did set up meetings with him and also some elders to broach the brokenness of his behavior and the way it was hurting more people than just us. We were following Jesus into wholeness, and we knew the only way there was to be honest about the distance between how we were being treated and who we already were to God—beloved.

Like I've said, my husband is a man of few words, but suddenly he needed to *talk*. Almost every night for about four months, we filled all of the space between ending work and putting our heads on our pillows with words. We witnessed each other's pain, because no one else could or would. In those long, lonely months, the personal cost of potentially leaving our church weighed heavy on our minds and hearts, but the cost of staying weighed even more. The cost of people whom God loves being further belittled and beleaguered was too high to ignore. We had to face the cost, because it was our calling as shepherds to care.

Over coffee and calls, we confronted our pastor and elders with as much grace and kindness as we could. Over and over, they kept saying they would do whatever it took to keep us. We loved our church, loved our staff, and even after everything we saw, we still wanted to stay, but we knew we needed a boundary that protected both our own wholeness and that of our coworkers. So we said that in order to stay at the church, we needed them to hire consultants or counselors to walk the entire staff through a long-term process of relational restoration and that the lead pastor needed to be in long-term therapy himself.

The next thing we knew, the church paid five figures for a sign to place outside their new multi-million-dollar building.[1] When we asked what was happening about the counseling process, we were told the church just couldn't afford it.

When we talk about choosing courage, we don't adequately honor the possibility of the cost. We all have bills to pay, bodies that need health insurance, stomachs that need filling, and hearts that can't thrive without community. When courage involves confronting injustice, it can cost you nearly everything.

Our livelihood depended on staying at that church and supporting its leadership regardless of how wrong we knew they were. Ryan worked there full time, and I ran my counseling practice out of the church's offices.

It's shockingly easy to dismiss red flags when doing so benefits you in some way. It's what we had been doing for years—mostly under the surface of our awareness—out of the need to keep our careers on track and to keep food on our table. But we couldn't stomach it anymore.

We were realizing that even though it could be easier to keep our livelihood and some relationships by staying silent and compliant, we would lose our *integrity*. Diane Langberg reminds us that the word integrity comes from *integer*, which means "whole."

---

1. We don't know if the money came from the general fund or if there was some donation for the sign that the staff was not made aware of. We just know that the church leadership decided an expensive sign was worth investing in.

She says that integrity "refers to something that is the same all the way through."[2]

Jesus called the Pharisees and teachers of the Law "white-washed tombs" that "look beautiful on the outside but on the inside are full of the bones of the dead and everything unclean."[3] A church that looks beautiful on the outside—has a stunning building, a talented band, great preaching, or a liturgy we like—but inside has domineering leaders who control and crush others has no integrity. A leader who looks wise and kind from a stage but yells at people in private is not the same all the way through. A family or couple who smile wide in photos but shame each other at home are living in a pretty tomb. The integrity gap between what we preach and project and what we do in private is the place where most of this world's harm happens. It is the place where wholeness lies decaying and entombed.

Congruence is a word that captured my imagination from the first moment I heard it in graduate school. One of the first classes you take in training to be a therapist centers around therapeutic communication. We spent a whole sweaty-palmed semester in triads, practicing the basics of reflective, empathic communication and typing up transcripts of everything we said along with the facial and bodily language that accompanied it. It was some of the best practice in courage I've ever had—blundering through training myself to ask open-ended questions in place of closed ones and often entirely missing the feeling my partner was expressing—but trying again anyway—all while knowing my every move was being

2. Diane Langberg, *Redeeming Power: Understanding Authority and Abuse in the Church* (Grand Rapids, MI: Brazos, 2020), 40.
3. Matt. 23:27.

106

videotaped and the dream of my whole career hinged on my ability to pass the class.

Our professor was like a blonde Yoda, an empath of empaths with an uncanny ability to intuit everyone's emotions. Being in her presence felt like getting the best hug of your life. Caroll taught us that congruence is when our body language and words match—what we feel and how we look match what we say. But more so, she showed me what it meant. Conversation by conversation, I saw Caroll reflect back the anxiety and insecurity buzzing under our smiling faces in a way that gave us permission to acknowledge the reality that stepping into this vocation takes courage. I started to grasp that my role as a therapist was to hold a gracious space for my clients to gain permission to be increasingly honest about what they experienced and felt.

In a world where we are told from almost the moment we can walk to be big girls and boys and stop crying when we fall, we learn to speak the language of emotional dishonesty to be accepted and belong. With chiding words and a lack of responsiveness from our caregivers, we learn to silence the sounds of our distress. And often without ever knowing it is happening, we internalize a script of success by shaming—complete with lines and blocking—that tells our bodies we have to shove all of our sadness, fear, and anger offstage if we're going to be protagonists in this story at all.

Incongruence becomes the currency of our belonging. The better we are at burying our pain behind positivity or productivity, the more it seems we're allowed to belong. If we want to please our parents or pastors or others in power, we often learn to shut down the internal sounds of anything that might make them frown.

So many of the Christian clients I see in my therapy practice essentially grew up learning incongruence as a spiritual discipline. They're well-practiced in burying, blaming, and shaming their emotions, but they come to my office because what they thought was biblical is breaking them apart.

When popular Christian teachers call things like empathy "an enticing sin," we learn to approach our emotions like enemies to conquer.[4] Dismissing empathy sure is a convenient cover for never having to be affected by another's person's pain enough to change.

Your emotions will remain part of your existence whether you call them bad names or not. You could keep burying or bullying them, but what if you could befriend them instead?

Empathy isn't the antithesis of the gospel. It's the incarnation embodied and extended, far as the curse is found. You are a friend of God—*all* of you. That which we have been silencing might be the substance of our greatest healing. When we compassionately pay attention to the parts of others and ourselves that have been silenced and shamed, we internalize a story of integrity. We learn to live like our whole lives and whole selves are being sought by a Shepherd who is determined to see us thrive.

In the last book he published before he died, pastor and scholar Eugene Peterson summed up the aim of the Christian life this way: "The Christian life is a lifelong practice of attending to the details of congruence—congruence between ends and means, congruence between what we do and the way we do it, congruence between what is written in Scripture and our living out what is written . . . the congruence of the Word made flesh in Jesus with what is lived in our flesh."[5]

When what is happening inside us doesn't match what's showing on the outside, we don't move into the story of redemption with

---

4. Joe Rigney, "The Enticing Sin of Empathy: How Satan Corrupts through Compassion," Desiring God, May 31, 2019, www.desiringgod.org/articles/the-enticing-sin-of -empathy.

5. Eugene Peterson, *As Kingfishers Catch Fire: A Conversation on the Ways of God Formed by the Words of God* (Colorado Springs: Waterbrook, 2017), xviii.

our whole selves. When the means we use to gain the end of giving God glory don't match the means Jesus modeled, we miss experiencing the wonder of being God's Beloved. When we don't notice and name that we are living our lives in states of stress, we miss out on experiencing the Shepherd being there to soothe and strengthen us. When Ryan and I were dismissing the red flags of incongruence in our pastor and church, we weren't just safeguarding our salary. We were slowly and subtly severing our consciousness of our bodies from our minds.

We had to wake up to and confront the cost of staying in an incongruent church system in order to gather the courage to choose a life of wholeness. Even though we could lose everything, our desire for integrity outweighed our wish to avoid being further wounded.

14. I WALK

I'VE BEEN A MEMBER OF A CHURCH since long before I had a driver's license. And we both know I was almost born in my church's parking lot. *Staying* was the virtue I knew best. Loyalty to the local church was the virtue I'd been practicing my whole life.

After doing everything we could to confront the incongruence in our church—waiting, praying, seeking wise outside counsel, and initiating bringing in a mediator to attempt one final time to have our concerns received by our pastor and elders—it was clear that we weren't going to be heard.

Jesus' words at the beginning of his ministry turn the purpose of holding power absolutely upside down. Drawing from the words of the ancient prophet Isaiah, Jesus announced, "The Spirit of the Lord is on me, because he has anointed me to proclaim good news to the poor. He has sent me to proclaim freedom for the prisoners and recovery of sight for the blind, to set the oppressed free, to proclaim the year of the Lord's favor."[1]

The kingdom of Christ is the place where power is given away freely to empower the poor, free prisoners, open the eyes of the blind, and set the oppressed free. If we are using the precious gift of

---

1. Luke 4:18–19.

our power for any reason other than cultivating the empowerment and flourishing of those with less power, we are extending loyalty to a kingdom other than Christ's.

Orthodox theologian Alexander Schmemann underscores the danger of loyalty: "Our belonging, our loyalty to anything in 'this world'—be it state, nation, family, culture, or any other 'value'—is valid only inasmuch as it does not contradict or mutilate our primary loyalty and 'syntaxes' to the Kingdom of Christ. In the light of that Kingdom no other loyalty is absolute, none can claim our unconditional obedience, none is the 'lord' of our life."[2]

Loyalty is not a Christian virtue or fruit of the Spirit. *Faithfulness is.*[3] Loyalty as we know it today has its roots in the medieval feudal system. Loyalty was an oath or pledge of allegiance sworn by a vassal (someone with less power) to their lord (someone with more).[4] Loyalty is about the maintenance of dominance and hierarchy. But faithfulness is about love that pursues the good of others.

Loyalty assumes the faithfulness of the system of which one is a part, whether that be a family, church, company, or organization. But faithfulness demands that we look closely for love and its fruits before we keep assigning goodness and giving trust to a leader or group. Faithfulness requires being loyal to Jesus first and foremost.

Being in a system where Scripture and Christian-sounding narratives have been used to justify maintaining a relational atmosphere of dominance, performance, and control is trust shattering. We knew we needed to leave, but spirituality was used against us to demean our maturity and discernment. When people you once gave

2. Alexander Schmemann, *Of Water and the Spirit: A Liturgical Study of Baptism* (Crestwood, NY: St. Vladimir's Seminary Press, 1974), 32.

3. Gal. 5:22–23.

4. John Kleinig, "Loyalty," *The Stanford Encyclopedia of Philosophy*, Winter 2020 edition, ed. Edward N. Zalta, https://plato.stanford.edu/archives/win2020/entries/loyalty/.

your trust treat you with derision, it poisons your trust in yourself. Before the courage of disloyalty frees you, the incongruence of being in a system that demands unswerving loyalty will lace your mind with fear. But even though fears that *you* might be crazy or blowing everything out of proportion will haunt your every step for a long season, with time and tenderness, you can untangle the lies.

Courage to seek wholeness brings clarity. Slowly. One step at a time.

When loyalty to a church meant forsaking our faithfulness to follow Jesus into wholeness, we had to summon the courage to walk away. It was terrifying. It was heart-shattering. And it was necessary.

We resigned on our eighth wedding anniversary. We were not treated well. And we lost almost everything we had.

We spent the next couple of weeks staring at moving boxes and our rapidly emptying apartment. We decided to sell nearly everything we owned—except my BFF books, of course—just to make some extra cash to survive. The church leaders had asked us not to share the news of our resignation until they made an announcement to members. The announcement itself made it sound like we had suddenly abandoned the church because we wanted more opportunities. But they reassured the members that the church was healthier and stronger than ever, just like they said at the member meeting after Josh resigned. It's sobering how many people just believed them.

They didn't make that announcement until the night before we were slated to leave town for good. So, with just a few exceptions, we didn't get to say goodbye to the people we spent five years shepherding.

We knew walking away was what following Christ needed to look like, but all the grief made it hard to see Christ by our side. People who were supposed to be safe didn't protect us. People who were supposed to have faith couldn't extend faith to us when we told our hardest truth about someone they adored. People who called themselves the body of Christ were content to see us walk away wounded and crumbling financially. We wanted to see Jesus, but we mostly saw pain.

Tunnel vision is real, both personally and in a group, and it drives the story we believe we have to keep living. When stress swirls around you, your vision constricts. Our eyes narrow to focus on the threat, just like prey in a large field zero in on the predator coming at them. When stressors come at us—from large ones like deciding what to do when you hear someone speak up about being wronged or you're the one having to leave a job and community you loved, to smaller ones like getting an unexpected bill or bit of bad news—we temporarily lose our peripheral view as our eyes focus on the threat in front of us.

The danger waves a red flag of alarm to our bodies, sending split-second instructions through our brainstem to put our bodily systems on ready-alert for attack, dropping us into a sympathetic nervous system state. Your body does this all the time.

While we're on the subject of stress: Next time you are scrolling on Instagram or Twitter because you might be trying to escape some stress, notice how your eyes lock in on the screen and how tightly your shoulders hunch up toward your ears. Notice what's happening with your vision as your eyes zone in on the screen. *That's* what I'm talking about here.

Stress can both swell and be soothed by sight. From the near-sighted vision of our fear focusing in on danger, discouragement, and perhaps some doomscrolling, shifting your sight up and out can shift the state of your nervous system toward calm and hope.

Directing your eyes to take in the panorama in front of you can turn off the switch in your brainstem that is flooding your body with too much vigilance and alertness. By directing our vision back to a wider view, we help our bodies remember where we are and who we are.

When you mindfully notice the green plant on the other side of the room or the blue sky peeking through the branches off to your right, your nervous system releases signals telling your body you're safe.

Looking up allows us to look out into a world where there is still one who remains so faithful to us that we don't have to attempt to make ourselves or our communities safe by silencing our hard stories and sensations.

We left Colorado with all that we owned stuffed into a five-by-eight U-Haul trailer and made our way north to Montana, where we could stay for free in—I kid you not—a windowless room with bunk beds in my parents' basement. I hadn't lived with them since I left for college at seventeen, and suddenly, at almost thirty, I was sharing a bunk bed with my husband in my parents' basement. You gotta do what you gotta do to survive.

The traffic dissipated as we got closer to Wyoming, and as we crossed over the border, thick clouds opened up to the sun stretching across a cerulean sky. We were speechless, absorbing a beauty that starkly contrasted with the constriction we had been living with for months. Behind us was everything we lost for the sake of walking with Jesus, and before us was a landscape of sage and hills, distant mountains, and open sky.

Ryan and I turned to each other with glances that silently said, *Are you seeing this?* I can't remember who spoke up first, but just

114

as we drove into the wide-open space of Wyoming, the words of Psalm 18 came into both of our minds.

> He brought me out into a spacious place;
> He rescued me because he delighted in me.[5]

My eyes had seen loss and the potential of loss for so long. But with that in the rearview mirror, God was showing us that in leaving a church, we were not leaving God's love behind. Love followed us like the sun chasing the horizon and the tears kissing our cheeks.

I grabbed my Bible from my leather tote on the floorboards and opened it to Psalm 18. With one glance at the words, I knew there was even more to our story than we realized. I held the Bible in my shaking hands and through tears read the whole psalm to Ryan as he drove us north.

David wrote Psalm 18 as his song of praise when God delivered him from being killed by King Saul. These were the words of a man whose goodness had once been prized by a person with more power than him, who eventually experienced that goodness being cursed, who had to flee the power of Israel's throne to live in exile in order to save his own life. These were the words of a man who knew what it felt like to be yelled at, cursed, and driven out to be alone.

"I love you, LORD, my strength," I read. "The LORD is my rock, my fortress and my deliverer; my God is my rock, in whom I take refuge, my shield and the horn of my salvation, my stronghold."[6]

Reading it aloud was like a confession of faith, an arrow of hope aimed at God's heart. Right at the moment our faith could collapse, God was pouring out the water of his Word alongside the water of our tears to nourish the parched plant of our faith.

David's song echoed the enmity we experienced: "The cords of

5. Ps. 18:19.
6. Ps. 18:1–2.

death entangled me; the torrents of destruction overwhelmed me."[7] My heart thundered inside me as I read what came next. David sang that God had heard his cries of distress and that God didn't just hear. God was moved by those cries into fury and action. "The earth trembled and quaked, and the foundations of the mountains shook; they trembled because he was angry."[8]

We had left our church quietly, entrusting justice to the Just One, crying out in private for a vindication that we knew might not come for decades. As we looked up to the sky before us and looked out to the spacious place God was bringing us through, we knew we had been heard by God, who was rising in anger on our behalf and moving to act in ways that, though hidden behind a cloud of mystery, were no less mighty than what was done for David. God weeps and roars over the harm done to the vulnerable.

As we kept reading, the words of Psalm 18 underlined our losses with the story of God's grace. We rested our longing for retribution in the reality of rescue. "He rescued me from my powerful enemy," I read.[9] The words were a realization. *He rescued us from people who had more power than us.* "They confronted me in the day of my disaster, but the LORD was my support," I continued.[10] *They called us contentious and cursed our faith as immature, but God was the steel in our spines to speak the truth anyway.*

We drove in silent amazement for miles upon miles, gazing at the spacious place God had brought us out into. In sky and sun, we felt the gaze of God shining upon us even though others had just looked on us with scorn.

He brought us out into a spacious place.
He rescued us because he delighted in us.

---

7. Ps. 18:4.
8. Ps. 18:7.
9. Ps. 18:17.
10. Ps. 18:18.

As we drove north, the spacious landscape was showing us that even though we had left a church behind, God was not leaving us behind.

And it would be through walking—actual walking—that God would keep lifting my eyes and heart to be welcomed into a world where I still belonged.

15. THROUGH

WHEN I THOUGHT OF EVERYTHING WE LOST, I felt angry. Anger came as quick as afternoon rains in summer, in the tone of a song registering memories of Sunday mornings, or while reaching for the phone to text a friend, only to realize I was no longer just ten minutes from their presence. There was a litany of losses in my brain's grey matter, and any sound, smell, flavor, touch, or image could blow a mess of memories forward.

One day when I was scrolling through Instagram and saw photos from a church gathering, I decided to unfollow all of Ryan's former coworkers and their spouses. Many of them were the people who had confided in Ryan about being mistreated and shared their concerns in the anonymous feedback process. But when Josh resigned, they fell back into placid silence.

In the months leading up to our resignation, it was like amnesia had settled over the staff, as though the pain of the past couple of years had never happened. Moving into our hip new church building served like a potent anesthetic, letting pain dwindle under the force of a much more pleasant narrative: God was clearly blessing us by allowing us to move into this amazing building. We were building the kingdom of God.

A woman we had seen weeping multiple times over being

bullied was now acting like everything was wonderful. Another woman who had felt crushed by how her gifts were being limited because of her gender suddenly seemed aglow at the awesome classrooms and nursery facilities. When we tried broaching the way our pastor had never been held accountable to change his behavior, we were met with downplaying and blank stares.

Now free from the heavy weight of pretending everything was fine, every tap of my finger against the unfollow button was like a prayer, a resetting of the boundaries around my life as a place where the truth of my experience deserves to be believed.

I felt like I could barely share online or in person about why we lost what we lost, because I'd be judged as being divisive or too judgmental toward the church. When church crushes you, Christians expect you to call it human error. When you try to lament your pain, Christians want caveats. It's like we're allergic to honesty, so anxious to keep our precious institutions powerful that we can't stomach hearing the truth that sometimes religion ruptures our society and souls.

Saying "the church doesn't hurt people; people do" is false comfort that keeps us all from facing our complicity in allowing and enabling the body of Christ to be a body that punches, crushes, and kills.

I was determined to hear my own pain, even if no one else could. In the silence of my head and the pages of my journal, I let myself list the losses: our career paths, the friends we opened our hearts to only to be shunned by later, neighbors we loved, all of our financial security, evening walks by the glowing ponds in our favorite park. Trust. Safety. Confidence. Hope that the community who calls themselves the people of faith wouldn't just harm us again. I let my tears well up like watery homing devices, pinging God to locate me in the wilderness of my sorrow.

In a vague but honest Instagram post from that day, I wrote, "For now, I think faithfulness is accepting the memories as they come, allowing the losses to be seen and counted. This kind of loss is a trauma, and I'm learning the contours of how it has and will shape me. So I welcome the flood instead of avoiding it altogether, because I know there is healing in remembering my story. I need not fear that which I have already lived."

I was welcoming the flood. And flooded I was.

Anger, Sadness, and Fear slouched their heavy bodies into the cushions of my parents' leather couch with me as I scrolled through Instagram. I knew from experience that if I didn't get up to do something soon, I might not work all day. I was still seeing a handful of clients by video, and I was writing the proposal for the book that became *This Too Shall Last*. I could tell I was sinking into a dark place, and if I didn't get up soon I could drown in the flood of my feelings all week long.

Look up.

The words whispered within me, like hearing the voice of a friend.

I put my phone down on the coffee table, listening. Light was pouring through the window, gilding the flecks of dust in the air into floating gold. From my cavern on the couch, I could see a sliver of sapphire sky beckoning me to get up with my grief, get out, and get on with my day.

How do we get up to walk again in a world that has so wounded us? How do we walk forward through the potential danger of another dark valley, when we're still aching and hobbling from the last one?

We begin where *we* begin.

At seventeen days after conception, the human eye begins to develop like a pinprick of light in the night. Five days later, this speck of a speck folds to become the optic cup and the retina begins to hatch like an egg. Scientists have compared the embryonic development of the human eye to a finale of Fourth of July fireworks.[1] Tissue and cells seem to explode into existence. From the tiniest dot comes the window through which we will see a whole world.

Did you know your eyes are part of your brain? During early embryonic development, the brain pushes the retina outward as an extension of the central nervous system.[2] Neuroscientists like Andrew Huberman have explained that sight emerges from the eyes' main purpose of regulating our overall state of arousal—how alert or sleepy our nervous system is.[3] You could say that the primary purpose of our eyes pertains to state rather than sight.

Our eyes offer the shortest route for our nervous system to travel back to safety. While our eyes are constantly regulating our bodies under the surface of our awareness, we can practice harnessing this regulating power to more quickly and frequently find our way back home to peace, connection, and joy. Or to say it another way, what we see determines what we will live.

The eyes tell the body how vigilant or vulnerable we should allow ourselves to be. Your sight can speak the kindest sermon, reminding your whole body that even though other shepherds and storms have shaken your sense of safety, in the presence of your Good Shepherd you are now safe and held. Sight paired with intentional movement and attention speaks a better story to your whole body, to move you into a life where goodness still grows.

1. Linda Conlin, "Embryonic Eye Development," *20/20*, November 2012, www.2020mag.com/ce/embryonic-eye-development-abo-and-7A85C.

2. Ching-Kang Jason Chen, "RGS Protein Regulation of Phototransduction," *Progress in Molecular Biology and Translational Science* 133 (April 16, 2015): 31–45, https://doi.org/10.1016/bs.pmbts.2015.02.004.

3. Andrew Huberman, "Dr. Andrew Huberman on How the Brain Makes Sense of Stress, Fear, and Courage," *Finding Mastery* 237, August 12, 2020, https://findingmastery.net/andrew-huberman/.

Looking up to see the sliver of sky and notice the dancing dust lifted my heart just enough to will myself to get up, to begin climbing the autonomic ladder. I pressed my hands into the wooden arms of the couch, walked my leaden legs to the closet, and strapped on my trusty chacos to make myself go outside. I still didn't quite *want* to go on a walk. It was more like an act of obedience, like answering a mother's call.

Beauty has a fiercer language than anger or fear. She speaks to our eyes, and she lifts our chins. And like a good mother, she calls us home for dinner to bring our fear-panged bellies with us to the table, where our hunger can be filled with food for our eyes.

I climbed over the fence behind my parents' house and started trudging up the hill. In the months of May through July, my parents' back yard is basically a scene from *The Sound of Music*. You can't be out there for too long before your anger softens with the sky and songs start welling up from somewhere deep inside.

As I stepped around knotty bushes of sagebrush, I looked to my left, where the still snowcapped peaks of the Bridger Mountains all but spoke Psalm 121 into my mind. "I lift up my eyes to the mountains—where does my help come from? My help comes from the LORD, the Maker of heaven and earth."[4]

I walked farther up the mountain, to the spot where I knew clumps of yellow arrowleaf balsamroot and purple and blue lupine sprout each year into a small sea of color. My pace became prayer, heavy steps like thunder, footfalls becoming faith to say the things to God that were crashing inside.

My legs lifted me to lament. I knew the rest of Psalm 121 by heart, and I ached in the space between its praise and my problems.

---

4. Ps. 121:1–2.

My mind rehearsed the lines like a litigator, a prayer of proof that God had abandoned us to be harmed.

"He will not let your foot slip—he who watches over you will not slumber."[5]

I spoke at the sky (grateful the closest neighbor was acres away) and duked it out with God. I was climbing the ladder, from freezing to fighting, letting the energy of anger lead me home.

So were you just asleep all this time while our feet were slipping? Where were you?

"The LORD watches over you—the LORD is your shade at your right hand . . . The LORD will keep you from all harm—he will watch over your life."[6]

All harm, God? Really? Because it really feels like we followed you straight into harm.

In the silence between me and the sky, another psalm came like a thunderclap on my lips. The words Jesus cried out on the cross, words first spoken by David.

"My God, my God, why have you forsaken me? Why are you so far from saving me, so far from my cries of anguish?"[7]

And with Christ's own words on my lips, I knew. Jesus—God himself—had stood in this silence. He had been exactly where I was. Stumbling up a hill to reckon with evil. Trudging through shame and sorrow in obedience to the beauty that would save the world.

"God's absence is always a call to His presence," poet Christian Wiman observes. "Abundance and destitution are two facets of the one face of God, and to be spiritually alive in the fullest sense is to recall one when standing squarely in the midst of the other."[8]

Every furious footfall I took was a step Christ had already

5. Ps. 121:3.
6. Ps. 121:5, 7.
7. Ps. 22:1.
8. Christian Wiman, *My Bright Abyss: Meditation of a Modern Believer* (New York: Farrar, Straus, and Giroux, 2013), 112.

taken. Every lament was a lament that had already been on his lips. My feet had taken me *there*.

In the autoimmune arthritis community we have a phrase: motion is lotion. Maybe the rheumatologists and physical therapists knew something good all this time and just didn't make the connections explicit, but the phrase has grown into something larger in my life. Moving our bodies moves our minds. We need the lotion of motion to move through stress.

It's said that Saint Augustine put it this way: *solvitur ambulando*. "It is solved by walking."[9] When our minds can't seem to grasp the threads of the truest story—that the Good Shepherd is with us—our bodies can walk us there. It's a process called optic flow. Optic flow is the experience of visual streaming that happens as we move continuously in one direction.[10] As we walk or run, circuits in our brains and bodies cancel out the speeds at which we are seeing objects go by so that we sense that *we* are moving past *them*.

Walking and running tell our bodies a truth beyond stress and shutdown. The sensation of self-generated optic flow sends signals throughout our bodies to simultaneously feel rewarded and relaxed.[11]

As we move our limbs, we release the weight of wrong from our minds. Optic flow quiets the alarm bells ringing in the circuits

---

9. Arianna Huffington, "Solution to Many a Problem: Take a Walk," *Baltimore Sun*, September 3, 2013, www.baltimoresun.com/opinion/bs-xpm-2013-09-03-bal-solution-to-many-a-walk-20130830-story.html.

10. John V. Forrester et al., "Physiology of Vision and the Visual System," *The Eye*, 4th ed. (Edinburgh, UK: Elsevier, 2016), 269–337.

11. Huberman, "Dr. Andrew Huberman on How the Brain Makes Sense of Stress, Fear, and Courage."

of our brains that trigger our stress response.[12] Self-generated optic flow suppresses the amygdala, the threat detection center of the brain.[13] Walking welcomes us into a world where we still have agency.

As I walked up the hills behind my parents' house—something that I did nearly every day while we lived there for five months job-searching—my eyes were telling my body that even though we were walking through a dark valley, we could still move through it into a life of love. Walking was training my autonomic nervous system to respond to movement to feel more calm and capable than I could by staying sedentary. I barely had words for what we had lost, but my body became my prayer.

Sight is how we get unstuck. Moving through space gives you the sense that you can better move through life. Our brains are artists of anticipation. They will keep painting the story our bodies are most used to telling, like *Stress means I'm stuck!* Or *Hoping means I'll only get hurt again!* We need the watercolors of walking and the brushes of beauty to teach our eyes to see a story of joy stretching across our lives.

When stress rises and anger or grief seem to block your way to hope, look up. Obey the beauty that beckons you to rise.

Let your faith have feet. Let your lungs expand with air. The sky tells a more spacious story than stress. And your feet can walk a prayer.

12. Mandy Erickson, "Setting Your Biological Clock, Reducing Stress While Sheltering in Place," *Scope* (blog), Stanford University, June 3, 2020, https://scopeblog.stanford.edu /2020/06/03/setting-your-biological-clock-reducing-stress-while-sheltering-in-place/.

13. Andrew Huberman, "Maximizing Productivity, Physical and Mental Health with Daily Tools," *Huberman Lab Podcast*, July 12, 2021, https://hubermanlab.com/maximizing -productivity-physical-and-mental-health-with-daily-tools/.

16. THE DARKEST VALLEY,

I KEPT WALKING OUT MY PRAYERS. Day after day, I climbed over the fence to the mountainside to forage for wildflowers and sing or scream at the sky, depending on my mood. But I started falling. More days than not, one of my ankles would just collapse under me, sending me straight into jagged rocks or gnarled bushes of sagebrush.

As each day passed, walking became harder. I woke up every morning with burning in my hands and cold fear in my heart. The inflammation in my body became so fierce that I had to crawl up the stairs from our basement bedroom. It took a couple of hours every morning before my spine could straighten.

When we left our church, we also left our insurance. My old specialists didn't coordinate care well to my new ones, and so, for the first time in almost a decade, I had to go without treatment for a month and a half.

In years past, sometimes when I injected my weekly neon-yellow chemotherapy into the fat of my stomach, I wondered whether I really needed to be on such intense immunosuppressive medications. Were all of the side effects and risks necessary? Now I was getting the cruel gift of no more doubt.

Without access to my weekly chemo shot, monthly immunotherapy infusion, and daily anti-inflammatory pills, my body became an incinerator. Fire in my fingers. Fire in my toes. Fire in my bones. Our decision to leave behind harm at our church seemed like it was burning through our whole hope.

We couldn't see a way forward. We didn't know where to look for a pastoral job that wouldn't just chew Ryan up and spit him out again. We knew leaving was the right choice, but the consequences were brutal. Each night, we headed down to our bunkbed room dejected, whispering the same fears and pains over and over to each other in the dark.

Then my hands started to shake. I was trying to write through the pain, working on the proposal for the book that would become *This Too Shall Last*, but I kept scratching out illegible sentences in my notebook and missing the right keys as I typed at my laptop. I spilled my coffee most mornings just trying to lift it to my mouth. The tremor in my hands was nearly constant. It was as though my hands were now shaking to make up for all the shaking I didn't have time to stop for in the fast fury of having to resign and leave town so quickly.

My body had gotten me through confronting wrong, leaving without defending ourselves or getting to tell our side of the story, packing up our life into boxes, and getting to a safer place. And now she was a bewildering bonfire of trembling and pain.

There was no way around my pain. I could not leap over the losses in our life. I could not burrow underneath the brokenness into belief again. The only way was through.

Psalm 23 paints a picture of a journey with a dark valley that cannot be circumvented. Israel is filled with places where streams have cut gaping crevices in the earth, and these are the dark valleys where shepherds guide their sheep to water, lush vegetation, and higher ground.[1] These dark valleys are also places of danger, with both predators and people who can harm the sheep, including bandits and robbers, hiding in the cleft of rocks.[2]

From a shepherd's perspective, Phillip Keller comments that this portion of the psalm parallels the journey many shepherds take their flocks on through the summer, away from home into the high country of the mountains and their meadows. "During this time the flock is entirely alone with the shepherd," Keller writes. "They are in intimate contact with him and under his most personal attention day and night. That is why these last verses are couched in such intimate first-person language."[3] David would have known these long trips through dark valleys well from years of experience tending flocks of sheep through dangers like "rampaging rivers in flood, avalanches, rock slides, poisonous plants, the ravages of predators that raid the flock, or the awesome storms of sleet and hail and snow."[4]

The way to the water the sheep most need is through the dangerous, dark valley. Psalm 23 shows us that our dark nights of the soul are not punishments or problems but places to walk closely with the Shepherd while all other comforts fall away. Here we are shown the daring path named Through. The only way to a life without lack is through the darkest valley.

Most of us don't know the way through our dark valleys because we've been discipled to believe we are supposed to rise above them.

1. Kenneth E. Bailey, *The Good Shepherd: A Thousand-Year Journey from Psalm 23 to the New Testament* (Downers Grove, IL: IVP Academic, 2014), 47.
2. George Lamsa, *The Shepherd of All: The Twenty-Third Psalm* (Amazon Direct Publishing, 2014), 37, Kindle.
3. W. Phillip Keller, *A Shepherd Looks at Psalm 23* (Grand Rapids, MI: Zondervan, 2015), 68–69.
4. Ibid., 69.

In Sunday school and sermons, we're taught to want faith like a kite, truth that liberates and lifts us above the weary world. We're discipled to tie up our painful emotions with string to the kite of Christ's resurrection, as though the string could sail us on the wind over this world's weaknesses, rising high into a cloudless sky, until our problems are out of sight.

Faith is not a kite. It is a long walk on a dark night.

The life of faith includes seasons through which we must walk alone with the Shepherd, far from the ease of our old certainties and communities. Jesus said, "Whoever wants to be my disciple must deny themselves and take up their cross daily and follow me."[5]

Faith without feet that follow Jesus' steps into the dark valleys of suffering is no faith at all. It's spiritual bypassing, a term coined in the 1980s by a psychologist named John Welwood. Welwood defined spiritual bypassing as our "tendency to try to avoid or prematurely transcend basic human needs, feelings, and developmental tasks."[6]

We Christians like to draw a straight line between the resurrection of Christ and the rejoicing we're supposed to feel all the time, but that line ends up crossing out all of the parts of Scripture that include having fears and crying tears.

Even Jesus wept *before* raising his friend Lazarus from the dead, even though he knew he was going to bring him back to life. The power to raise Lazarus from the dead emanated from Christ's energy of compassion, which in Greek could be translated as Christ being

---

5. Luke 9:23.
6. John Welwood, "Principles of Inner Work: Psychological and Spiritual," *Journal of Transpersonal Psychology* 16, no. 1 (1984): 64, www.atpweb.org/jtparchive/trps-16-84-01 -063.pdf.

full of "anger" or even "rage."[7] And even Jesus protested drinking from the cup of his suffering before choosing to drink it anyway.[8]

Why do we race past our pain and anger and grief when they are what fueled Christ's compassion? Why do we silence grief when God incarnate paused to feel it? Why do we push down our protests when Christ himself prayed through his? Why do we attempt to be holy without allowing ourselves to be human first?

Grief, fear, and anger can be fuel in the fire of redemption, but we're over here dousing it with all our churchy expectations to quickly jump from hurt to hope and pain to praise.[9] We pass out platitudes like kleenex, anxious to wipe each other's tears away. We use Scripture on ourselves and each other as a silencer instead of a solace. We subconsciously take scissors to all the parts of Scripture that show us that our crying, confusion, and even contempt are central parts of prayer—preferring to keep the picture of our faith more pleasant and tidy than the psalms and Christ do.

Romans 8:28 isn't a pill to pop like aspirin to make the headache of your hurt pass in thirty minutes or less. Like too much sugar destroys kids' teeth, a faith of spiritual bypassing rots our souls.[10]

I could not avoid the pain ravaging my body. I could not ignore the fraility of falling in parking lots or just walking through a door. I

7. Kelly M. Kapic, *Embodied Hope: A Theological Meditation on Pain and Suffering* (Downers Grove, IL: InterVarsity, 2017), 84.

8. Luke 22:42.

9. My favorite author has long been Kathleen Norris. In *The Cloister Walk*, Norris reflects at length on how we jump from pain to praise too quickly and the way the psalms offer us a way *through* instead. Kathleen Norris, *The Cloister Walk* (New York: Penguin, 1997), 94.

10. I initially shared a version of these thoughts in a foreword for the book *With Those Who Weep*. See S. A. Morrison, *With Those Who Weep: A Theology of Tears* (Austin, TX: GCD Books, 2021).

could not pray my way past the truth my body was telling about how terrorized I felt. My body wouldn't let me bypass my brokenness, and for her feral wisdom, I give her thanks.

Nourishment starts with our needs. And life starts in the dark. Priest and author Barbara Brown Taylor reminds us that "whether it is a seed in the ground, a baby in the womb, or Jesus in the tomb, it [new life] starts in the dark."[11]

When we bypass the darkness, we kill courage.[12] When we avoid our anguish, we bypass our healing. When we anesthetize our ache, we end up letting wounds fester that could be the place of our greatest healing and hope.

We cannot heal what we will not feel. Remember, the only way back home to the top of the autonomic ladder is by climbing each rung. We might want to jump from distress or doubt to delight in God, but unless we tend to our emotions and sensations, we'll just be pretending at praise. We cannot grow if we will not go—through the dark valley—with Jesus, walking the same well-trod path he walked before us, that thousands upon thousands of saints before us have walked as well.

In the middle of my darkest valley, physically trembling and afraid that whatever was happening in my body was a harbinger of even more darkness to come, I started looking to Christ not as the conclusion to my courage but my companion within in. I didn't know what we'd find in the darkness, but I was resolved that the only way home was through.

---

11. Barbara Brown Taylor, *Learning to Walk in the Dark: Because God Often Shows Up at Night* (New York: HarperOne, 2014), 129.

12. Brené Brown puts it this way: "The problem is that when we imprison the heart, we kill courage." Brené Brown, *Dare to Lead: Brave Work. Tough Conversations. Whole Hearts.* (New York: Random House, 2018), 73, Kindle.

17. I

I WAS FALLING SO OFTEN I started to fear some fire had taken up residence in my brain. About 25 percent of autoimmune patients develop multiple autoimmune diseases, and my own sister has three.[1] It wasn't a hypochondriac thought; it was a realistic estimation of the odds.

My new rheumatologist was worried about my symptoms and sent me to a neurologist, who promptly ordered an MRI of my brain and whole spine. I swallowed back a swell of nausea as I signed a form acknowledging my financial responsibility to pay the $1000 copay—more money we didn't have, another rude reminder that we had left a salary and insurance where I'd already met our deductible for the year.

In the changing room, I peeled away layers of clothes and glanced at my naked body in the mirror—the curve of my slumped shoulders spoke the language of defeat. I hung my head in resignation as I pulled on the pair of blue scrubs the medical tech had handed me like a ritual of reduction from being a person to a problem to diagnose.

I padded my socked feet across the cold hospital floor, through

---

1. Benaroya Research Institute, "Mystery of Multiple Autoimmune Diseases," May 17, 2018, https://www.benaroyaresearch.org/blog/post/mystery-multiple-autoimmune-diseases.

the thick metal door of the MRI room, to the massive magnet that could tell me why my body was betraying my desire to thrive. I laid back onto the chilly table and let the tech fasten a plastic cage over my head, willing myself into immobility because a small part of me had hope that this would help return me to me.

Alone in a tunnel of noise, trying to keep my tremor-filled body from shaking in a test that would be ruined without stillness, I broke. In the cacophony of the MRI machine, the sounds of fear in my body finally became so loud I could no longer breathe. My heart pounded through my chest and I felt lost to space, lost in the cold, cold chamber of the MRI, immobilized by a power greater than my own, soul stripped and stuck.

Until I pushed the call button cradled in my sweaty palm. Until I remembered I can say, "Stop." Until I remembered there still is no power greater than the personhood within me.

Out, out of the cold, loud dark, I came. And I breathed and breathed until I felt sane.

I kept pushing back the blackout curtains of thoughts of the lesions that the radiologist might have found on my brain, trying to see past a potential dark future into today, waiting to discuss the results with the neurologist. I brought Ryan to the appointment, determined to have an advocate ready in case I was called crazy or got no answers but was still clearly unwell. I needed the physical presence of someone in my corner, who knows who I am even when pain or problems seem to overshadow me.

The neurologist greeted us with warmth, and I felt my shoulders unclench by an inch. This was a person who would treat me like *a person*. Before pulling up my scans, he asked what had been happening in our lives. What stress had we been under? We let the story spill out—the stress of the church system where we had served, the bullying and impossible expectations of our pastor, the way we confronted it and were unheard, how we left our jobs and lost everything, and were now job searching and living with family. We told it with as much composure as we could, but the more we talked, the more my hands shook. Under the pressure of shame, my tears escaped, running down my face, willing this man—begging *someone*—to see how terrible things had become.

"I don't tell many patients this," the doctor said. "But my wife is a complex trauma survivor, and what you've just shared with me, what you two have lived, is trauma. I believe you are experiencing post-traumatic stress."

He looked from Ryan to me and said, "I think the farther you both get away from this system and experience, the better your body is going to feel."

He proceeded to gently show me how my tremor wasn't present before we were talking about our trauma but had emerged as we let the story out. He showed me scans of my "beautiful brain" and told me I wasn't crazy. I just had a body that was showing me that what we had lived through mattered.

Silence can soothe us and silence can scar us. I was raised for reverence, to sit still and silent in church, and to give people in leadership, especially men, unquestioning respect and honor for their "God-given" authority. I learned to raise my voice when grace amazed me but relegate it into silence when harm alarmed me.

Silence is the arbiter of scarcity, the force of coercion and control that those who hold the most power wield to maintain the status quo. If power can be held only in the hands of a few, then pleasing them is what buys us belonging. So we learn to fold our hands and cross our legs and put a smile across our faces to hide our hearts' frown, all the while absorbing the bad, bad news that God is actually a power who must be pleased and love is just a reality we receive when we are good enough.

I was taught reverence for the sound of a preacher's voice and the pages of my Bible, but I was never taught to reverence the sounds of my own body and soul.

Consequently, when we felt the creeping sense that something was horribly wrong in our church, when our hearts pounded at the sound of our pastor yelling at other staff in his office, when I felt shame in my skin when the pastor made comments about my weight, when going to work felt like walking into an exam where only perfection passes, we instinctively silenced the alarm bells of our bodies. To listen to the clanging bells of chaos in our bodies would have countered the subconscious belief that belonging means being loyal and obedient, good little girls and boys.

But our bodies kept bearing witness to the broken system we were in and the way the community that was supposed to bring freedom was burying us under a heavy burden. We slowly crawled out from under the dirt of doubt and self-dismissal and let our confusion form into words. We wrestled with the gospel we believed and the gospel we received. We felt crazy for questioning our pastor's behavior as bullying, but seeing it happen to more than just ourselves was leaving us breathless.

And when we broke the unwritten code of Christian silence, we were met with verbal violence. We were shamed and scorned by the pastor, co-pastor, and church elders in the mediation meeting we had requested ourselves, with our maturity maligned and our character questioned. But because we were no longer anesthetizing the ache in our bodies from being in such a domineering system, because we were no longer silencing ourselves, we didn't fall back into amnesia about what we had experienced.

We said, "Stop." And we left. We walked away, wounded and confused but determined that the gospel of Jesus Christ shouldn't crush our souls.

When harm happens, the senselessness and powerlessness of suffering overwhelms our bodies and disconnects us from our brains' innate capacity to name and tame the truth of our experience. Trauma steals our tongues. It disconnects us from being able to readily access the language centers of our brains, as we dip down the autonomic ladder to survive. Silencing ourselves is part of how we survive in a community, system, relationship, or situation where our attempts to seek safety are shamed or shut down.

Giving pain a name and a voice is a giant act of courage in a subculture that privileges positivity. I can't tell you how many clients I have seen who struggle to name how people they love hurt them, especially parents or others in authority. Naming harm can feel like a betrayal of love. And when the source of our pain is someone who stands as a symbol of our Good Shepherd, naming hurt and harm can feel like a threat to our connection to God.

When we cry from the crosses where we were crushed or betrayed, we're often treated with extreme awkwardness or even flat-out spiritualized shaming, as though Christ's resurrection means that nothing hurts now. When we feel silenced spiritually, cut off from the song of the saints and confused about why church hurts so much, our wordlessness, doubts, and darkness are treated like a lack of resurrection faith. But before Christ was raised, he was cold and silent in a grave for a whole day.

The Word who spoke the world into being went to the wordless place of death. He sank into silence.

Courage doesn't begin on the bright day the Spirit raised Christ from the grave. Courage is in the shadows of Saturday, where the Word became wordless for your sake.

When religious power was used against me and my spouse, shutting us down, making us question our sense of reality, and overwhelming our nervous systems into collapse and chaos, it was the wordless Word who was with us in the shadows and the silence. It was the crucified God who gave us courage to see that even the place of powerlessness is a place where God is present.

I often tell my clients, "Tell the truth—beginning with yourself." Hearing that neurologist name what we had experienced as trauma gave us courage to keep naming our experience and its effects with honesty and accuracy—beginning with ourselves. We couldn't deny or dismiss the truth my body kept telling. What we had experienced in church had harmed us in body and soul.

My body wasn't betraying me by falling and shaking. My body was begging me to tell the truth about what we had lived, even though the church hadn't been willing to hear it.

I needed to hear the cries of the lost and crushed parts of myself in order to heal. I needed to find the silenced parts of myself and rename them as parts that God is in solidarity with. And Ryan did too.

Walter Brueggemann says that "the cry that breaks the silence is the sound of bodies becoming fully aware of what the predatory system has cost and being fully aware as well that it can be otherwise."[2] It was hearing the way our bodies had been silenced and shut down that led us into healing. Honoring our wordlessness, overwhelm, and loss of agency to protect ourselves and those we

---

2. Walter Brueggemann, *Interrupting Silence: God's Command to Speak Out* (Louisville: Westminster John Knox, 2018), 16, Kindle.

love is part of how we come back home to the place where we are ever and always named Beloved.

To remember our name, we had to name the harm.

We were spiritually abused.

Pastor David Johnson and counselor Jeff VanVonderen define spiritual abuse as "the mistreatment of a person who is in need of help, support or greater spiritual empowerment, with the result of weakening, undermining or decreasing that person's spiritual empowerment."[3] All abuse and oppression is about power, domination, and control—allegiance to a story of scarcity where goodness and life for one person or group depends on taking it from someone else. It is in the language of our groans and sighs, our racing minds and pounding hearts, and our nightmares and knotted stomachs that our bodies speak the truth that communities and people who are supposed to build us up are tearing us down instead.

This book is not meant to be a primer on spiritual abuse. But experiencing, confronting, leaving, and healing from spiritual abuse has been the landscape where my husband and I have most learned to walk with courage. I've included some additional information about spiritual abuse and abuse dynamics in the appendix to this book.

But long before the groans and grief, there is the allure of growth. Spiritually abusive churches and leaders don't set out to be abusive. They set out to be *amazing*. Spiritual abuse happens under the shiny guise of believing that the end of building God's kingdom is worth whatever means it takes.

At its core, abuse is about using a person rather than encountering them as someone to love. Philosopher Martin Buber describes

---

3. David Johnson and Jeff VanVonderen, *The Subtle Power of Spiritual Abuse: Recognizing and Escaping Spiritual Manipulation and False Spiritual Authority within the Church* (Minneapolis: Bethany House, 1991), 20.

the heart of human relationships as an encounter between an I and a Thou.[4] We were made for mutual reverence. But in our churches and families, we often replace encounter with effectiveness. We reduce relationships to transactions. We, as Buber writes, subtly come to each other as though we are an I meeting an It.[5] Our time, effort, vulnerability, tithes, and stories can be packed down into blocks to build someone else's kingdom, leaving us with less joy, internal safety, and hope than before we ever walked through the church's doors.

When people are not encountered, they are exploited. Our belonging in the body of Christ becomes bound to our utility. Our place among our people becomes contingent on being compliant. Our security requires taking scissors to any part of ourselves that doesn't fit the church's idea of what is true and good and right. For me and Ryan, having to give our allegiance to that kind of relational system diminished our sense of safety, autonomy, and agency as image bearers of God.

What if we encountered those with trauma histories as bearing costly truth? It is from the shattered and the silenced, we whose words have been forged in the fierce night of wordlessness, that the whole church can hear that the heart of our faith is not doing anything for God; it is being with God. We who have been used know the truth: if we are not cultivating reverence for every human we encounter, every part of this world we touch, and every moment we meet God, we will reduce all that is sacred to a resource to use. Buber underlines the damage of our unexamined addiction to utility: "One cannot divide one's life between an actual relationship to God and an inactual I-It relationship to the world—praying to God in truth and utilizing the world. Whoever knows the world as

---

4. Martin Buber, trans. Walter Kaufmann, *I and Thou* (New York: Scribner, 1970), Kindle.
5. Ibid., 56.

something to be utilized knows God the same way. His prayers are a way of unburdening himself—and fall into the ears of the void."[6]

On the other side of shattered agency, this is what I know:

God doesn't love you to use you. God loves you because you are you.

You are not a product to use. You are a person to love.

I encounter so many clients and readers who are afraid of and even allergic to giving their pain from other Christians a proper name. We fear doing so will cut us off from any belonging we have, so we minimize the harm with nicer-sounding names and narratives like "church hurt" and "a difference of opinion."

My clinical and personal experience tell me that usually we don't just "get hurt." Often, we're harmed. And if we can't name the injury, how will we apply the remedy?

The truth is, I didn't just skin the knee of my spirituality. I didn't just "have a misunderstanding" and hold a grudge like a shield over my heart. I wasn't unteachable. I just was no longer willing to give the precious gift of my faithfulness to anyone other than Jesus Christ.

Spiritual abuse and religious trauma are terms that give us courage to rightly name just how deep these wounds go and, thus, how far the healing needs to reach.

I still believe in the Holy Spirit, the holy catholic church, the communion of the saints, and the resurrection of the dead. So I also believe the church cannot be a communion that crushes. We cannot be people of the resurrection when we're silencing anyone who says, "Your behavior is bullying me to death."

---

6. Ibid., 156.

People can dismiss the cries of the crushed all they want. They can decry deconstruction until someone gives them an award. But don't for one second think they are saving the church from those who would tear her down.

The truth is, people like me and my husband have been and are being torn down, kicked around, gaslit, and slandered all over town.

It wasn't until I named that I experienced spiritual abuse and religious trauma from pastors and church folk that I found the courage and commitment to heal my little limb of the body of Christ.

I'll never stop loving the church. So I also won't stop being honest about the harm that happens in her midst.

Whatever your pain, may you have courage to name your injury, because you are more than worthy of the remedy. Break the silence, beginning with yourself.

18. WILL FEAR

AT THE TIME OF WRITING THIS BOOK, more than 1.7 million posts on Instagram have been tagged with the hashtag #faithoverfear. By the time this book is in your hands, that number will be much higher. One quick scan through the top #faithoverfear posts shows open Bibles, sweaty gym selfies, a bunch of cheesy-as-hell quotes and hand-lettered Bible verses, and even a girl who appears to be no older than twenty-one proudly holding up an assault rifle. (First, I am *not* making this up. Second, *what* in the actual hell is she planning on doing with that gun?) One thing is apparent: droves of people believe fear is something that ought to be fought.

I fear we have been discipled to rise above the places where God most wants to meet us. We need security we'll never get from a gun store. We need truth we can't buy at Target on a flowy-font sign from the dollar bins. We need a Savior who went to the depths of fear itself so that even our most painful emotions are places where we can partake in his life.

You don't need to fight your fears. You need a Friend who draws near.

"Do not fear" (and other versions of the phrase) is one of the most repeated refrains in Scripture. When something is repeated in Scripture, we need to pay attention. Scholars have shown that repetition is one of the primary ways meaning is constructed in biblical stories.[1] Repetition primes us to realize something is important, cueing us to pay attention to its place and purpose in the larger narrative, allowing the meaning we derive to well up from the phrase's place and purpose within the nested narratives of the immediate story and the larger narrative of God's people throughout the ages. "Do not fear" is most often uttered in Scripture as an imperative statement—but one of comfort, not chastisement. (But goodness, we *love* to use it to chide and correct ourselves and others!)

"Do not fear" almost serves like a chorus in the song and story of God's love. It is a refrain that is repeated over and over to people about to embark on risky endeavors who will endure uncertainty, possible judgment, and danger, predicated on the promise that God *will* go with them. The words echo from cover to cover of the Bible, across landscapes and losses, around perceived limits and problems, penetrating story after story with an undeniable assurance of grace.

A homeless and people-less Abraham in the wilderness. A destitute and abused Hagar in the desert. Moses' words to the Israelites fleeing Egypt. Samuel to the people of Israel after they realized the horror of what they had gotten themselves into by wanting a king other than God. The angel of the Lord to Elijah before he confronted the king. King David to his son Solomon about to undertake the monumental task of building the temple. Isaiah's words of comfort to the exiled people of Israel. God's charge to Ezekiel in calling him to be a prophet whom the people would despise. A man in a vision to Daniel as he stood up to the king of Persia before being thrown into the lion's den. The angel Gabriel's words to a pregnant Mary, about to bring the Son of God into the world.

---

1. See especially chapter 11, "The Structure of Repetition: Strategies of Informational Redundancy," in Meir Sternberg, *The Poetics of Biblical Narrative: Ideological Literature and the Drama of Reading* (Bloomington, IN: Indiana Univ. Press, 1987), 365–436. See also Edward L. Greenstein, *Essays on Biblical Method and Translation*, rev. ed. (Providence, RI: Brown Univ., 2020).

We need to read Scripture on Scripture's terms, not cherry-picking prooftexts to solve our problems but carefully and continuously placing ourselves within the story of seeing that God goes with us. In other words, we cannot pluck the phrase "do not fear" off the tree of love. Rather, faith is finding that we are limbs and branches on this eternal tree, forever tended by the Farmer, forever found in his care, forever fruitful because of his love. Our fears find rest in God's hands, watchful eyes, and tender heart.

The power of the phrase "do not fear" is found in participating in the story where the presence of God goes with and before us everywhere we go, all the days of our lives.

I cannot help but wonder if a reason this phrase features so prominently in Scripture is that God knows that *we will feel fear until the day we die.* Fear is a facet of being human. Fear emerges from a physiological state of stress that God made to protect you from danger and bring you to safety. At its core, fear is not a lack of faith. It is a lack of perceived safety. Your tight shoulders, pounding heartbeats, and even your panic attacks are all prompts to treat yourself like someone who is truly worthy of safety, love, and belonging. Fear is a physiological prompt to seek safety in the presence of Christ and remember your place in his heart.

Fear is like a carbon monoxide detector ringing in the house of your body. It's one of your body's ways of telling you it is picking up on excessive levels of danger and not enough safety. Feigning that fear isn't happening or only telling yourself, *Don't fear! Just trust God!* is like turning off your carbon-monoxide detector and throwing it in the dumpster. It's not exactly the smartest way to stay alive.

"Faith over fear" is a mantra that peddles toxic half-truth. I'm willing to call this out, even though it might piss you off, because the stakes are simply too high to tiptoe over our precious platitudes. Lives are at stake. Suicides happen because of this toxic theology. We stay in abusive relationships, churches, or jobs, dismissing our sense that it's not safe because we should just "trust God." Depression worsens. Disease proliferates. Shame spirals us into dark corners of separation and death, all because we think we're supposed to treat a normal function of our bodies like an enemy to fight and kill.

By buying into popular Instagram tropes and clutching uprooted Bible verses, we basically jump from "do not fear" to "do not be human." What happens when you can't overcome your fears? What are you left with if your anxiety disorder doesn't go away or your feelings of depression or suicidal thoughts never fully lift? With a "faith over fear" theology, what happens is shame and separation. When we don't allow ourselves to be human, we don't create space to grow strong. We end up amplifying the very feelings we most wish to conquer. We end up corroding "the very part of us that believes we are capable of change."[2]

I have never been more afraid in my life than in the long months of writing *This Too Shall Last*. There I was, supposed to be proclaiming good news, and all I felt was fear that none of it was true for me anymore. Regardless of my theological position on the matter, I still wasn't sure I could trust a God who seemed to only bring us more suffering.

In the immense stress of moving across the country and starting totally over in both finances and friendship, I reverted to my oldest ways of coping. I am a master of the stealthy shutdown. I grew up hiding my feelings under a smile and a book. I tuned out the stress

2. Brené Brown, *I Thought It Was Just Me (But It Isn't): Making the Journey from "What Will People Think?" to "I Am Enough"* (New York: Gotham, 2008), 197.

swirling around me with better stories than mine, turning pages to propel me past my pain.

It should come as no surprise that I did the same thing as an adult, but this time instead of reading books, I protected myself from pain by writing one. But as my fingers tapped the keyboard, fear always itched inside me, trying to crawl its way out of my body, where it remained trapped inside.

After a few months of pushing fear away, my body forced me to face it. Sometimes she speaks through the stress of my autoimmune disease, with joint pain or fatigue asking me to find rest. This time she spoke in the dark tones of depression and the sharp screeches of persistent anxiety.

If we do not reckon with fear, it will reckon with us. I was submerged in despair and then apathy, which I now recognize as my body's protest against the flood that had too long raged in my life. I didn't know it then, but deep sadness, despair, and feeling entirely stuck are often symptoms of sinking into a dorsal vagal nervous system state of shutdown because the flood of fear has simply become too exhausting for our bodies.

My body was protesting, and she stopped me in my tracks. I called my agent and told him I wouldn't be writing for a while, not until I really believed what I was writing again—even though my deadline was fast approaching. I decided I would not walk any farther until I knew that God went with me. Being honest about my fear and hopelessness ended up being my first step back toward courage and hope.

It was when fear shrouded my life that I encountered Christ most intimately.

He finds us in our fear, *because he has gone there already.* In the garden of Gethsemane, Jesus felt the stress of his imminent death on the cross so intensely that his sweat was like drops of blood.[3] This isn't just a figure of speech. It's a rare phenomenon called hematohidrosis, which physicians have noted is caused most frequently by "acute fear and intense mental contemplation."[4] A medical journal article describes it this way: "The severe mental anxiety activates the sympathetic nervous system to invoke the stress-fight or flight reaction to such a degree as to cause hemorrhage of the vessels supplying the sweat glands into the ducts of the sweat glands."[5]

Be careful you don't try to dehumanize Jesus here, desperately trying to cling to the whitewashed image of the pristine, peaceful Jesus you've seen in paintings.

Jesus kneeled on the ground of that garden, allowing himself to feel the utter depths of fear itself—anxiety so severe it made his sweat ducts bleed—so that there can be no depth of darkness we experience that is outside the reach of his empathy.

Can you stomach a Savior who felt fear and stress so intensely he sweat drops of blood? Do your theology and anthropology include an incarnate God who felt anxiety so intense it ruptured his blood vessels?

If we cannot see Christ as fully human, we will not experience him as Lord. And if we cannot accept our own full humanity, we will not feel the full friendship of our suffering Lord.

A Jesus who felt such fear is a Jesus who is able to meet me in mine. Indeed, as the author of Hebrews reminds us, "we do not have a high priest who is unable to empathize with our weaknesses, but

3. Luke 22:44.
4. Hemangi R. Jerajani et al., "Hematohidrosis—A Rare Clinical Phenomenon," *Indian Journal of Dermatology* 54, no. 3 (July–September 2009): 290, www.ncbi.nlm.nih.gov/pmc/articles/PMC2810702/.
5. Ibid.

we have one who has been tempted in every way, just as we are—yet he did not sin."[6]

We cannot equate faith with never feeling fear, for fear is knit into our body's wiring to respond to threats. We can, however, increasingly experience the stress of those threats *differently* because we have someone standing with us in them. Christ's empathy is our empowerment.

I will not allow myself to be less human than Christ. I will not cut myself off from receiving empathy in the very place Christ stands ready to meet me.

In my darkest valley and deepest need, I dared to approach the throne of grace with confidence, asking for the very power that sustained and raised Christ to reconstitute me in resilience. And this is what I found:

Fear is but courage's fuel.

---

6. Heb. 4:15.

19. NO EVIL,

WE WHO HAVE SUFFERED THE PSYCHOLOGICAL EVIL of spiritual abuse may not have visible scars on our bodies, but we bear them on our souls. Psychological trauma, of which religious trauma is a part, disrupts the homeostasis of the body and can cause both short- and long-term damage to the body's systems and organs.[1] The harm is real.

And yet thirteenth-century German theologian and mystic Meister Eckhart says, "When the uncreated God is your Father, nothing on earth can really harm you."[2] As Jesus prepared his friends for his death, he told them that they would be persecuted, put in prison, betrayed by the people closest to them, and even put to death. "But," he reassures, "not a hair of your head will perish. Stand firm, and you will win life."[3]

If the harm we experience in life because of evil is both real *and* not final, where does fear belong?

Our answer to that question determines how much belonging

---

1. Eldra P. Solomon and Kathleen M. Heide, "The Biology of Trauma: Implications for Treatment," *Journal of Interpersonal Violence* 20, no. 1 (January 2005): 51–60, https://doi.org/10.1177/0886260504268119.

2. Quoted in Mark S. Burrows and Jon M. Sweeney, *Meister Eckhart's Book of Secrets: Meditations on Letting Go and Finding True Freedom* (Charlottesville, VA: Hampton Roads, 2019), 90.

3. Luke 21:18–19.

we will experience in life. The place we put our fear will determine how much we experience the fact that no evil can ever separate us from the love of God in Christ Jesus our Lord.

Trauma is about the suspension of time and the separation of the self inside, wherein our bodies struggle to differentiate between past and present. Small reminders or rising states of stress can make us feel lost in space and time. Even though we might be technically safe and heard right now, inside we feel silenced and stuck, trapped in the place where we were harmed. As Walter Brueggemann says, "the taproot of violence is surely silence,"[4] of our voices being so shut up and shut down that our bodies carry fear that we no longer have any say in the future of our stories.

Psychologist Francine Shapiro reminds us that "by dictionary definition, trauma is *any event that has had a lasting negative effect.*"[5] Trauma can also include the absence of attunement. When we haven't received enough soothing and support from those who were supposed to give it, we often experience that lack as traumatic. Whether you've experienced a massive traumatic event or bear the load of a lack of attunement, the presence of long-term abuse or rigidity and control, please remember Shapiro's definition when you are tempted to discount the effects of evil in your story and body.

4. Walter Brueggemann, *Deep Memory, Exuberant Hope: Contested Truth in a Post-Christian World* (Minneapolis: Fortress, 2000), 7.

5. Francine Shapiro and Margot Silk Forrest, *EMDR: The Breakthrough Therapy for Overcoming Anxiety, Stress, and Trauma*, updated edition (New York: Basic, 2016), 1, Kindle.

As a content warning, the following is a painful part of my story that might be hard to read if you've struggled with suicidal ideation or someone you love has.

Even though we had walked away from spiritual abuse, we carried the hypervigilance of the resulting trauma with us. The truth was, I was trying to write a book but trauma had stolen my words. Trauma had filled the soil of my days and relationships with landmines. I was tiptoeing through life, terrified that my trust and hope were about to be blown to smithereens again by things I couldn't see.

The next job Ryan took seemed like a great fit. Our nearly two-month-long interview process led us to believe we were joining a more open and simple church community focused on relationships. But when I heard the click of the landmine of realizing that Ryan's job was in yet another image-conscious, performance-based, megachurch-aspiring church, I froze in fear. And then despair. After that is when I called my agent, because the truth was I couldn't deal with trying to string together words to put in a manuscript when I was busy feeling like I wanted to die. If life was mostly a series of landmines, my body felt like just giving up might be better.

I was in an all-out dorsal vagal collapse, and I wish I would have known then what I know now. When the energy of fighting to survive becomes too much for our bodies to bear, we shut down to stay alive. The paradox of the pain of being in a state of dorsal vagal shutdown is that it can feel so hopeless that you want to die. Our shutdown state doesn't always look like severe depression and suicidal ideation, but it can.

In the throes of that traumatic state, I couldn't think straight. As I collapsed into bed, contemplating cramming my mouth full of the pills on my nightstand, I couldn't recall some memorized Scripture or pray a prayer beyond muttering *help*. Ryan's face finding my eyes and then his arms wrapping around my shaking body is what made me rise. His physical presence offered co-regulation right in the place I felt crushed. When we are at the bottom of the autonomic ladder, we need the compassion of co-regulation to climb.

It took me weeks to be able to find my way back to the top of the ladder with enough trust that it was still my home. I ascended not by reframing my thoughts about the situation we were in—it was truthfully a rough situation—but by offering my terrified and stressed body compassion. During that season, we both had started seeing new therapists, and Ryan's therapist taught him tapping as a way to release the energy of trauma and stress.

Tapping, or the emotional freedom technique (EFT), is a body-inclusive tool to turn toward yourself in stress with compassion and courage to shift your autonomic state through energy release through the body's meridian points. Researchers have found that EFT effectively improves the symptoms of post-traumatic stress disorder.[6] EFT has also been found to lower pain, increase feelings of happiness, and improve blood pressure and cortisol levels.[7]

One day during these weeks, I found myself flooded with fear about the future again. I could barely breathe. I kept repeating, "I'm just not okay. I'm just not okay," and started to rock back and forth. Ryan helped me slow my breathing and taught me what his therapist had taught him. The center of my chest still ached with anxiety, like a coal had burned a hole through my heart. But as I tapped through specific points on my body, acknowledging aloud what I was experiencing along with the truth that I was safe, I felt my body return to peace.

---

6. Brenda Sebastian and Jerrod Nelms, "The Effectiveness of Emotional Freedom Techniques in the Treatment of Posttraumatic Stress Disorder: A Meta-Analysis," *Explore* 13, no. 1 (January–February, 2017): 16–25, https://doi.org/10.1016/j.explore.2016.10.001.

7. Donna Bach et al., "Clinical EFT (Emotional Freedom Techniques) Improves Multiple Physiological Markers of Health," *Journal of Evidence-Based Integrative Medicine* 24 (2019): https://doi.org/10.1177/2515690X18823691.

Turning toward my body in stress changed the story I believed about myself in that season. Our life remained stressful. Our circumstances got worse. But day by day, my body and soul became stronger.

In his 1974 book on the liturgical theology of baptism, Alexander Schmemann writes that modern Christians do "not know what to make of the 'destruction of death' and 'the resurrection of the body.'"[8] The resurrection is the reality that we can renew our lives right in the middle of stress, but most of us reduce the resurrection to a mere future hope. I believe we don't know how to receive the resurrection in our breathlessness and brokenness because we've inherited a gnostic legacy of dichotomizing body and soul.

The most damaging story in the world is not of a creatorless creation but a creation that must be transcended.

We pit our souls against our bodies, even though God strangely chose embodiment as the artistry of salvation. As my mentor, theologian Kelly M. Kapic writes, "The doctrine that the Word became flesh means that God himself affirms our flesh as good."[9]

So many of us are fighting a civil war with our bodies even though they are the place God has most made peace possible. The heresy of gnosticism is a large reason why.

The gnostics elevated the soul over the body, and the early church fought their heresy with fierceness. In the gnostic version of the story of God, humanness can't be part of holiness. In this story, our pesky bodies and their limitations and needs—of sleep and food

8. Alexander Schmemann, *Of Water and the Spirit: A Liturgical Study of Baptism* (Crestwood, NY: St. Vladimir's Seminary Press, 1974), 62.
9. Kelly M. Kapic, *You're Only Human: How Your Limits Reflect God's Design and Why That's Good News* (Grand Rapids: Brazos, 2022).

and sex and soothing—are the part of us that is sinful and weak. In this story, pleasing God requires reaching beyond our ordinariness to be extraordinary.[10]

Irenaeus was one of the fiercest contenders against this lie during the second century, and his chief charge against those teaching it was their dissatisfaction with the pace of God's grace, their preference for more, better, and faster (temptations just like the ones Christ resisted). It turns out that our expectation to be able to jump from pain to praise is quite ancient. "So," theologian Julie Canlis writes, "Irenaus threw down the gauntlet: if you downgrade creation, you downgrade Christ. If you downgrade the physical ways that God meets us, then you lose the means of redemption."[11]

The story you may have swallowed in church or in our culture that your body is bad is not the gospel story but the gnostic story. It's a counterstory to Christianity, one that keeps us from rising to the very heights it claims to reach.

Whenever our ordinary emotions and physicality are demonized or dismissed, some form of gnosticism is at work. When my pursuit of God excludes kindness toward my ordinary body, gnosticism is there, gnawing at my goodness. When my pursuit of peace in God sidesteps seeking peace in my physicality, gnosticism is slicing me in two. When my worship of God does not include welcoming my neighbors or sitting with the suffering, I am succumbing to a gnostic form of spiritual autonomy. When ordinary shepherding and ordinary sacraments don't seem relevant enough to build a church

---

10. Julie Canlis, *A Theology of the Ordinary* (Wenatchee, WA: Godspeed Press, 2017), 20. Canlis's summary of gnosticism is one of the best, most succinct summaries I have encountered. This chapter is deeply influenced by her insights and scholarship.

11. Ibid., 22.

or reach the world, gnosticism is our god. When we try to enact a Christian story that is more epic than the weekly witnessing of Christ's transforming presence in bread and wine, we want a gnostic god more than the one who let Thomas touch his side.

Evil is always trying to dress up lies in the dazzling clothing of dichotomies. Good and bad. False and true. Soul and body. The ancient gnostic dichotomy of the mortality of the body and the immortality of the soul drives us farther into death and disconnection by shaming or attempting to shut down our stress. We end up practicing faith by fighting the very parts of us that most need love. We try to preach our way out of pain, not realizing our emotional pain is our bodies' cry for care.

"Preaching to yourself" can easily turn into punishing yourself. When I was having an anxiety attack, I didn't need to preach myself to feel peace. I couldn't have heard it anyway, because when we are in states of stress, we are disintegrated from the parts of our nervous systems that enable us to connect through words.[12] I needed to pay compassionate attention to my body to move my nervous system there.

Prescribing a strategy of hypervigilance and violence toward our fear is never going to produce the fruit of security. Only presence can take us there.

Courage is practicing integrity, embracing that beautiful wholeness that refuses to slice apart body and soul, physical and spiritual, ordinary and extraordinary—the wholeness embodied in the person of Christ, who brought heaven and earth *together*. Courage is resisting the hurried pace of modern life and embracing the slower rhythm our bodies need to regulate and rise. Courage is refusing to dichotomize that which Christ has dignified.

When your body sinks into states of stress or you are stuck in

---

12. Deb Dana, *The Polyvagal Theory in Therapy: Engaging the Rhythm of Regulation*, Norton Series on Interpersonal Neurobiology (New York: Norton, 2018), 66.

a season of inexplicable suffering, you cannot just think or preach yourself into faith. You cannot *should* yourself into being soothed. You cannot shame your way out of stress. You have to love your way there.

Courage begins by being a compassionate witness to your own stress.

In our union with Christ, "do not fear" comes to mean "do not only fear." We can authentically say with David, "I will fear no evil," because fear is always a place Christ has gone before us and is able to sit with us. He empowers us to rise.

In the presence of Christ, the symptoms and scars of our stress dignify us rather than disqualify us. The only prerequisite to receiving Christ's presence of love is being a person who needs it.

Contempt for your fear will never create courage. You have to set down your sword.

Pick up, instead, the practice of courage, being willing to receive the present risenness of Christ in your ordinary body right now.[13] Because Christ has gone before us into the depths of fear, because we have been united to Christ and are inextricably bound up in his belovedness, the same Spirit who raised Christ from the dead now lives within our very bodies, joining together the compassion of Christ with our self-compassion, energizing us to live resurrection lives.

Whether you are facing a bully, feeling burned out, or going to bed brokenhearted, everything you are and do is an invitation to see Christ working out his wholeness in and through you. Your entire life—including your fear—is an opportunity to bear witness to the wonder that Christ who made your body good is also making this world whole.

---

13. I'm borrowing the phrase "the present risenness of Christ" from the fierce words of Brennan Manning in *Abba's Child*: "For me, the most radical demand of the Christian faith lies in summoning the courage to say yes to the present risenness of Jesus Christ." Brennan Manning, *Abba's Child: The Cry of the Heart for Intimate Belonging* (Colorado Springs: NavPress, 2015), 80.

20. FOR YOU
ARE WITH ME;

P SALM 23 IS JUST FIFTY-FIVE WORDS IN HEBREW. There are exactly twenty-six Hebrew words before the phrase "for you are with me" and twenty-six words afterward. *This is the heart of the psalm.*

The climax of the psalm is the crux of our shared story:

When we are stepping through the shadows of fear, how do we sense that God is still with us?

How can we hear God calling us Beloved when evil has labeled us too broken or brash?

We listen.

I wrote the final chapters of my first book while living through one of the most daunting chapters of my life. We were jobless, technically homeless (without long-term, secure housing of our own),[1] and nearly moneyless, and I showed up at the public library

---

1. It's called "hidden homelessness," and the experience carries hidden stresses that most can't see. "Hidden Homelessness," Homeless Link, www.homeless.org.uk/facts/homelessness -in-numbers/hidden-homelessness.

in Bozeman, Montana, every single day it was open for five weeks straight, determined to finish what I had started.

I arrived at the library each day with a backpack full of supplies—a thermos of black coffee, a handful of meds, kleenex for the sinus infection that *would not* go away—and a body buzzing with fear that I might not be able to make my deadline, let alone step into a life that might hold more disappointment than it already had.

The protest of my body in the months before had made me adamant about one thing: I would not write unless I knew God went with me. I was unwilling to write good news for others unless I could keep receiving it as good news for me first. I knew the only way I could make it through the marathon of each day, the only way I could emerge with both an intact manuscript and an intact psyche—while wading through problems that couldn't get solved quickly—was to anchor myself in a peace that passed all possible understanding.

So before I worked, I paused. Before I wrote, I listened.

I'd walk straight from the car to the library's sculpture garden and sit down at the same bench day after day, bulging backpack at my feet and the sharp Montana sun on my face. It was my act of acknowledgment, to pay attention to the presence of the God I knew loved me but feared had forsaken me.

I started by reading a prayer by Peter Traben Haas, one I still pray almost every day: "Living Life and Sustaining Love, help me feel your attracting grace in the universe, which keeps everything from coming apart. May the Word of Christ hold me together with wisdom and love. I give thanks for your Word and consent to being held by it, so as to remain at center with you."[2] And then, holding my travel mug of hot coffee between my hands, I sat in silence for twelve minutes, practicing being held by the God I could not see.

---

2. Peter Traben Haas, *Centering Prayers: A One-Year Daily Companion for Going Deeper into the Love of God* (Brewster, MA: Paraclete, 2013), 248.

Any moment my mind would wander to the mountain of words I still needed to write or the possibility that Ryan wouldn't find a job soon, I'd simply repeat one word in acknowledgment that God's presence was holding me and my future together in ways I could not comprehend.

Held.

Held.

Held.

That sacred word was, and still is, my anchor, returning my whole self to a story where I can remain grounded with God because God has made a home in me.

Every single day, I showed up to the library determined to pay attention to God's presence before paying attention to making progress. It wasn't magical. I didn't always feel amazed or embraced. But day by day, I was strengthened to walk up the stairs of that library confident in the truths I would write. It was as though sitting with the pit in my chest transformed it into a well, and once I saw it, I could trust I already had all I needed. I was finishing a book about our union with Christ in suffering, and by acknowledging that Christ was holding me together and filling me when it seemed like everything had fallen apart, I grew more resilient and radiant with joy. Every day, I watched as God drew up words and peace and energy from deep within my soul.

Former Archbishop of Canterbury Rowan Williams gives language to what was happening in me. "Christians pray because they *have* to, because the Spirit is surging up inside them."[3] Further, he writes that the life of being baptized as beloved "is characterized by a prayerfulness that courageously keeps going, even when things are difficult and unpromising and unrewarding, simply because you

---

3. Rowan Williams, *Being Christian: Baptism, Bible, Eucharist, Prayer* (Grand Rapids, MI: Eerdmans, 2014), 8.

cannot stop the urge to pray. Something keeps coming alive in you; never mind the results."[4]

Something kept coming alive in me, never mind religious trauma. Someone still stirred me, regardless of religion's harm.

Something beautiful came out of me, even when I was most broken, because I was learning to be still enough to hear the silent voice who already and always calls me Beloved.

We most often cannot hear we are beloved because our bodies are burdened by the sounds of stress. We want the sound of love, but we don't realize we may need to shift our autonomic state to be able to hear it.

Our autonomic state serves like a negotiator between brain, body, and the surrounding world. It intervenes in our capacity to listen, absorb and understand information, and respond socially. Different autonomic states support different behaviors. A sympathetic stress state, for example, *is* effective if you need to protect yourself from danger! But it's ineffective at producing a sense of connection, confidence, and joy.

One of the chief challenges in being courageous is how our bodies become stuck in states of stress from months and years of loss, chronic pressure, and trauma. Many of us struggle to feel connected to God not because we lack faith but because we are carrying a heavy burden in our bodies.

The cumulative burden of chronic stress is called allostatic load, and it's likely part of what is making you feel inadequate to cope with your life or step into your calling.[5] When our nervous systems

---

4. Ibid., 11–12.
5. Jenny Guidi et al., "Allostatic Load and Its Impact on Health: A Systematic Review," *Psychotherapy and Psychosomatics* 90, no. 1 (2021): 11–27, https://doi.org/10.1159/000510696.

have sensed more cues of danger than safety for extended periods of time, we experience allostatic overload. Our bodies become stuck in states of stress not because we are bad people or don't try to believe hard enough but because the load is heavy.

If we want to feel connected to God and more courageous in our calling, we have to practice unburdening our bodies by shifting our autonomic state back to a place where we are able to hear we are loved. We can't cut fear out of our faith, but we can allow our sensation of fear to awaken us to the reality of the stress underneath it. In this way, fear can fuel faith. We can look up to Christ who always *wants* to climb down to us at our lowest to lift us up and carry us home.

One of the trauma-informed modalities I integrate into my counseling practice is the safe and sound protocol (SSP), which was developed by Stephen Porges, the founder of polyvagal theory. In the training for SSP, Stephen says, "Listening is a pathway to change neural state."[6] While SSP offers a passive way of retraining the vagus nerve through the middle ear, the practice of centering prayer offers a similar benefit through the simplicity of silence. Porges teaches that lowering auditory stimulation helps the nervous system develop trust. When it comes to developing trust, less is more. Less noise. Fewer words. Less effort. As Porges has said, "'Less' enables the nervous system to catch up."[7]

Centering prayer is the practice of tolerating the presence of a God who doesn't require our performance to be pleased with us. We don't even have to say anything *to* God to be loved by God. God is always glad to be with you, and centering prayer is practicing a willingness to receive God's kindness as yours, right in the midst of days and seasons where life is telling you a different story.

Before I can tell myself what to believe and become, I must

---

6. Stephen Porges, "Foundational Safe and Sound Protocol Certification" (Unyte web-based training, 2021).
7. Ibid.

listen to my body telling me where I need to go. Prayer is learning to listen, and it's the listening that pulls us, even physically, out of stress and into a place of hearing we are God's Beloved.

Centering prayer heals the violence of silence by returning attentive presence to the silenced and stressed parts of our souls. Centering prayer sometimes feels strange and even too simple to be doing anything, but as we practice simply *being with God*, God is restoring our bodies and souls to be able to hear the voice of Divine Love everywhere we go. It is what the wise priest and author Cynthia Bourgeault calls an "interior rearrangement" and "interior awakening."[8] In the silence, our bodies learn to trust that God is more near than we feared and we are more loved than we imagined.

Christ names the reality of the evil and trouble we will experience, the real dangers we will face that make our blood pump and feet freeze as our nervous systems sink into stress and self-protection. In John 16, as Jesus prepared his disciples for his coming death and their coming suffering, for a time in which they would need great courage, he told them two things to expect suffering and to expect his Spirit.

God is not a gaslighter. Christ extends an example of acknowledging distress, not dismissing it. Before his death, he took time to acknowledge the distress his friends would feel. And then he identified himself as the source of their peace, saying, "I have told you these things, so that in me you may have peace. In this world you will have trouble. But take heart! I have overcome the world."[9]

---

8. Cynthia Bourgeault, *Centering Prayer and Inner Awakening* (New York: Cowley, 2004), 6.

9. John 16:33.

In John 16, Jesus is telling us, *Peace is found only in my presence. And I will not leave you alone.*

And then Jesus says to "take heart," which can also be translated as "have courage," telling us that our future is secure because he has already overcome the world.

Fear is just courage's preamble. When we practice remembering that the Spirit of Christ is our companion, fear simply becomes one more prompt to pay attention to the voice and presence of Love. Fear doesn't have to be an enemy to conquer. It can be a place to be companioned by Love.

When we felt exiled from our community, far from financial security and the certainty of old beliefs and habits, it was when I stopped running and practiced sitting that I realized God was still speaking the words I most longed to hear. *I am with you.*

This God continues to speak the words that false shepherds of scarcity would most like to stop, because if we know God is with us, we won't need a powerful person or institution's approval to feel secure. People who befriend their fear cannot be so easily manipulated and controlled.[10]

---

10. Walter Brueggemann's words in *Deep Memory, Exuberant Hope* infuse me with hope in my experiences of exile. "This is an intimate word of assurance. It is an intimate word on the lips of the creator of heaven and earth, the one who authorizes oddity, the one who speaks the words the empire would most like to stop, because people mothered beyond fear are not so easily managed or administered or intimidated." Walter Brueggemann, *Deep Memory, Exuberant Hope: Contested Truth in a Post-Christian World* (Minneapolis: Fortress, 2000), 12.

21. YOUR ROD AND YOUR STAFF,

YOUR ROD AND YOUR STAFF, THEY COMFORT ME." This line of Psalm 23 may have cued the proverb "spare the rod, spoil the child"[1] to begin to stomp through your brain. Maybe it kicked up the dust of memories of soap in your mouth and a belt on your butt. (Just me?) Don't worry. You are not about to read a whole manipulative chapter asking you to consider how all the hard things that have happened to you are just God's good rod of discipline.

This line of Psalm 23 is not a baptism of brutality as kindness. The Lord disciplines the one he loves,[2] but this psalm's immediate context is the shepherd's readiness to protect and guide the vulnerable sheep in his care.

Sheep have almost no ability to protect themselves from predators. Even when they survive an attack and avoid sustaining injury, they can still die from panic.[3] As grazing animals, sheep have an innate instinct to seek protection by banding together and running

---

1. Prov. 13:24.
2. Heb. 12:6.
3. Paula Simmons and Carol Ekarius, *Storey's Guide to Raising Sheep* (North Adams, MA: Storey Publishing, 2001).

164

from danger. They have sharp peripheral vision, with slit-shaped horizontal pupils that allow them to see behind themselves without fully turning their heads, enabling them to scan for danger better than you or I could. But other than being able to deliver a swift kick to anyone who gets too close to their lambs, sheep entirely depend on their shepherd to protect them from harm.[4]

A shepherd's rod and staff have historically been used to protect the flock and guide them into safety, not as tools for punishing them for their vulnerabilities.[5] A shepherd's staff is used to rescue sheep who are isolated and in danger. As theologian Timothy Laniak describes, "Sheep have a way of getting caught in pits, fences, bushes, and crevices. They can get stuck in mud or, worse, swept off by a flash flood. The staff becomes an extension of a shepherd's arm, reaching carefully around the isolated creature and pulling it back to safety."[6] It's used to separate sheep when tensions rise and to bring them back together when they need grouping. *The staff is used as an extension of the shepherd's voice*, lightly tapping the shoulder or laying the staff across the side of a special sheep, as though to say, "I'm here."[7]

Likewise, in traditional shepherding contexts, the rod is the shepherd's "primary offensive weapon for protecting the flock from enemies, be they wild animals or human thieves."[8] While the "rod" is mentioned in other parts of Scripture to describe discipline, in the context of a shepherd's attentive care, the rod's primary purpose is protecting the vulnerable sheep against *external threats*.[9]

---

4. William P. Shulaw, *Sheep Care Guide* (Englewood, CO: American Industry Sheep Association, 2005).

5. Kenneth E. Bailey, *The Good Shepherd: A Thousand-Year Journey from Psalm 23 to the New Testament* (Downers Grove, IL: IVP Academic, 2014), 53.

6. Timothy Laniak, *While Shepherds Watch Their Flocks: Forty Daily Reflections on Biblical Leadership* (Franklin, TN: Carpenter's Son Publishing, 2007), 96.

7. Ibid., 96.

8. Bailey, *Good Shepherd*, 50.

9. Ibid., 53.

A rod likely was a carefully chosen sapling, uprooted and then carved and shaped with patience to perfectly fit the shepherd's hands.[10] It would typically be about two and a half feet in length, with a rounded, mace-like end with bits of sharp iron embedded.[11] Traditionally, shepherd boys would carve their own rods and spend hour after hour practicing how to throw them to develop precision like that of a master archer and force like that of a warrior.[12] A shepherd would train himself to use the rod as his primary weapon to protect his valuable and vulnerable sheep as well as he possibly could. The lives of the sheep depended on his accuracy, strength, and readiness to stand up to predators.

Placed in the context of the psalmist's life, the rod mentioned in Psalm 23 is best understood as a description of the shepherd's willingness to rise up to defend the vulnerable. David would have chosen his words with care, knowing how often he had to use his own rod to protect his flock and remembering well the day he stood up against all odds to protect his people.

When Israel was fighting the Philistines, their enemy sent out a giant named Goliath to defeat them. Goliath towered outside the Israelite camp, taunting them, "Choose a man and have him come down to me. If he is able to fight and kill me, we will become your subjects; but if I overcome him and kill him, you will become our subjects and serve us."[13] The Israelite army and their king, Saul, spent forty days straight quaking in their tents, terrified of Goliath and the imminent enslavement he had threatened.

---

10. W. Phillip Keller, *A Shepherd Looks at Psalm 23* (Grand Rapids, MI: Zondervan, 2015), 80, Kindle.

11. Bailey, *Good Shepherd*, 50.

12. Keller, *Shepherd*, 80, Kindle.

13. 1 Sam. 17:8–9.

That's when David—just a boy—showed up with some food from home for his brothers in the army. As he was catching up with them, Goliath's voice thundered out over the valley with his daily display of defiance. Every time Goliath taunted, the Israelites fled in terror. Like sheep without a shepherd to reassure them, the Israelites had the same flight instinct as terrified sheep.

But David was indignant. He hated the way Goliath was shaming "the armies of the living God."[14] His oldest brother scoffed at him, calling David conceited for coming to the battle just to watch, as though David was shirking his shepherding duties at home. But his brother's shaming didn't stop him. David kept saying that someone needed to stand up to Goliath, and kept speaking up until someone told King Saul about the boy and his bravery.

Saul sent for David, and when David arrived at the king's tent, he volunteered himself for the task none of the grown men were willing to do.

"Let no one lose heart on account of this Philistine," David said. "Your servant will go and fight him."[15] Saul probably looked him up and down in disbelief. Compared with a giant, David's stature was nothing. Saul wasn't about to shame the whole army and himself by sending out someone impossibly young.

David defended his courage with his history of shepherding. He told Saul how he'd tended sheep for his father, how whenever a bear or a lion came to take a lamb from his flock, he'd run it down, strike it with his rod, and deliver the lamb out of its mouth. King Saul's eyes had been full of fear for forty days, and I imagine David looking into them with his own fierce, clear eyes, saying, "Look, lion or bear—it didn't matter. I killed it. It was after my sheep, and I did what needed to be done to protect them. And I'll do the same to this Philistine pig who is after the army of the living God."

---

14. 1 Sam. 17:26b.
15. 1 Sam. 17:32.

And then, with the kind of faith that comes from experience, David declared the most audacious thing yet: "God, who delivered me from the teeth of the lion and the claws of the bear, will deliver me from this Philistine."[16]

Theologian N. T. Wright has written that virtue is what happens when courageous choices have been practiced so repeatedly they become our instinct.[17] Courage is what happens when we've made a thousand small, hard choices requiring our attention and effort, risking embarrassment and even failure, to honor the vulnerable within our care, including the vulnerability within our own souls. Courage is what comes out of you when you've practiced standing up to the giants of shame, lions of lies, and bears of brokenness so repeatedly that it becomes second nature. The truth is, David's courage wasn't just his audacity to believe God would save him that day; it was every choice he made to become the kind of person who would risk believing it.

Don't think that David was some kind of superhuman, immune to feeling fear. He had a body just like yours, wired to respond to threats by fleeing or fighting. The difference between fleeing and fighting is the choice we make to protect what we love. David's fear didn't extinguish his courage; it fueled it.[18] When the object of fear threatens what we love, courage is our practice and choice to honor that love.

David didn't want to be mauled by a bear, but his love for his sheep outweighed his fear of danger. He had practiced, day after day, remembering he had a protector with him always, that he could

16. 1 Sam. 17:37 MSG.

17. N. T. Wright, *After You Believe: Why Christian Character Matters* (New York: HarperCollins, 2010), 20–21.

18. I would be remiss to overlook that even David, who was once well practiced in the virtue of courage, eventually used his power to take advantage of others, raping Bathsheba and having her husband killed on the battlefield to cover his tracks. The darkest chapters of David's story remind us that we must continue to cultivate the practice of courage our whole lives, especially as we grow in influence, privilege, and power.

risk doing hard things. And the choices he made to protect his vulnerable sheep built up courage in his nervous system, overshadowing the terror he felt with truth that love is worth risking it all. Eugene Peterson writes of David, "He had practiced the presence of God so thoroughly that God's word, which he couldn't literally hear, was far more real to him than the lion's roar, which he could hear. He had worshiped the majesty of God so continuously that God's love, which he couldn't see, was far more real to him than the bear's ferocity, which he could see."[19]

Courage is the practice of wanting to protect what is good and true and beautiful more than we want to avoid being wounded. Courage is not the absence of anxiety but the practice of trusting that we will be held and loved no matter what happens.[20]

So David risked his life again, this time for an entire nation of people instead of a flock of sheep. He took his shepherd's staff, found five smooth stones from the nearby stream, and with his sling in hand, walked toward the giant no one else had the courage to face.

Goliath mocked him as he approached, "Am I a dog, that you come at me with sticks?"[21] He mocked the rod and staff that David had long used to protect his flock on those long days and nights alone in the wilderness, the small tools through which God had always provided what he needed to fight massive lions and bears, growing within him the very courage that had brought him to that day.

David met Goliath's defiance with dignity, calling on the name of the Lord Almighty as his deliverer and strength, naming the way God would save him—without sword or spear but with the weapon

---

19. Eugene Peterson, *Leap over a Wall: Earthy Spirituality for Everyday Christians* (New York: HarperOne, 1998), 40.

20. K.J. Ramsey, *This Too Shall Last: Finding Grace When Suffering Lingers* (Grand Rapids, MI: Zondervan, 2020), 213.

21. 1 Sam. 17:43.

least expected. And just as he ran at the lions and bears bullying his sheep, he ran at Goliath, readied his sling, and killed the giant with one small stone.

This is what David had to have recalled when he wrote, "Your rod and your staff, they comfort me." David's attestation that God's rod and staff comfort him is a description thick with proof of how the Shepherd comes to deliver the vulnerable from the bondage of fear.

This line isn't about being punished or disciplined by God. It's about the promise of deliverance. It's about the intimacy of belonging to a Shepherd who fights for us, who runs down lions and bears to keep us alive, who rescues us out of briars and bushes of bullying, who stretches out his staff just to remind us he is near, who is relentlessly determined to bring us home.

22. THEY
COMFORT ME.

THE HARDEST ASPECT OF PRACTICING COURAGE is developing our capacity to hold hurt and hope in our hearts at the same time. David didn't forever remain the conquering hero. He lived with the hope of becoming Israel's king, as God had secretly anointed him for that role through the priest Samuel. But in the years after standing up to Goliath, David instead became hunted and hated, living in constant danger of harm.

King Saul grew jealous of David's growing acclaim. He hated David's goodness—his bravery on battlefields, his constant melodies of God's majesty. But most of all, he feared losing his own power. The thought of the people giving David the power and praise that Saul saw as his own possession filled him with fear. *Saul's fear* fueled rage and a scarcity-shaped storyline where he felt the need to throw spears at others to secure his own kingdom. Saul hoarded power, believing that there was only enough room in the kingdom for one man's acclaim.

Saul tried to kill the very man to whom he owed his kingdom. Yet David escaped, leaving Jerusalem and his close proximity to the royal family in order to save his life. The hero became the hunted. David lived for many years in the wilderness, hiding in caves and hills while Saul hounded him. Saul was determined to kill and destroy the man who seemed primed to take what he would never give. But the same man who had killed lions and bears, the man who had believed in God's protection and defeated the giant, continued to carry the hope of God's deliverance in his heart, even as he held the constant threat of harm in his head.

David's prayers show us how to hold hurt alongside hope. Writing from one of the caves where he hid, David prayed words like, "Look and see, there is no one at my right hand; no one is concerned for me. I have no refuge; *no one cares for my life*."[1]

Prayer is not constant positivity. It is honesty held in our hands and hurled at the sky. Strangely, honesty about our hopelessness is what revives our hope. David's dejection widens the space available for our worship. Our worst self-pity and loudest wails are welcomed prayers.

He let his lament become longing, continuing in prayer:

> I cry to you, LORD;
>> I say, "You are my refuge,
>> my portion in the land of the living."

> Listen to my cry,
>> for I am in desperate need;
> rescue me from those who pursue me,
>> for they are too strong for me.
> Set me free from my prison,
>> that I may praise your name.
> Then the righteous will gather about me
>> because of your goodness to me.[2]

---

1. Ps. 142:4, emphasis added.
2. Ps. 142:5–7.

David's honesty—held in tandem with his hope—empowered him to trust that the harm threatened by Saul would not be the end of his story.

Honesty about our hurt empowers us to hope in the God who stretches out a staff to comfort us. Courage is a continuous choice to be honest about the reality of harm while reaching for hope, even when it is inconvenient and even when it bristles against cultural and religious expectations that equate goodness with niceness.

Evil pits hurt and hope against each other on the balancing scales of scarcity. Evil welds our well-being to the balance of those scales, pressing the weight of dichotomies to pull us into discouragement, distraction, and despair.

When hurt and hope are pit against each other, evil holds the reins, yanking us right and then left, as though hustling to have more, be more, and do more will finally bring us home to less hurt and more belonging.

If evil can convince us to stay stressed (by shaming, silencing, or sermonizing our stress!), it can keep us stuck in neural states of self-protection. Some find safety in telling a story with the hard parts cast as footnotes. Others, who feel silenced by those stories, might find safety in recasting suffering in a leading role. We both end up living out stories of searing solitude, feeling like the truth of the story as we see it isn't being fully heard.

Evil plays in the poles of both our pain and positivity. It demands or defeats, miring us in the muck of either overfunctioning or underengaging in our good lives. Evil sings in the chorus of cheer, demanding through smiles, happy-clappy out-of-context verses, and heavyhanded expectations that we throw away the weight of hurt to feel the comfort of hope, as though our willpower to worship is the only thing standing between us and joy. Yet evil also defeats us in dark caves, convincing us a speck of light is not worth seeking at all.

Because Goodness made his home in the middle of humanity's hurt, Divine Love is always meeting us in the middle of what seems diametrically opposed to knit us back together by kneeling at the foot of the cross.

Bearing witness to the truth of our wounds welcomes us to see the larger truth that the Wounded One is with us. Just as Christ walked outside the gates of Jerusalem's power to his cross, Jesus is always walking outside the places of expected power to meet us in the paradoxes of our pain. He pulls us into redemption right where life seems to be ripping us apart.

The paradox of having a shepherd whose rod and staff comfort us is that we live in a world where a rod and staff are needed. It is a painful thing to enfold our faith into the expectation that we live in a world where we will need to be rescued.

David might not have expected his king to be the person who would most threaten his life. I didn't expect my church to be the place that would crush my sense of safety.

After we left, I wanted nothing more than the comfort of communion again. Church had been our safe place once before, and we wanted it to be that again. I wanted to wrap my wounds in worship. I wanted singing next to other saints to serve like salve on my scars. I wanted to taste assurance on my tongue. I wanted the bread and the wine to bind up my brokenness. I wanted to swallow solidarity with Christ and his body whole.

So we went back to church, even though it was church that had wounded us.[3]

Even though it was a different church community, as soon as we sat down that first time, I instinctively scanned the room, looking for people from our previous church. Enemy mode was activated (but I didn't have language for that quite yet). I couldn't sink into my seat until I had cleared the room of potential threats—people who might approach me to ask awkward questions with answers they weren't entitled to hear. I found myself cynical and critical, judging every announcement and song choice like I was sorting the substance of church into boxes of "harmful" or "helpful" to determine whether I could be safe there. As soon as the pastor stepped to the pulpit, I dropped into my own world, scratching out the start of a poem in my journal instead of listening to the sermon.

Halfway through the service, my spine suddenly screamed in pain. So I retreated to the back with the mothers rocking their wailing babies. I stood separate, shifting in the shadows of the sanctuary, where my pain couldn't disturb the worshiping crowd. I rejoined Ryan for communion at the end and as soon as the last words of the benediction left the pastor's mouth, I nudged Ryan to leave before anyone could make us have conversations I was not ready to have.

This went on for weeks. Finally, I decided to just leave before the sermon started and sit on a bench outside until it was time for communion. I gripped the armrests to slow the swaying sense that the world was a sea in which I was sinking. And in the quiet, I

---

3. By the way, I wish I had a dollar for every time I've heard a Christian correct someone who's been crushed by saying something like, "It wasn't the church that wounded you. *It was people.* No church is perfect!" It's funny how we cast aside ecclesiology when it's convenient, eager to individualize that which is inseparably systemic. Individual Christians make up the body of Christ (see Rom. 12:4–5 and 1 Cor. 12:12–31), and pretending that a hand stabbing a foot isn't an action done by the body is a false comfort that only further confuses our relationship to the body long-term.

realized: every week for a month my disease symptoms had suddenly started to flare up fifteen minutes into the church service. As a therapist who sees so many clients with trauma, it was undeniable. *My mind wanted to be at church again, but my body didn't feel safe there.*

Spiritual abuse braces our bodies for harm where there should be help. It twists the sacred into a sword, leaving us subconsciously on alert in case Scripture or a sermon or a small group interaction suddenly becomes sinister. Diane Langberg agrees: "Spiritual abuse involves using the sacred to harm or deceive the soul of another."[4] Spiritual abuse ruptures our bodies' sense of trust that being in the Body won't brutalize our souls.

Ignoring my body's sense of things being off was what had put me in a position to be spiritually abused in the first place. I decided then and there that I would no longer silence the truth my body was telling me. I knew I needed to hear and honor the honest truth that my body didn't feel safe if I was ever going to cultivate hope to feel safe inside a church again.

So, for the first time in my life, I stopped going to church. As a trauma-informed clinician, I knew that my body needed space to regain stability and a sense of safety before I'd be able to tolerate the stress of church and its corresponding triggers again. Ryan still felt like he wanted and was able to attend sometimes, but we agreed that for me a season away was best. We knew that my complex childhood trauma made my body more sensitive to stress than his, and we didn't want our church trauma to exacerbate my autoimmune disease. I knew I needed space to learn how to feel safe with God and myself again before trying to feel safe with his people.

---

4. Diane Langberg, *Redeeming Power: Understanding Authority and Abuse in the Church* (Grand Rapids, MI: Brazos, 2020), 127.

At that point, we were back in Colorado, living temporarily with our friends Josh and Rachel, who were giving us space to get back on our feet while job searching. Their generosity is a grace I still can't adequately express with words. When the church pushed us out, our friends welcomed us in.

Every Sunday of that summer, instead of putting on a sundress, I'd pull on shorts and my chacos, gather up a quilt, water bottle, and a book, and sit for hours in our friends' back yard in the dappled shade of a giant cottonwood. Week after week, I caught my breath reading Eugene Peterson's *As Kingfishers Catch Fire*, a collection of sermons he preached over twenty-nine years of pastoring the same congregation. Every Sunday, my body learned to relax in the rhythm of a pastor's voice—one that was kind, safe, and more attuned to presence than accumulating power and prestige.

I let Eugene become my pastor through the page. I let my heart be shepherded outside of a sanctuary. I let the tension of my pain and God's promises stretch me. And in the space between my hurt and hope, I started to sense a slight pressure on my shoulder, the Shepherd's staff reminding me that even outside of a church, God remained beside me.

In the place where fear had wriggled its way inside me and rewired my nervous system into a pattern of hypervigilance, God was coming to find me. Honoring the hurt manifested in my body—the symptoms of post-traumatic stress that were shouting each Sunday I tried to go to church—ended up being the choice that helped me learn to hope again. The trauma of spiritual abuse had isolated me from the flock of God's people, but Christ was extending his staff to me, scooping me up out of the briars where my body had gotten stuck in scarcity.

I needed the comfort of communion, but I needed to experience the Shepherd bringing it *to me*. He knew where to look, because it was a place he knew well. Jesus Christ was the first Christian casualty of religious abuse. I needed to see the Savior that religious folks had killed was the same God coming to save me. I didn't need to push through my pain to sense the Savior's solidarity at church. I needed to choose the courage to honor my pain as something he will go any length to seek and soothe.

Faith positions itself in the middle of paradox, unwilling to allow evil to pull us away from the place the person of Christ is coming to find us.

God in Christ made himself into a paradox.

> God—with skin.
> God—with us in our sin.
> God in Christ—who became like us,
> so we can always be with him.

Christ's arms stretched out on the hard wood of the cross hold every paradox of our personhood and every promise of our redemption. Only the Paradox himself can hold the entirety of your story, with all of its wounds and wonders.

I often remind my clients that two things can be true at the same time. Grief does not cancel out goodness. Hurt does not silence all hope. Our wounds bring us to the intersection of grace, where hurt and hope are held in the scarred and tender hands of Christ. Jesus holds the paradoxes of your past, present, and future in indivisible love.

Every paradox in your life is an invitation to be held, for it is in sensing Christ's scars that we learn to rise with ours. Held in the center of his encompassing grace, you are being made capable of beholding the center of everything.

23. YOU PREPARE

PARADOX IS THE ONLY TABLE LARGE ENOUGH TO HOLD TRUTH.[1]

That summer I didn't receive communion from the hands of a pastor or priest; I received it from the hands of my friends. On more evenings than not, we closed our days together, gathered around a table in the fading heat of Josh and Rachel's back yard, as they joined with Ryan and me, and our mutual friend Mish. Together, we found our way to the table, where we talked out our troubles over whatever was searing on the grill.

We prepared a space for each other simply by showing up as we were and sharing what we had. We were a circle of misfits and mourners, where everyone had bruises, so no one had anything to hide. Josh and Rachel were still reeling from resigning from the church six months before we did. Ryan and I were jobless and untethered, still stinging and confused from our own abuse and losses. And one week before we moved back, out of nowhere Mish's husband told her that he no longer wanted to be married.

We triaged around the table, piecing together the fragments of our faith and our families. We asked our hardest questions to

---

1. The priest Robert Farrar Capon put it similarly: "Paradox is the only basket large enough to hold truth." Robert Farrar Capon, *The Supper of the Lamb: A Culinary Reflection* (New York: Modern Library, 2002), 155.

each other and ourselves. Why did God allow a pastor to spiritually abuse us? How do you live with being rejected by the person who was supposed to love you till you die? What role did our sin and shame play in getting sucked into others' egos? Will we ever heal?

We left a seat for Curiosity and told Certainty to give her a turn to talk. We held forbearance for each other like the glasses of wine in our hands. We let each other unburden and unravel with every bite of bread, our ears tuned with silent trust that like the wheat that was once cut and crushed to become food, our breaking would become bread.

After dinner was finished, we kept talking as the blue sky turned to tangerine and peach. The sunset stretched around our sorrow—a symbol of hope we could not spark ourselves. Often, we'd grow quiet, spellbound by the wonder of the sun's fading strokes across the sky. I remember one night being gripped by the beauty of the growing darkness—violet shading into cobalt and the deepest navy. "Even the darkness is not dark to you," I silently prayed in realization.[2]

It was at the table of the bruised and the broken that I most felt held. Without even meaning to, we prepared a table in the wilderness where every person had a seat and every story could be told. Our pain had a place. Our hurt was heard. Our hope was held—by each other. Only the table of the rejected could hold enough room for our hurt to sit by our hope. At that table, the space between our hurt and healing became sacred ground.

At this point, you've probably realized that I believe metaphors make faith come alive. Eugene Peterson loved them too, writing,

---

2. Ps. 139:12.

"A metaphor is a word that carries us across the abyss separating the invisible from the visible. The contradiction involved in what the word denotes and what it connotes sets up a tension in our minds, and we are stimulated to an act of imagination in which we become participants in what is being spoken."[3]

The dissonance that a metaphor creates in our minds stimulates our attention, asking us to draw near in order to follow the author or speaker. It's only in being pulled into a sentence or paragraph that we become participants in the story being told.

At this point in Psalm 23, David asks us to come closer by changing up the central metaphor of his story. While some argue that "you prepare a table" refers to the shepherd seeking out a flat plateau for the sheep to graze,[4] others note that interpretation simply does not fit with the geography of Israel.[5] Here David shifts from speaking of a sheep's hunger being quelled and thirst being quenched to God providing food and drink for a person, David himself.[6]

This shift gives us a sense of who God is, but in a way we might not expect. In the ancient middle eastern culture in which David was writing, a man's honor increased by means of his hospitality rather than his possessions.[7] If you wanted your community to know you had been blessed in acquiring more wealth, you didn't buy a fancy horse; you held a lavish meal with three times more food than anyone could possibly eat.[8] Psalm 23 isn't just the story of a good shepherd. It's also the story of a *good host*.

---

3. Eugene H. Peterson, *The Jesus Way: A Conversation on the Ways That Jesus Is the Way* (Grand Rapids, MI: Eerdmans, 2007), 25.

4. W. Phillip Keller, *A Shepherd Looks at Psalm 23* (Grand Rapids, MI: Zondervan, 2015), 92.

5. Kenneth Bailey, *The Good Shepherd: A Thousand-Year Journey from Psalm 23 to the New Testament* (Downers Grove, IL: IVP Academic, 2014), 53.

6. Ibid., 54.

7. George Lamsa, *The Shepherd of All: The Twenty-Third Psalm* (Amazon Direct Publishing, 2014), 43, Kindle.

8. Bailey, *Good Shepherd*, 54.

Theologian Kenneth Bailey shows us that in this ancient society, to "prepare a table" would have meant "to prepare a meal," since people did not eat from individual plates and with utensils but from common dishes with flatbread and their own hands.[9] Bailey also notes that while the Hebrew verb "you prepare" is masculine in this text, we are clearly shown a male engaging in activities which, in that culture, only a female would do.[10]

I've heard Psalm 23 my entire life. Yet *no one* ever taught me the feminine aspect of God in David's prayer. I didn't encounter it until researching for this book. I wonder what comfort we cut ourselves off from by putting God in a box marked male.

Jesus taught us that "God is spirit."[11] God is not made in humanity's image; humanity is made in God's. Both male and female characteristics reflect God, who is neither male nor female. Yet in every church I have been part of, the accepted way to speak of God has been with primarily masculine pronouns. In Psalm 23, we are given an undeniable picture of God that is both masculine *and* feminine—a strong shepherd *and* a generous host.

I'm visiting my parents right now, and every time I come to their home, my mom has stocked her kitchen with my favorite bread and chips, sour cream for French onion dip, and tri-tip to serve smoked alongside mashed potatoes. There is more food in her kitchen than we could possibly eat in a week. *This* gets at what David was describing.

God seeks us like a good shepherd. *And* God feeds us like a mom who is glad her daughter has come home.

9. Ibid., 55.
10. Ibid., 56. The phrase "prepare a table" is also clearly attached to women's work in Prov. 9:2–5.
11. John 4:24.

The Good Shepherd story arcs through the pages of Scripture over a thousand years, beginning with David's words in Psalm 23, thundering through the prophets Jeremiah (23), Ezekiel (34), and Zechariah (10), culminating in Christ (Matthew 18; Mark 6; Luke 15; John 10), and carried out into the church by Peter (1 Peter 5). Though David gave us the dual picture of a good shepherd and good host in Psalm 23, the "inclusion of both male and female components in the 'good shepherd psalm' disappears for a thousand years and then dramatically reappears in Jesus' matching parables of the good shepherd and the good woman (Lk 15:3–10)."[12]

In Luke 15, Jesus gives us a picture of his understanding of himself through these two linked parables.[13] The good shepherd leaves his ninety-nine sheep to find the one who was lost. And the good woman, who has ten silver coins, searches relentlessly to find the one she lost inside her house. Upon finding what they lost, both the good shepherd and the good woman prepare a feast for their friends and neighbors to rejoice over the recovery of their precious possessions. Through both stories, Jesus is redefining who belongs in his flock, what real lostness is, and what repentance means— through a shepherd and a woman. Jesus is the one who takes God out of our small boxes.

The welcome of the table God prepares for us is striking, but to see it clearly we have to first recognize the walls of control the Pharisees had built around their table. Before we consider *who* Jesus saw himself as and what table he was preparing, we need to consider *why* he is telling these stories.

---

12. Bailey, *Good Shepherd*, 57.
13. Ibid., 130.

The scene in Luke 15 opens with "tax collectors and sinners" thronging around Jesus to hear him teach. The Pharisees are standing nearby like the policemen of God's promises, ready to pounce on Jesus for departing from *their* laws of faith. Seeing the crowd, they mutter with contempt, "This man welcomes sinners and eats with them."[14]

The Pharisees' entire practice of religion centered on ritual purity. They had placed themselves above other Jews in the practice of their faith, believing that as long as they never shared a table with the "unclean" common people and sinners, they would maintain their ritual purity to please God.[15] It would have been detestable to them that Jesus not only ate with the common people but also was called "rabbi" by them.

Jesus overhears their insults, but instead of defending himself, he redefines the center of their religion—repentance. In theologian George F. Moore's exploration of Judaism around the time of Christ, he describes repentance as "the Jewish doctrine of salvation."[16] The repentance the Pharisees practiced hinged on *separation* from people and things considered unclean. Theirs were tables prepared to welcome only a select few. In the parables of the good shepherd and the good woman, Jesus reverses repentance, showing himself as the one who *seeks out* the separated.

"We can discover who Jesus is," Bailey writes, "by looking at how he takes images and stories about God from the Old Testament, retells them and 'writes himself into the story.' That is,

---

14. Luke 15:2. The Greek here is more literally translated "This . . . receives sinners and eats with them." The missing word is a connotation of contempt, like saying "this fool" or even "this asshole." Judge me if you want, but it's important we stay close to the text to feel how much contempt the Pharisees felt toward Jesus. See Bailey, *Good Shepherd*, 115, for a description of the Greek translation and its connotation of contempt.

15. Bailey, *Good Shepherd*, 114.

16. George F. Moore, *Judaism in the First Centuries of the Christian Era* (1927; New York: Shocken, 1971), 1:500.

in the retelling of the story he places himself at its center as he acts out the role of God."[17]

Jesus—God incarnate—decides to position himself at the center of these stories by casting religiously "despised" and culturally "inferior" characters as the protagonists who most describe who he is. He positions repentance among these "separated" people and places the religious elite of his day among those judged by God.

While the rabbis of his day considered shepherding a "despised trade," Jesus makes a shepherd the hero in his story.[18] While Jews and Romans alike viewed women as inferior to men, Jesus wittingly centers a woman as his exemplar.[19] Jesus dares to disturb the world of religion and the empire of Rome by positioning people society scorned as those who hold the most honor *and* who most reveal his heart for the lost. In the parable of the good shepherd, Jesus shows us those whom religious folks disdain are so precious they are worth rescuing at great personal cost. And in the parable of the good woman, Jesus shows us that you can be lost right in the middle of God's house. Both the sheep and the coin are so valuable, it's worth holding a feast to rejoice over them being found.

Don't miss this.

God is preparing a table for you—in places you might not expect, by the people religious folks might judge.

---

17. Bailey, *Good Shepherd*, 130.

18. Joachim Jeremias, *Jerusalem in the Time of Jesus* (Philadelphia: Fortress, 1976), 304.

19. Ben Witherington III, *Women in the Ministry of Jesus* (Cambridge: Cambridge Univ. Press, 1984), 10. Rebecca McLaughlin, "Jesus Changed Everything for Women," Gospel Coalition, March 22, 2021, www.thegospelcoalition.org/article/jesus-changed -everything-women/.

24. A TABLE

YOU ARE NOT JUST A HEARER OF CHRIST'S STORIES. His parables and life aren't a book of fiction you can set down when you are sleepy or put back on the shelf when you get bored. This isn't some saccharine story, sentimental and sweet but having no bearing on your actual eating, breathing, brokenhearted life. The stories of Scripture are not meant to simply be read. They are meant to be lived.

Your life is inside this story. You are the Pharisee giving Jesus side-eye. You are the sheep who wandered into the wilderness. And you are the coin—inert, lifeless, and lost in the cracks on the ground of God's house. You are the friend and neighbor being invited to a celebration feast. But above all, you are the one being found.

Here is courage: to dare to be found in the story of grace healing everything. Courage hinges on our willingness to shift—right here and now, in our ordinary, fractured lives—from being observers or gatekeepers of God's story to active participants in it.

Grace is seeking you, but will you let all the parts of yourself be found?

Just as Jesus took the threads of David's story and wove himself into its center, your story can be held between these strands. Let's look at both of the parables in Luke 15 again to trace how Jesus positions himself in them—and where he places us.

Notice: both parables end with a celebration at a table. But before you can celebrate, something precious that is lost must be sought and found. May we find ourselves caught between the threads of these stories, found in the crosshairs of Christ's compassion for the precious parts of us some have said we should silence.

Something valuable has been lost.

Jesus refuses to litigate his love to the prosecuting Pharisees. Instead, he begins a story that ripples dissonance through every ear in the crowd.

"Suppose one of you has a hundred sheep and loses one of them," he says.[1] Like we would know the chorus to a song we've heard covered by the best bands, the Pharisees would have recognized that Jesus was deliberately retelling his own version of the good shepherd story, the story first told by David in Psalm 23.[2] They would have been on edge, waiting to evaluate how this rebel was about to reshape such a sacred story.

While it escapes our Western ears, untuned to the subtleties of a shame and honor culture, Jesus is beginning his story by implicating the shepherd for losing his sheep. In doing this, he is gently and boldly weaving the prophetic tradition of judgment against Israel's bad shepherds into his rebuke and invitation to the Pharisees.[3] This precious sheep has been lost because the religious folks have let it wander.

---

1. Luke 15:4a.
2. Kenneth Bailey, *The Good Shepherd: A Thousand-Year Journey from Psalm 23 to the New Testament* (Downers Grove, IL: IVP Academic, 2014), 113.
3. Ibid., 124.

Jesus goes on, "Doesn't he leave the ninety-nine in the open country and go after the lost sheep until he finds it? And when he finds it, he joyfully puts it on his shoulders and goes home. Then he calls his friends and neighbors together and says, 'Rejoice with me; I have found my lost sheep.'"[4]

In the space of four sentences, Jesus has informed the Pharisees that the sinners they so scorn are not only *part of their flock*, they are of such significance that the loss of even one is worth leaving all the others to go rescue.

"I tell you," Jesus presses, "that in the same way there will be more rejoicing in heaven over one sinner who repents than over ninety-nine righteous persons who do not need to repent."[5]

Bailey explains that "heaven" was a common rabbinic way to talk about God without saying God's name.[6] Jesus is saying that *there is more joy in the heart of God* over one sinner who repents than ninety-nine people who don't think they need to be found.

Ibn al-Tayyib, a Syrian Orthodox monk writing in Baghdad around 1020 AD, remarks that in this text Jesus was making it clear to the Pharisees "that the reasons for which they despised him, and for which they complained about him, were the very reasons that led him to come into this world and were the very focus of his ministry."[7] Jesus was placing the people the religious folks judged at the center of his story. The shamed and scorned sinners are of such value to Jesus that the recovery of even one is the source of his biggest celebration.

---

4. Luke 15:4b–6.

5. Luke 15:7.

6. Bailey, *Good Shepherd*, 136.

7. Ibn al-Tayyib, *Tafsir al Mashriqi* (Cairo: Towfiq Press, 1910), 2:262, as translated by Bailey in *Good Shepherd*, 115.

Next, Jesus shows another layer of David's good shepherd story—this time with a woman as the hero. He chooses to redefine repentance in front of members of the guild of Pharisees—in which no women were welcome—*by centering the story on a woman.*[8]

"Or suppose a woman has ten silver coins and loses one," Jesus expounds. "Doesn't she light a lamp, sweep the house and search carefully until she finds it?"[9] One silver coin, a *drachma*, would have been an entire day's wages for a working man.[10] And the woman has lost it inside her house.

At that time, most houses north of the Sea of Galilee were made of basalt—a volcanic rock as dark as charcoal. The only windows were slits for ventilating cooking fires. A coin lost between the cracks of basalt stones would have been incredibly hard to find in such darkness.[11] The woman would have had to get on her knees, holding a lamp near the ground, running her fingers over every inch of the floor to find the valuable coin.

Just like the shepherd, Jesus describes that the woman has such joy in finding her lost possession that she gathers her friends and neighbors around a table to celebrate.[12] And then he explains that she too is a metaphor for himself. "In the same way, I tell you, there is rejoicing in the presence of the angels of God over one sinner who repents."[13] If Jesus wasn't afraid to liken God's heart to a woman's, we don't need to be so violently opposed to seeing the feminine in the divine.

In the parable of the good shepherd, the lost sheep has wandered far from the flock. In this parable, the valuable possession is *lost inside the house itself.* Jesus is redefining and relocating lostness.

---

8. Bailey, *Good Shepherd*, 145.

9. Luke 15:8.

10. Arland J. Hultgren, *The Parables of Jesus* (Grand Rapids, MI: Eerdmans, 2000), 66.

11. Bailey describes a typical house in this region in some detail. Bailey, *Good Shepherd*, 147.

12. Luke 15:9.

13. Luke 15:10.

You can be lost in the wilderness of exile. You can wander far from the center of religion's power and practices. But you can also be lost right inside God's house.

You can sit within a stone's throw of the temple studying Torah and yet be lost from the heart of God![14] You can fall between the cracks of control and certainty, lost in the darkness of the place most symbolizing light. You can be just as lost inside the house of God as the "sinners" who are seen as too unclean to come inside.

Theologian Mary Ann Beavis believes it is even appropriate to interpret the lost coin in this passage as the innocent victims of injustice, over whose vindication God rejoices more than the repentance of those who have abused them.[15] Her words bring to mind the continuum of crushing and confusion that happens right inside the church's walls—from sexual and spiritual abuse to heavy yokes of shame around purity and politics.

The lack of specificity in Jesus' description of the coin begs us to notice our own lostness. Whether we have been crushed by control or are the ones doing the crushing, Jesus is saying:

You are lost.

You are valuable.

You are worth being found.

The hardest question to answer in life is not "Does God exist?" but "Is God kind?"[16]

14. Bailey, *Good Shepherd*, 149.

15. Mary Ann Beavis, "Joy in Heaven, Sorrow on Earth," in *The Lost Coin: Parables of Women, Work and Wisdom*, ed. Mary Ann Beavis (New York: Sheffield Academic, 2002), 44–45.

16. In the foreword to my first book, my mentor wrote, "I believe the hardest theological question is captured by three simple words: is God good?" Kelly M. Kapic, foreword to *This Too Shall Last: Finding Grace When Suffering Lingers* by K.J. Ramsey (Grand Rapids, MI: Zondervan, 2020), 13.

TABLE

By echoing David's prayer in its fullness, Jesus is revealing his identity as the one whose pursuit is relentless, whose table is welcoming, and whose heart is kind.

God is like the shepherd, and God is like the woman. God leaves behind the ninety-nine pretty and perfect-seeming parts of you to find and restore the one part of you that feels too broken and lost. There is no part of you that the Good Shepherd will not seek and follow to extend goodness and love.

There is no distance you can go that is beyond God's willingness to search. There is no road too rocky or trail too long for God to travel to pursue and gather up the hurting parts of you. There is no part of you that is too broken, too angry, too anxious, too judgmental, too traumatized, or too lifeless for God to seek. God's very heart is to seek and save the lost.[17]

God gets on the ground to find the part of you that has slipped through the cracks. Like a woman on bended knees on her grimy floors, God is resolved to keep rummaging for your return. There is no crack or corner too dark or dirty for the Good Woman to trace with her own hands to ensure that you are found.

Your worth is not diminished by your lostness. Your preciousness is not annulled by your pain. You are pursued through both the dangers of the wilderness and the darkness within God's house.

God's goodness and love are fierce to find the parts of you that have gotten lost or that others have left behind or pushed to the side. God is too kind to leave you behind, too possessive to let you stay in the cracks, and too generous to not celebrate when any part of you is found.

And when God finds the most shamed and scorned and sad parts of you, like a shepherd, he lifts you up—he gets that you might be too weak to even walk home on your own. The Good Shepherd

17. Luke 19:10.

places you across his strong shoulders and carries you all the way home, rejoicing the whole way. Because what he loved was lost, but what was lost, he found.

Count on it.

God rejoices over recovering the most weak and wounded parts of you more than anything else about you. God is preparing a table to celebrate your return, where every part of you has a spot, every story has space to be told, and every guest has more food than they could possibly eat.

Count on it.

God is determined to never leave the most broken and hurting parts of you behind.

25. BEFORE ME

THERE IS A TABLE PREPARED BEFORE YOU, where all of you is welcome, every part of you has a seat, and Christ sits at the head. Your whole life is an invitation to feast at this table.

Too often, though, we live like bullies and beggars before God's table. We've grown accustomed to being banished by the bossy parts of ourselves or others. We sense deep down that parts of us aren't welcome or wanted at the table—sitting in timeout in the corner for speaking up or grounded to our room while everyone else eats, just because we started to cry.

If we are allowed to show up, sometimes we feel like we have to make part of ourselves small, shrinking into the middle, being as quiet as we can to avoid being the object of anyone's ridicule or shouts. Part of us wants to speak up and another part says, "Shut up!" There are parts of ourselves that seem to be at war within us, and often, certain parts seem to be the only ones who are allowed to have power and a voice.

A modality of therapy called internal family systems (IFS) reveals the distinct parts that make up who we are and surround our truest self.[1] IFS helps us turn on the light over the dinner table

---

1. Richard C. Schwartz and Martha Sweezy, *Internal Family Systems Therapy*, 2nd ed. (New York: Guilford, 2020).

in a house that's usually dark. Suddenly, we can see the table within us has a family around it. *This* is the family of your soul—the parts that make up you, who each need the love, curiosity, and compassion of your truest self for you to become whole.

IFS shows us that in addition to our true self, we each have three kinds of parts that make up our inner life, who have been dictating how we show up in the world—managers, firefighters, and exiles.[2] Some of these parts act like parents or even bullies to the others, the parts of us who feel lost, buried, or left behind.

One astounding thing we need to realize is that every part of ourselves has a purpose. We are always seeking safety, and some parts of us have been working overtime to find it. As somatic IFS therapist Susan McConnell writes, "One of the most unique and transformational assumptions of IFS is that all parts have a positive intention."[3] From the parts of yourself that you hate to the parts that call all the shots, each part has a purpose.

To become whole—secure in the core of who we are—we must intentionally practice replacing shame and blame with a love that calls our name.

Parts exist because pain happens. And our bodies spring into action to protect us from being harmed by it—sometimes banishing or burying the most vulnerable parts of ourselves to a place that seems far from danger. Throughout this book, we have considered the ratio of cues of safety to cues of danger. Parts are formed, often early in our lives, that respond to being inundated and overwhelmed by too many cues of danger. Our bodies are always seeking safety

---

2. While a full overview of IFS is beyond the scope of this book, you can learn more through the following books. Cook and Miller's book provides an accessible overview from a Christian perspective: Alison Cook and Kimberly Miller, *Boundaries for Your Soul: How to Turn Your Overwhelming Thoughts and Feelings into Your Greatest Allies* (Nashville: Thomas Nelson, 2018); Susan McConnell, *Somatic Internal Family Systems Therapy: Awareness, Breath, Resonance, Movement, and Touch in Practice* (Berkeley, CA: North Atlantic Books, 2020); Schwartz and Sweezy, *Internal Family Systems Therapy*.

3. McConnell, *Somatic Internal Family Systems*, 32.

and survival, and we develop parts *and* often live bound to their roles, because we are doing our best to survive. When we seek out the pain that broke us into pieces, we can move into our lives more wholeness than before.

Manager and firefighter parts have taken on the role of *protectors*. These parts are often overfunctioning, trying their darndest to safeguard our security, belonging, and worth. Protectors usually develop as your body's best possible attempt at protecting you from overwhelming pain in impossible circumstances.[4] Protectors are resourceful, using whatever they can to do their job, including your body. Even though our protectors might be harming us and hurting others now—through the presence of behaviors like addictions, chronic pain, disorders, tension, and weight loss or gain—they once were your best way to survive. Viewed through a polyvagal and IFS lens, you can begin to encounter the part behind your fear as a protector springing into action in stress, a part who needs safety and your support.

Managers protect us by pushing us "to perform, produce, perfect, and please."[5] They mobilize us to avoid emotional and physical pain, preemptively positioning us to avoid being corrected, judged, or rejected. Managers think if we can critique, correct, or reject ourselves first, we can avoid the pain of being critiqued or rejected by others. And firefighters rush in to slow the blaze when it seems like we are burning. Firefighters douse pain with the water of distraction, dismissal, and even dissociation to get us back to believing we're okay.

Exiles are the most vulnerable parts of us, who hold the painful emotions and memories of those times we have experienced rejection, abandonment, trauma, and even misattunement.[6] We all

4. Ibid., 33.
5. Cook and Miller, *Boundaries for Your Soul*, 33.
6. McConnell, *Somatic Internal Family Systems*, 9.

experience fragmentation. We all have exiled parts of ourselves, even if we have not experienced major traumas. Growing up with screens in front of our faces and those of our caregivers', with stress pumping through our veins, in a culture where emotional repression is still our norm, we all experience a scarcity of the attunement we need to develop into fully secure selves.[7] Our exiles are the parts who have been banished to the dark rooms of our souls or shamed into silence at the table in an attempt to sequester the pain of the past from disrupting the present. Managers and firefighters have been trying to protect your exiles. The thing is: the way they protect often also belittles.

For most of us, protector parts have long sat at the head of the table, bossing and bullying everyone else around. Our managers often scold everyone else to shut up. They might glare at another part of you when you take a second helping of potatoes. The firefighters might overlook the exile at the end of the table, shouting over their quiet attempt to tell a story. The managers come to the table eager to find affirmation. The firefighters come ready to fight for scraps and significance. And the exiles—if they come at all— believe shrinking into the shadows is the best way to survive it all.

In chapter 6 we discussed how our bodies often go into enemy mode when under stress. While Wilder and Hendricks were describing how we drop into enemy mode with others, the critical thing to realize is that *we go into enemy mode toward ourselves too.* We treat the wounded, vulnerable parts of ourselves like enemies to vanquish. We're often more comfortable being at odds with parts of ourselves than being friends with them. We end up exiling parts of

---

7. Psychiatrist Dan Siegel writes that youth today are often accustomed to high levels of stimulus-bound attention, "with little time for self-reflection or interpersonal connection of the direct, face-to-face sort that the brain needs for proper development. Little today in our hectic lives provides opportunities to attune with each other." Dan Siegel, *The Mindful Brain: Reflection and Attunement in the Cultivation of Well-Being,* Norton Series on Interpersonal Neurobiology (New York: Norton, 2007), 4.

ourselves far away from the table of our souls. Noticing and naming our parts and how they are attempting to keep us safe can help us find our way back to the table—where every part of us can feast in peace.

God speaks peace over every part of you that clashes and clings for control. Your greatest joy, deepest belonging, and eternal safety no longer need to be safeguarded by striving or shutting down. Your worth is welded to Christ's finished work on the cross.

Jesus seeks the exiled parts of yourself at the cost of his own life. When Jesus redefines repentance before the Pharisees by telling them the story of his lost sheep and lost coin, he is *including* our lostness and lifelessness.

The only way the Shepherd could have found his lost sheep was to call out with his own voice. A sheep might cry out for a while when first lost, but it quickly uses up its energy keening and must wait for rescue, partly as a protective instinct to not be found by predators. The shepherd continues to call, and when the sheep hears his voice, it will use up the last remaining bit of its energy to bleat again. It is the faint bleating of the sheep that allows the shepherd to locate it and bring it home. Remember, repentance both in Psalm 23 (*shuv*) and Luke 15 (*metanoia*) means to be brought back.[8]

Even your cries are part of repentance.[9] Your fear, shame, and anger are cries of your soul asking to be sought.

Repentance is not reprimanding yourself for getting lost; it is

---

8. For an examination of how *metanoia* in Luke 15 is a direct translation of *shuv* from Psalm 23, see Kenneth E. Bailey, *The Good Shepherd: A Thousand-Year Journey from Psalm 23 to the New Testament* (Downers Grove, IL: IVP Academic, 2014), 134.

9. Bailey says that in Luke 15, the shepherd's pursuit of the sheep as well as the sheep's participation in being found by the shepherd together make up Jesus' redefinition of repentance. Ibid., 136.

turning toward yourself as someone who is always worthy of being found.

In the story of the good shepherd, the sheep must accept being found. Day after day, you can practice allowing the vulnerable parts of yourself to be found by paying attention to the shifts in your nervous system and acknowledging where you are emotionally. Your protectors need the relief of hearing that their best rescue isn't in their strength but in the shepherd's. The vulnerable work of hearing the cries of your own soul is the very substance of repentance and the source of the joy in God's heart. In fact, out of the entire New Testament, the word joy (*chara*) is applied only to God here.[10] Your cries are not a source of shame to God; they are the beautiful sound of your soul being found.

Repentance also stretches beyond even our capacity to cry for help. In the parable of the good woman, her coin cannot cry for help.[11] It can be found only through her relentless pursuit. When life has brought you too low to even cry for help, silent and inert as a coin, stuck day after day in a dorsal vagal state of despair, you are not beyond the reach of God's hands or the reality of repentance as defined by Jesus. Even in your lifelessness, God is seeking you.

Here is repentance: the willingness to be held where we feel unloved and unlovable and the courage to be found.

God is preparing a table before you, ready to rejoice over every lost part of you being found.

May you practice seeing even the presence of your hardest emotions, bossiest protectors, and most wounded exiles as lost sheep in need of rescue. May even your darkest thoughts and bleakest days

10. Ibid., 139.
11. Ibid., 151.

sink into the silver of being one of God's treasured coins. You are being brought back to the table of the Lord.

The only wonder greater than your worth is that you have been hidden with Christ in God.[12] Your truest self is seated with Christ at the head of the table of your soul. *You have been united to Christ.*[13] Your truest, wisest self—your ventral vagal self, who can access all the courageous, regulating strengths of your social engagement system and prefrontal cortex—is presently united to Christ and seated with him at the right hand of the Father, ready to search for and rescue every lost part of your soul. Your Shepherd stands with love in his hands, and he wants to bring your whole self home.

Standing with Christ, empowered by the Spirit, there is no wilderness in your soul too treacherous to tread. Every single day of your life is an invitation to walk with the Shepherd to seek the lost parts of your soul. Every day, when we start to sink onto the lower rungs of our autonomic ladder, we can descend there with compassion along with Christ. You will find other bleating sheep along the way; they too can belong in this fold. With the Shepherd by your side, you can trust your search will end in joy.

Every day, you can come home to a crowded table, where Christ sits at the head of your soul and every part has a seat. Your protectors can learn to listen. Your exiles can tell their stories. And there's more than enough space and time and food for every story to be told and every stomach filled.

12. Col. 3:3.
13. Eph. 2:13.

26. IN THE PRESENCE
OF MY ENEMIES.

PART OF WHAT KEEPS US FROM SITTING at the table of courage and communion is a refusal to identify the reality of enmity. I love that David uses the word *enemies* in his prayers. I love that he does not pretend away the pain of being condemned and chased. Instead, he dares to name something our contemporary Christian niceness generally leaves vague or even venerated. The experience of enmity is embedded in our bodies, wringing our hands into fists and hearts into hiding when others threaten our safety.

When David delights in the table God has prepared for him in the presence of his enemies, David is affirming that Love is so completely on his side that God is willing to absorb the hostility being hurled at him.[1] I love that David does not hide his pain behind platitudes, because platitudes can never penetrate our pain. Only God can take the weight of enmity. In a world full of harm and hatred, only God's presence can give us peace that reaches every part of our souls.

The symbol in which we most witness where God positions

---

1. Kenneth E. Bailey, *The Good Shepherd: A Thousand-Year Journey from Psalm 23 to the New Testament* (Downers Grove, IL: IVP Academic, 2014), 57.

our enemies is the Eucharist, the ultimate place where enemies are made friends. But far too often, Christians prefer to dilute the wine of Christ's sacrifice into the grape juice of niceness. Wherever wrong has been done or experienced, someone is following close behind with the paintbrush of platitudes. "There are two sides to every story," they say. "There are no perfect churches," they chide. "All things work together for good," they paint and paint and paint. Sometimes it seems that Christians like to put lipstick on lies instead of fighting to remove their stain from our souls and communities. It is easier to dismiss pain than deal with changing the circumstances that produce it.[2] We forget that noticing and naming enmity is a prerequisite to knowing whom and what to love and protect.

Neutrality is the nicest kind of evil. Not taking a side *is* taking a side. Neutrality shows victims that their health is worth less to you than avoiding awkwardness or not having to make relational changes. Neutrality tears open the wound of trust over and over again.

If we cannot name our pain, it just remains a chain. If we will not name the reality of evil, we will remain defenseless to defeat it.

David's prayers are like dialysis for Christians who have been drinking the sugary-sweet preaching of platitudes for so long that we've become diabetic to the dissonance at the heart of the cross. "You prepare a table before me *in the presence of my enemies*," David prays.[3] "Because of all my enemies, I am the utter contempt of my neighbors," he laments. "I am forgotten as though I were dead . . . For I hear many whispering . . . They conspire against me and plot to take my life."[4]

Alexander Schmemann writes that "evil is not to be 'explained'

---

2. And, yes, I *am* talking about systemic racism and poverty in addition to abuse.
3. Ps. 23:5a, emphasis added.
4. Ps. 31:11–13.

but faced and fought. This is the way God dealt with evil. He did not explain it. He sent his Only-Begotten Son to be crucified by all the powers of evil so as to destroy them by His love, faith and obedience. This then is the way we must also follow."[5]

The summer we moved back to Colorado, I found refuge inside David's psalms and at our friends' table. We all had been treated like enemies—shamed and shunned by church leaders for naming evil instead of just playing nice. Evil had clawed at each of us with others' contempt and condemnation, trying to wound and weaken our confidence and joy in belonging to Christ.[6] When we face and fight evil, it fights back—often through the words of people who are most supposed to bless. Pastors. Parents. Friends.

I knew that if I wanted to be able to come back to the table of communion within the doors of a church again, I needed to experience God's lovingkindness around tables where we would not be cursed for confronting evil. Jim Wilder asserts that we can learn to trust and extend lovingkindness, the *hesed* love of God, only in groups that practice love with us.[7] The only antidote to enemy mode is empathy. It was during those long evenings over our friends' crowded table, among the rejected and ruined, where God was most rebuilding my trust and the truth of who I am.

Our sense of safety and joy in God's love had eroded from years spent in a community that practiced power accumulation more than it practiced *hesed*. My husband wrote a poem about that season,

5. Alexander Schmemann, *Of Water and the Spirit: A Liturgical Study of Baptism* (Crestwood, NY: St. Vladimir's Seminary Press, 1974), 23.

6. James Wilder describes this as being especially true of narcissistic abuse, which my friends and I had all left behind. E. James Wilder, *The Pandora Problem: Facing Narcissism in Leaders and Ourselves* (Carmel, IN: Deeper Walk International, 2018), 174.

7. Ibid., 26.

and one line often reverberates in my mind: "We watch our faith collapse into seedbeds."[8]

It's become vogue in conservative circles to decry deconstruction.[9] It strikes me that leaders who prefer dominance and control to shepherding and serving hate deconstruction because it crumbles the power structures under which they hide. While the term has become both overused and over-judged to the point of losing its meaning, this is what I know: sometimes the frame of a house becomes rotten. Sometimes a collapse of certainty is simply the necessary demolition of curses that have long been eating away at the structure of our faith and the functioning of our nervous systems.

Our faith felt like it was collapsing around that table, but it was only the collapse of all the curses that had been hurled at us. Control and certainty had to be removed from the house of our faith for us to be rebuilt into real resilience. Our friendships became our renovation. We were making a space where we could relax into the truth that no enemy could disinvite or excommunicate us from the table of the Lord. During those long evenings breaking bread and drinking wine together, our broken hearts were being rebuilt by the fact that in each other's faces, as in God's, we could be nothing but beloved.

When Jesus reveals himself as the realization of David's Psalm 23 story, he does not just flaunt his love in the presence of enemies; he invites them to the table too. In Luke 15, when Jesus tells the story of the good shepherd and the good woman who, upon finding what was lost, prepare a table with a feast and invite their friends, the Pharisees present would have heard their names called. The "friends" or *haberim* were an elite group of Pharisees who were even more intense in their separation from common folks—not

---

8. Ryan Ramsey, "Listens for Shadows," *Fathom*, May 17, 2021, www.fathommag.com/stories/listens-for-shadows.

9. Joshua Ryan Butler, "Four Causes of Deconstruction," Gospel Coalition, November 9, 2021, www.thegospelcoalition.org/article/4-causes-deconstruction.

visiting them, not traveling with them, not studying the law with them, and definitely never eating with them.[10] Jesus calls his *friends* and neighbors to come celebrate with him, to move toward the lost ones they have spent their whole lives judging.

I eventually felt strong enough to return to church, and we visited an Anglican church ten minutes away from our new apartment. I felt a familiar fear walking with me through those wooden doors, but I also had a growing awareness of the blessing I carried inside. A blessing I didn't need to give away to the first pastor who saw my gifts and asked me to serve. A blessing no one could revoke, coerce, or control.

When we came to the front of the church to receive communion, my memories came with me. As the priest placed a small piece of bread into my open hands, I saw myself serving communion at the church where we were harmed. With the sun streaming through the small Anglican church's stained-glass windows, I saw myself standing at the front of the shadowy room of the sanctuary where we had once worshiped.

The year before we resigned, we had convinced the pastor to allow leaders to serve communion instead of congregants getting it themselves from the back of the room like a Jesus vending machine—probably our best legacy. As Ryan and I walked to the front of the church that Sunday before we resigned, I sensed that this was it, the final time I would ever serve communion at that church and the final time I would ever worship within those walls. I was broken but steady, ready to offer one final blessing to the people we had loved, in the place we had been crushed.

The last person to walk toward me to receive bread and wine that morning was the pastor who had most harmed us. As he made his way toward me, I thought, *Jesus, broken for me, was broken for him*

---

10. Bailey, *Good Shepherd*, 111.

too. After months of naming the way he had harmed us and privately praying angry, imprecatory psalms,[11] somehow on that morning, communion gave me the courage to see and extend Christ's compassion for him. It wasn't kindness I mustered up myself; it was like water surging up from within me. Communion made me a conduit to a forgiveness and compassion beyond my capacity.

I gave him the bread as a blessing and a prayer. "The body of Christ, broken *for you.*"

Ryan offered him the wine, "The blood of Christ, poured out *for you.*"

Communion did not rescue me from the trauma of being cursed and condemned by a man called to bless us, but it did carry me into compassion.

We were equalized at the foot of the cross.

After not being able to even step foot inside a church for months after that, it was compassion that carried me back. As I swallowed the wine-dipped bread, I looked up through my teary storm cloud eyes and found the priest's eyes looking back into mine with kindness. This was resolution. This was absolution. This was the circle of communion enfolding my hurt and hope with love.

Communion was giving me courage to trust there could be compassion in church again. Cognitive neuroscientist Thomas Fuchs writes that as we reenact the Lord's Supper together, the church's collective body memory of receiving Christ's presence renews our participation in Christ's life.[12] When we suffer or are abused, evil scrawls *forsaken, forgotten,* and *unloved* all over our neural pathways, coiling our bodies with contempt and contention. The sound of Christ's words in our ears, the texture of the bread in our

---

11. Thank the living Lord those prayers are in God's Word. We need room to cry for vengeance in order to rest our revenge in the final judgment of God.

12. Thomas Fuchs, "Collective Body Memories," in *Embodiment, Enaction, and Culture: Investigating the Constitution of the Shared World,* ed. Christoph Durt, Thomas Fuchs, and Christian Tewes (Cambridge, MA: MIT Press, 2017), 333–49.

hands, the taste of red wine on our lips, the scent of candles, and the sight of kind eyes meeting ours can bring our whole bodies and minds back into a story where we are beloved. The communal practice of communion gathers our grief with grace at the foot of the cross, enfolding us together into the life of the world to come.

The table of communion is the place where curse meets blessing. As we long for and seek the justice and reconciliation of the world to come, we can take our place at the table, even in the literal or figurative presence of our enemies, daring to believe that in Christ all that has been cursed can come back to life.

27. YOU ANOINT MY HEAD WITH OIL;

WHEN DAVID ENVISIONED God's feast and welcome, where God anoints him with oil, I imagine his heart swelled with remembrance of the day he was first anointed, chosen by God not just to be an honored guest but to be Israel's king.

Chief in the tradition of self-protective leaders, Israel's first king, Saul, had decided his means of achieving God's ends were better than the means God had instructed. The details of that story aren't critical for ours—but what we need to see is that Saul chose to ignore God's instructions to lead his people, just like so many leaders do today in choosing expediency over obedience, taking on business models of growth instead of honoring Jesus' words that the kingdom of God comes like the smallest of seeds and only grows with the self-sacrifice of being split open.

Because of Saul's disobedience and arrogance, the Lord regretted making Saul king and instructed Samuel to anoint another.[1] He sent Samuel to the house of Jesse in Bethlehem, where he consecrated Jesse and his sons who were present. Samuel took one look

---

1. 1 Samuel 15.

over the oldest, who probably looked tough and tall, and thought, "Surely this is God's chosen king." But the Lord nudged Samuel to look farther than what shines, instructing, "Do not consider his appearance or his height, for I have rejected him. The LORD does not look at the things people look at. People look at the outward appearance, but the LORD looks at the heart."[2]

One by one, God rejected all of Jesse's sturdy, strong sons, until finally there was no one left. So Samuel asked Jesse if these were all of his sons, and Jesse replied that there was one more, the youngest, who was out tending the family's sheep.

The baby of the family, overlooked and left out in the field to watch the flock—David was the one God chose. Samuel took his cone of oil and let it drip over David's skin, tan from days spent in the sun watching the family's flock with devotion.

Before David had done anything amazing—before he slung a stone to slay a giant or led armies to advance in victory—God decided to anoint him as king.

We are anointed, not for what we have done but for who we will become.

Like Christ in the Jordan, consecrated as God's Beloved Son before he did a miracle or gave up his life, we are named Beloved before courage comes. Scripture is one long story of ordinary people being named into extraordinary courage for the sake of love.

Before they had any children, beyond the time when anyone could have imagined they even could, God renamed Abram and Sarai as a mark of who they would become—Abraham and Sarah, the parents of a nation through whom the whole world would be

2. 1 Sam. 16:7.

blessed. Before their unbelief, before the terrible ways they tried to coerce the promise to come by abusing Hagar. Naming precedes the courage to trust that God's promises will come. When scarcity ripples fear through us that God's goodness may never materialize, naming stretches past our self-sufficiency and self-protection.

Our naming enfolds our brokenness into the beauty of who we and this world will become. When Simon the disciple recognized Jesus as the Messiah, Jesus renamed him Peter, meaning "rock," and said he would be the rock on which he would build his church—a church whose foundation is so sturdy not even the gates of hell can overcome it.[3] Jesus named Peter the rock, even though he knew Peter would betray him not once but thrice. Jesus saw the whole of who Peter would become, and he named him for this wholeness.

Courage himself names us with a love so strong that even our weakness and wounds are woven into the irrevocable goodness of who we will become.

Evil assaults us in the place of our anointing. It is always leveraging the pride and pain of others to curse our confidence that we are beloved by God.

We need rituals to remember our true name, to hear past our shame, to, like David, relish the memory and scent of anointing oil on our skin in a way that strengthens us to stand stronger than all pain.

At the end of that summer after we moved back to Colorado, while sitting around our shared table, Mish told us her husband finally decided he wasn't willing to stop his affair and come back home. He betrayed the married name they chose together, and decided it was

---

3. Matt. 16:15–19.

easier to love someone else instead. Mish had wanted to fight to keep their marriage alive, but she had to accept this final, deadly blow.

She never imagined her story would include divorce. She never imagined committing her life to someone who would reject her. The death of her marriage was a loss no one knew how to grieve, and she struggled to know how to share it with others. She tried to find her way over all the rocks her ex had thrown at her to take out her confidence and joy. She wanted to step into remembering the goodness of who she really was.

So Mish decided she needed a witness. Like Samuel's anointing of David, like Jesus' naming of Peter, like our baptism as beloved—we receive our true names only from beyond ourselves. We are held and heard and named into who we will become.

Mish dreamed up a ritual to grieve the death of her marriage and asked a few of us women who are closest to her to plan a marriage funeral. Women, like those who were faithful to stay with Christ to his final breath and who went to anoint his dead body with perfume, have historically been the ones who prepare bodies for burial. She was asking us to be her witnesses to mourn and give dignity to what had died.

One warm night that next June, after the divorce papers were signed, the money split, and many tears cried, a small group of us women crested a nearby mountain to grieve the death of Mish's marriage and rename the life that would rise.

The cleansing scent of sagebrush greeted us as we sat down and watched as Mish knelt to bury the remains of the flower crown she had worn five years before on her wedding day, letting the joy of that day rest with the dirt. Behind her, a rainbow stretched across the sky. When Mish sat back down, we placed a new flower crown on her head—such beauty is not only for brides. And as the graphite-blue sky bloomed into peony pink, we each named the goodness we saw growing in Mish.

Before she knew what pain might come next to press her heart back into the dirt, before seeing how God would bring her into joy in the coming year, Mish let us grieve the way she fell and grace the goodness of who she would become.

Jesus' story shows us that those who are faithful to witness death become the first to witness resurrection. We became witnesses to the death of Mish's marriage. We honored the body of the union that dissolved. We made space—together—for the hopelessness of being abandoned. We laid dirt over the dreams that had died. And we anointed her as a person with a goodness that no betrayal could break.

This past spring, Mish bought her first house. On one of the first nights after she moved in, I sat at her table in wonder of how in honoring the death in her life, God had made *her* into a home for hope. As we clinked glasses of champagne, I thought to myself, *These last two years, I've been witnessing resurrection.*

But it started when Mish bore witness to what had died. It was sown in her risk to ritualize the grief others hide. It rooted as she received our anointing over the life that remained. It bloomed as she carried the burden of the mystery that she still could become who she always was—Beloved. And from the seeds of her sorrow and strength, trust took root in my own life that out of grief, joy can grow.

Evil will always try to convince us to live numb and nameless. Evil will always curse us as too small, too young or too old, too wounded, or too unwanted.

David imagines in Psalm 23 that God anoints his head with oil in a display of lavish welcome. God so welcomes you, even when others have chased you away or exiled you, as Saul did to David.

Just as David was chosen when everyone in his family counted him as too unimportant to introduce to the prophet Samuel, you are not too small to be significant. Just as Peter was named the rock before he would struggle to stay faithful, even your struggles cannot stain your name. Your anointing is a gift given not for what you have done but out of God's love. Divine love ensures who you will become.

This is what I know: the betrayal of another cannot take your belovedness away. Darkness cannot steal your inheritance. Evil cannot revoke your anointing.

The kingdom of God is here. This is still your Father's world. Beautiful and brutal things will happen to you and those you love. But do not be afraid. God never leaves us without a witness or a name.

28. MY CUP
OVERFLOWS.

SOMETHING DEEP WITHIN US kept drawing Ryan and me to that small liturgical church. Songs still stung. Sermons still prickled our spines with anticipation of arrogance and abuse. But the pastor's "wisdom" wasn't the focus. We were finding safety in the centrality of the bread and wine.

On our first Sunday, the connecting pastor reassured us. "No one will expect anything of you here. You don't have to serve—not until you feel ready. You can just come and heal here for as long as you need." She wasn't lying.

Just a few months before we started attending the Church of the Advent, the church's founding priest, Rob, died from brain cancer at just forty-seven years old. Grief sat in every pew. Sorrow sang in every song. While we couldn't make it through a church service without tears because of the tenderness of our own trauma, I quickly realized this was a place where my tears could belong.

Within the liturgy, we found space to rest. Our participation was not bound to belief, enthusiasm, or loyalty to the party line—which was good, because we had little to muster. We only needed to offer our willingness to let Christ's love be our sign. When my heart was heavy, my bended knees could pray. When my mind was stormy, the creed could hold all I struggled to say. When I felt lost, my hands could still find the sign of the cross.

This community was becoming a place we felt safe to share our loss.

When Father Jordan (the same priest who had served us communion our first week there) announced there would be a class for those who were discerning whether they wanted to "belong" in this community, we were curious. The language of belonging was disarming. We had seen church membership laid on people like a heavy yoke, but belonging felt like a gracious invitation to come as you are. The language of belonging felt like widening a space in our lives to let this community hold our wounds and hopes with us—slowly, with grace.

For me and Ryan, choosing to belong with Advent was a step of courage and faith to see God make the church a safe and spacious place.

After attending the class, we decided that before we signed any papers or participated in the church's liturgy of belonging, we needed to share our story with Jordan. We wanted our new pastor to know whom he was pastoring. We didn't want to test him, but we wanted him to hear our losses. We set up a time to get coffee a week before we were due to be publicly received into belonging in the church.

The coffee shop was closing early when we arrived, so we walked together down the block through the bitter December air to a pub. We huddled in our down jackets in a booth, and the three of us started talking over glasses of cider and beer as the room grew dark. As we warmed up, we peeled off our thick layers of coats and vests while we started peeling back the layers of our story.

Before we met with Jordan, Ryan and I had committed to each other that we would tell our story as plainly as possible. We had become familiar with having our pain interrogated by most pastors and leaders we encountered. Many only partly heard our pain before quickly asking us to prove its validity. Most people reflexively push pain away, afraid of being stained by what spills out when we tell our stories of suffering. Spiritual abuse and religious trauma, or what many give the politely dismissive name "church hurt," is often judged as cynicism. Often without ill intent, pastors make themselves into judge and jury instead of shepherd and surgeon, separating themselves from the anxious possibility that you might be a source of criticism to *them* in the near future too. The sharing of a painful story should always be a moment to suture and soothe rather than size up or sermonize.

It takes courage to practice believing yourself when others might meet you with suspicion. No one can give you the depth of belief and respect you desire, but *you* can give yourself the dignity of holding your story as something so sacred it deserves to be shared with care. The only way for us to learn how to do this was to try.

So we spilled out our story drop by drop, offering Jordan an unadorned summary of our experience of Ryan being a pastor— how he was pushed down, underappreciated and bullied, and then pushed out when he couldn't stand himself or anyone else being pushed around anymore. We were not looking for permission or pardon for our pain. We just knew it was part of our personhood that walked with us through the church's doors—a part we would not justify, judge, or ignore.

I watched Ryan with pride as he shared. We have a habit of watching each other as we talk, taking in each other's faces. Then I made myself look across the table to Jordan, afraid of what I might find.

There were tears running down his face.

When darkness falls on the end of Shabbat, Jewish families gather around a braided candle, cup, and a box of spices for the ceremony of *havdalah*. As they face the work and worries of the week ahead, havdalah offers a sensory way of welcoming the week while carrying the joy of sabbath with them into it. "Behold, God is my unfailing help," they profess. "I will trust in God and will not be afraid."[1]

I've seen folks on Instagram call the start of a new week the Sunday Scaries. We can feel the hurried hands of Monday reaching for us with each passing hour of the weekend, pulling us back into hustling to have what we need. Wouldn't it be beautiful to resist that narrative with a liturgy of abundance, to give ourselves room to remember there are Hands that will hold us all week?

In the space between the abundance of Sabbath and the anxious scarcity of the coming week, many Jews practice cultivating their imagination to carry the blessing of Sabbath into the future. They inhale the aroma of the spices, savoring the sweetness of Shabbat, and then carry their sense of connection and responsibility for the earth into the week. They light the braided candle as the first light of a new week, reflecting the call to create again like God—who first spoke light into being and whose presence gathers the scattered parts of humanity together in Sabbath rest.

The cup is then filled with wine as a symbol of sanctifying joy. Rabbi Julian Sinclair teaches that "there is a common custom to fill the havdalah cup with wine all the way to the brim . . . so that a little spills and overflows when you pick up the cup. The symbolism

1. Susan Silverman, "Havdalah: Taking Leave of Shabbat," My Jewish Learning, accessed November 2021, www.myjewishlearning.com/article/havdalah-taking-leave-of-shabbat/.

of the custom is that we wish for a week with an overflowing abundance of blessing."[2]

When David says "my cup overflows," he is describing this kind of abundance. He is relishing being a guest at a table where the host is so determined to offer lavish welcome that the cups keep being refilled to the brim. Keep the image of a full cup in your mind. Think of the last time you held a cup so full you spilled a little bit of what was inside.

When a brimming cup is lifted or bumped, you quickly find out what's within. When Jordan was bumped by our inconvenient story, his tears showed us the compassion that filled him. The glistening drops running down his cheeks were evidence that Love was what had filled him up inside.

On the night Jesus was betrayed, tears fell down his face in a garden as he begged the Father to remove the cup of his suffering. But before the begging, before he let anxiety fill his body to the brim so that we can become like him, he gathered his disciples around a table, took bread, blessed it, broke it, and gave it to them saying, "This is my body given for you."[3] Then he took the cup of wine and raised it before their eyes—perhaps spilling it over the sides. Maybe he held it as in havdalah, which is traditionally recited at Passover, letting that cup of wine be an image of the life that would soon flow from his side. In time, they would look back on that bread and cup and see that he is the resurrection and the vine.

Later, after they had feasted, Jesus turned to face his coming doom. He walked to the garden of Gethsemane, where his grief

2. Rabbi Julian Sinclair, "Spilling Wine at Havdalah," The JC, July 16, 2015, www.thejc.com/judaism/jewish-ways/spilling-wine-at-havdalah-1.67618.
3. Luke 22:19.

grew like a womb. He cried aloud to the star-flung sky. *Take this cup from me. I don't want to die.* God incarnate howled in fear, yet he held the cup and let the Spirit steer. He swallowed death whole and drank every last drop of sin and shame and abuse. Full stop.

The cup he swallowed is what has brought us near. For that is the riddle, the paradox, and the art of God's kingdom coming true—drinking the cup of grief is what makes us new.

My cup overflows now, and I'm seeing a what is true. Christ's courage to drink his cup is what changes mine too. Christ takes our poison and turns it into possibility. He takes trauma and transforms it into tenderness. He takes all the harm meant to bend and break and shapes us into a new fate. His life is the pattern. His cup is the rhyme.

We must swallow the cup of sorrow to overflow with the compassion of Christ's wine.

Do we not realize? *We are living liturgies.*

We are containers for God's care. All that is needed is to practice staying there. At the table. Ready to be refilled. We have only to try trusting that goodness comes from this host's hand. He who drank the dregs of death is here to stand. He serves us mercy. He gives us grace. His very Breath fills us to make this table a spacious place.

A few moments ago, I stepped outside to eat a plum. The moment my teeth pierced its skin, juice shot into the air like a fountain. I leaned forward with my hands outstretched, relishing every bite of the coral-veined fruit as sticky sweetness dripped down my hands into a puddle on the pavement.

We hold an abundance that announces itself like ripe fruit. We are cups that can be continually filled with Christ's courage. So filled, we will spill. Even our sorrow will stream into compassion. Even our sadness will become a container from which others can drink care.

When we are bumped, it will be love that flows down the edges of our cups. Kindness will drip from our fingers like the plum juice in my hand. Gentleness will leave a residue of resilience on everything we touch. Empathy will be the water that turns to wine. Tears will tell the truth that in us, Love resides.

GIVEN

*Joy is the gift of love. Grief is the price of
love. Anger protects that which is loved. And
when we think we have reached our limit,
wonder is the act that returns us to love.*
—Valarie Kaur

*Joy is the emotional expression of the
courageous Yes to one's own true being.*
—Paul Tillich

29. SURELY

THE WORD *SURELY* is translated from the Hebrew word *ak*. Just as it sounds, *ak* is like saying, *Ah! Now I see it!* As the *Brown-Driver-Briggs Hebrew Lexicon* describes it, *ak* is a way of exclaiming a truth newly perceived.[1] From the panoramic view of God's table, now David can see that the whole time he was wandering in the wilderness, hungry and in need of water and rest, confronting dangers and enemies, God was seeking him and providing for him. "Surely" is David's realization that in every preceding line of the psalm, God was holding him together.

Hebrew Scholar Jeff Benner notes that the ancient pictograph of *ak* shows an open palm alongside a seed, revealing both provision and possibility.[2] *Ak* moments can be like the opening of a seed, a realization that roots us into growing strong and enduring long.

A seed must open for the roots to grow. We need *ak*-like glimpses of God's presence and story to strengthen us into trusting

---

1. F. Brown, S. Driver, and C. Briggs, *The Brown-Driver-Briggs Hebrew and English Lexicon: With an Appendix Containing the Biblical Aramaic; Coded with the Numbering System from* Strong's Exhaustive Concordance of the Bible (Peabody, MA: Hendrickson, 2014), 36.

2. Jeff A. Benner, *Ancient Hebrew Lexicon of the Bible: Hebrew Letters, Words and Roots Defined within Their Ancient Cultural Context* (College Station, TX: Virtualbookworm .com Publishing, 2005), 149.

that Love, like a rich soil, is where we are planted. Our lives rest in the loam of God's love.

Ak moments remind us that being strengthened by Love's presence requires lifting our eyes to something outside of ourselves. David uses the word *ak* in a way similar to Psalm 23:6 in a few other places, including Psalm 139:11 and Psalm 140:13. But one place I find particularly intriguing is when it is used in 1 Samuel 25.

David has just been chased into the wilderness by Saul. He isn't there to take in the vistas or smell the wildflowers. He has gone to the wilderness to escape Saul's abuse. And the place has shaped his vision. He now sees both this world and its inhabitants differently. Most of David's psalms were written out of his years in the wilderness, and they reveal a heart that holds together both profound pain and awe.[3] The harsh setting of the wilderness was a place where David hid himself in the holiness of God and grew in his capacity to behold and respect the holiness hidden in every living thing.

Including his enemy Saul.

The wilderness isn't just a place we go; it's a critical context for who we will become.

Right before chapter 25 of 1 Samuel, David had spared Saul's life in a cave in the wilderness of En-Gedi because he knew it was not his place to take the life of God's anointed. He recognized the holiness of God's anointing on King Saul and respected it as something real, even when the anointed one was abusive. That day, David set down the surging story of revenge and instead clung to the camouflaged story of God's care.

Yet in the very next chapter, we read that David nearly lost his

3. Eugene Peterson, *Leap over a Wall: Earthy Spirituality for Everyday Christians* (New York: HarperOne, 1998), 77.

capacity to see. He and his men were in the wilderness of Paran, helping protect the massive herd of sheep and goats of a rich man named Nabal, a man we are told was surly and mean.[4] When the time came for Nabal's sheep to be sheared, there would have been a grand feast with banquet tables loaded with food and drinks, much like the table mentioned a verse earlier in Psalm 23.

David, reasonably, sent some men to ask if they could be included in the festivities and share in the bounty of their table. They had protected Nabal's shepherds all year and were probably living on meager rations. They justly deserved to be included, yet Nabal acted like he didn't even know who David was, treating David as nothing but a common criminal.

David was furious. In the space of a moment, we see the man who spared Saul's life—his real enemy—filled with rage and ready to release his revenge on Nabal. "*Surely* in vain have I guarded all that this fellow has in the wilderness," David shouted. "God do so to the enemies of David and more also, if by morning I leave so much as one male of all who belong to him."[5] The *surely* David speaks here is the same Hebrew word, *ak*, but this time, David uses it to justify his actions. He is about to root himself into a story of retaliation,[6] about to become just like Saul, crushing anyone who doesn't give him the space he thinks is rightfully his.

We can so easily become that which has harmed us.

Nabal's wife, Abigail, heard about David's protection of their herd and his plan to kill her husband. She secretly gathered up more food than David was asking for and intercepted him before he reached her husband. As soon as she saw David, she jumped off her donkey and threw herself on the ground, begging David not to be as foolish as her husband. Eugene Peterson wonderfully paraphrases

---

4. 1 Sam. 25:3.

5. 1 Sam. 25:21–22 ESV, emphasis added.

6. Brown, Driver, and Briggs, *Brown-Driver-Briggs Hebrew and English Lexicon*, 36.

Abigail's words to David: *"Remember who you are. Remember God's anointing. God's mercy. Don't stoop to fighting grudge battles; your task is to fight the battles of the Lord."*[7]

And then Abigail says this: "Your life is bound up in the bundle of the living in the care of the Lord your God. And the lives of your enemies will be flung aside like a stone from a sling."[8]

Abigail calls forth David's memories of God's faithfulness, using poetic words to position his heart back into the story where God had miraculously defeated Israel's enemies through David's own sling and stone. Her words cut through his hardness of heart. And we see another miracle, perhaps more mundane, but beautiful all the same: David listens to her.

In a world where patriarchy held all the power, a woman's words shifted the story of the man who would one day be king. *Her* courage to approach David, defenseless but indubitable in the story of God's care, changed the course of his life and Israel's history.[9] Just as David once saw the holiness hidden in Saul behind layers of envy and cruelty, Abigail saw the holiness hidden behind the hatred in David's words. Her sight and speech called him back to being who he was. God's anointed.

That day, David remembered who he was, who God was, and what he was doing in the wilderness—and in the next chapter of 1 Samuel David spares Saul's life *again*. Abigail speaks David back into becoming the man who would later pray, *Ak!* "Surely your goodness and love will follow me all the days of my life." Her words rooted him into the soil of his true story, where love, not revenge, gets the final say.

---

7. Peterson, *Leap over a Wall*, 84.

8. My paraphrase of verse 29.

9. And hers! When Abigail's husband died, David married her.

Like David, we often develop hard shells around the seed of our soul to protect the precious life inside. We build these shells by cursing those who have hurt us or flinging contempt their way, choosing to stay in enemy mode, believing we have to protect ourselves because no one else will. We grow hard shells around our hearts in a million different ways.

Many species of plants develop tough shells to keep contaminants like bacteria and gases out, to prevent infection and rot. In the wild, animals chew these seeds, piercing through the shell and allowing them to germinate. Botanists and gardeners use the term scarification to describe the necessary damaging of a seed that must occur for it to grow. Sometimes gardeners will take a knife to their seeds to make a small nick, allowing moisture to get in. Other times, they might rub sandpaper on the edges or even boil the hard exterior away.[10]

All the ways we've tried to protect ourselves like seeds from enemies both large and small make it necessary for an outside intervention, something or someone who can open the husk of hardness around our souls.

I'm not saying that being hurt means we are hard of heart. Most of us have been harmed, and it is in hearing and being heard that we discover how our roots can grow into a new story, one where we're held by another. Like David, we need to be broken open by beauty through the courageous words of another to become beautiful ourselves.

In the last chapter I mentioned seeing tears spilling down our new priest's face. That was an *ak* moment for me. Seated at the table with

---

10. "How Scarification Brings Stubborn, Slow-Germinating Seeds to Life," The Seed Collection, June 30, 2018, www.theseedcollection.com.au/blog/our-blog/how-scarification -brings-stubborn-slow-germinating/.

Jordan and Ryan, like David at his table in Psalm 23, I glimpsed a more panoramic perspective of our painful story. I saw how God had always been intercepting us with grace, like the kindness on our priest's face. His tears evoked my memory of the day another pastor and his wife blessed us with their tears and, in so doing, gave us courage to rise up from our fears.

Pat did not attend our former church, but he had witnessed the control and contempt we had experienced there. At one point, as we were still wrestling with whether to leave, he invited us over to his house to talk. So we came, but with our guard up, not certain what to expect from the meeting.

Having the courage to flee into the wilderness to escape abusive or controlling relationships and systems does not only involve leaving. It also means rooting ourselves in the story of how God sees us, while uprooting every weed of self-contempt and shame others might try to sow as we grow and go.

We sat in the shade of a tree's sweeping branches in Pat's back yard as he poured us each a large glass of red wine. The setting was peaceful, but I was still protecting myself, with my arms folded tight against my chest like a shield. Pat asked if he could share some of what he had been observing in our church. "Okay," one of us said. "Of course." At that point, we wanted freedom and healing, but— goodness—we just wanted to be believed.

Without our saying a word to prove our pain to him, this man we barely knew named the reasons we were not insane. He pieced together patterns that had taken us years to see. We were shocked, in the best kind of disbelief.

Then Pat said something I'll never forget.

"You have done everything you could at that church. You are free to leave."

His words broke through the thick layers of fear and self-protection that were covering something important in our souls—our agency to choose wholeness. His courage to speak honestly about the reality of what he saw binding us, leaving us feeling small and stuck, gave us courage to become more.

We were free to leave.

Soon after, Pat's wife, Sarah, joined us and we spent the whole evening drinking wine and swapping stories, alternating between crying and laughing, like we had known each other for ages and weren't decades in age apart. We learned things about their story, *ak* moments that had broken them open to become the kind of people who were courageous and tender enough to help split apart our own seeds.

Between a desire for reconciliation and the fear of losing our income and insurance, we had been struggling for months to summon the courage to leave that church. That evening, Pat and Sarah conferred on us the courage we needed.

A psychologist named Annie Rogers has a study published in the *Harvard Educational Review* on the loss of voice, resilience, and confidence among adolescent girls. In it, she says that an older definition of courage that dates back to the 1300s is "to speak one's mind by telling all one's heart."[11] That night Pat and Sarah pierced the shell condemnation had grown around us by speaking their minds and their hearts with the same conviction with which Abigail spoke to David. In their words, we started to realize (*ak*) that even though we needed to leave our church behind, God would never leave us behind.

Courage is not something we can cultivate on our own. It is something we hold in common, a gift we confer on each other. It is the communion we offer with our faces, in safe spaces, with words that break the bondage of yesterday's shame and harm, rooting us

---

11. Annie Rogers, "Voice, Play, and a Practice of Ordinary Courage in Girls' and Women's Lives," *Harvard Educational Review* 63, no. 3 (September 1, 1993): 271, https://doi.org/10.17763/haer.63.3.9141184q0j872407.

in the reality that Beloved is who we are. With words aptly spoken, we break the bonds of evil that try to keep us stuck in our shells and burst forth in the boldness of belonging—bound up in the care of the living God.

Welcome the words when they come. Let them split open the husk of yesterday's harm. Let the view from the table change how you see your whole story. *Ak. Surely God's goodness and love will follow you.* Let this be the moment you burst into life.

30. YOUR
GOODNESS
AND LOVE

IN PSALM 23, Goodness and Love have feet. They become people who come behind the psalmist. In Goodness and Love, God walks on stage and becomes personally present, part of the play.[1] David is describing our greatest longing for each day.

In Hebrew, goodness is the word *tov*. It is the first description that God gives of this world. In the creation liturgy, the world begins with void and chaos and God speaks life into existence with the creative energy for its continuance. Life within life.

Seven times God saw what he made as good, *tov*. Light, land and sea, plants and seeds, day and night, sea animals and birds, land animals and birds—and then, in summary, all of it: *tov*. As Walter Brueggemann says, this liturgy invites us to respond "in the recital of the repeated formula, 'It is good! It is good that order defeats chaos! It is good that the world is ordered for fruitfulness . . . It is

---

1. Kenneth E. Bailey, *The Good Shepherd: A Thousand-Year Journey from Psalm 23 to the New Testament* (Downers Grove, IL: IVP Academic, 2014), 60.

very good indeed!'"[2] Life begins with a blessing in which we are invited to participate.

The love mentioned in Psalm 23 is the Hebrew word *hesed*. *Hesed* is a word that fleshes out *tov*; it is God's goodness on display in kindness that is both a faithful response to God's covenant love and a grace that is freely offered to the undeserving.[3] Put another way, it is kindness that cannot be and *does not have to be earned*. Jim Wilder describes *hesed* as attachment love.[4] Like God's *tov* rising out of chaos, *hesed* is given throughout Scripture in the context of human weakness and need—the chaos we carry from the fall of sin.

Take your finger and draw a circle in the air. Psalm 23 is like this circle, composed in a literary structure in which two truths uphold and strengthen each other.[5] Like a radial line connecting across the circle of the psalm, the first and seventh cameos form a pair. When David names God as his shepherd, in whom he lacks nothing because of God's protection (cameo 1), he is saying that God's *tov* and *hesed* are why and how his deepest needs have been met (cameo 7).

When Jesus presents himself as the Good Shepherd in John 10, he deliberately traces himself into the literary circle of Psalm 23, with poetic prose in the same ring composition as the psalm.[6] Jesus is revealing himself as the center of this circle, the long-anticipated shepherd of David's song coming to set things right. His words in John 10:11 bring the one-thousand-year good shepherd tradition to their climax: "I am the good shepherd," Jesus proclaims. "The good shepherd lays down his life for the sheep."

2. Walter Brueggemann, *Sabbath as Resistance: Saying No to the Culture of Now*, rev. ed. (Louisville: John Knox, 2017), 28–29.
3. See *The Brown-Driver-Briggs Hebrew and English Lexicon* and Bailey, *Good Shepherd*, 61.
4. E. James Wilder, *The Pandora Problem: Facing Narcissism in Leaders and Ourselves* (Carmel, IN: Deeper Walk International, 2018), 16.
5. Bailey, *Good Shepherd*, 24.
6. Ibid., 227.

The goodness and love relished by David and longed for by Jeremiah, Ezekiel, and Zechariah are finally brought together and embodied in the person of Jesus Christ. *Tov* and *hesed* meet in Christ's bones, breath, heart, and hands.

Jesus speaks in concert with the deliberate parallelism rooted in David's ancient song. Just as in Psalm 23, the first and seventh cameos in this scene form a pair, but here the literary climax comes when Christ says that the good shepherd gives his own life for the sheep.[7] Jesus, the one by whom the whole earth was spoken into being and through whose Spirit all Scripture was breathed, positions himself as the culmination and center of God's people's greatest longing.

Not only did Jesus say he would give up his life for the sheep, but he said that he knows his sheep and they know him, just as the Father knows him and he knows the Father.[8] He encompasses the culmination of David's song in the offering of his own life to *include us* in his relationship with the Father.

Jesus came so that his sheep might have life and have it fully—that our very life would be God's life—and he was determined to do whatever it took to give us this. He offered himself as a sheep to be slain. He felt his bones break. He allowed his breath to become nothing. His heart gave up its pace to give us space.

His goodness and *his* love come in the place where life meets death, making new life. Death was defeated by his willingness to drink it down. The Spirit raised him to life three days after he died, and he ascended into heaven, where he rules and reigns at the right hand of the Father. And the apostle Paul says *we have also been raised with him and seated in the heavenly places.*[9]

Our truest selves—the selves not bound by time and space or

7. Ibid., 229.
8. John 10:14–15.
9. Eph. 2:6.

any scarcity—are seated with Christ where *tov* and *hesed* are already ours. And it is as witnesses of Christ's costly love that we become witnesses of his life filling ours, bringing *tov* where there is chaos and offering *hesed* where there has been harm. We become bound up in this mystery as martyrs, the truest meaning of which is *to be a witness* of Christ's death and life as ours. "A martyr," Alexander Schmemann reminds us, "is one for whom God is not another—and the last—chance to stop the awful pain; God is his very life, and thus everything in his life comes to God, and ascends to the fullness of Love."[10]

In the Good Shepherd, everything in this world "has become an ascension to and entrance into this new life."[11] Will you be a witness of it? Will you listen for *tov* and *hesed*? Will you watch for their presence, savor their yeast, and swallow their wine?

Scarcity sings a siren song. It is always alarming our attention, turning us in on ourselves to self-protect and other-reject. Sin is the siren stance of scarcity, bent in on ourselves with our hands over our ears or rushing past others as though our lives are the emergency and no one else's matters.[12] Our bodies display the bending and breaking of scarcity in the effects of stress—skyrocketing cortisol levels, high blood pressure, chest pain, chronic pain, illness, cancer, poor sleep, and the list goes on.

Christ restores our capacity to witness and welcome the life of

10. Alexander Schmemann, *For the Life of the World* (Crestwood, NY: St. Valdimir's Seminary Press, 2018), 124–25.

11. Ibid., 124.

12. Kelly Kapic says that sin bends us in on ourselves, *homo incurvates in se.* Kelly Kapic, *God So Loved, He Gave: Entering the Movement of Divine Generosity* (Grand Rapids, MI: Zondervan, 2010), 37. Here Kapic is referencing Martin Luther's perspective on original sin.

God in the world, and the world wants to sing us into sensing that God's goodness and love are restoring us to life.

I know that hate is loud and people are proud, but quiet streams still sing and mushroom stalks talk. Anger and anxiety will howl no matter what. But there is a beauty that beckons—but never yells. Amazement asks for your attention, gently tugging at your hand to get off that couch or set down that spreadsheet, put down your phone, and return to the rhythm of reverence singing through Christ in every living thing. As Florence Williams writes in *The Nature Fix*, "Our nervous systems are built to resonate with set points derived from the natural world. Science is now bearing out what the Romantics knew to be true."[13]

When our bodies are full of fear and we feel like there must be someone to blame, we need beauty to bring us back to hearing Goodness and Love calling our name.

Remember this ratio: *Your body needs more cues of safety than cues of danger to rise.* Stress releases its grip on our bodies when we notice the presence of goodness.

Your nervous system needs cues of safety to come back home to feeling like yourself, and there is a world of it waiting nearby. Within a polyvagal framework, we talk about needing to find glimmers of goodness to balance the presence of triggers. Triggers happen when something has overwhelmed the flexibility of your nervous system.[14]

Triggers aren't failures; they're invitations. Triggers take us to the edge of our window of tolerance for stress and ask us to become larger—not through clenching or controlling but through compassion. They take us to the place where grace can soothe our

---

13. Florence Williams, *The Nature Fix: Why Nature Makes Us Happier, Healthier, and More Creative* (New York: Norton, 2017), 5.

14. Deb Dana, *The Polyvagal Theory in Therapy: Engaging the Rhythm of Regulation*, Norton Series on Interpersonal Neurobiology (New York: Norton, 2018), 67.

stress, where the Shepherd still stands with goodness and love in his hands, ready to reach toward us with glimmers of his kind plans. Glimmers are cues of safety that bring us back to our ventral vagal selves, calming our nervous systems out of survival mode back into connection and joy.[15]

This world is not a distraction that keeps us from God. It is the wonder that will delight us into the worship of God. One of my clients, who suffers from severe anxiety, recently shared that she was never taught God could be found in nature. So many of us, myself included, have been discipled by distrust. We've been missing the miracle of the majesty that reveals itself in the most mundane things—in leaves and streams and bees and the flutter of a butterfly's wings. This world will be a witness to us of the wonder of God's goodness and love, if we will watch for it.

When stress screams, we quickly stop feeling like ourselves and instead feel frustrated, even forgotten and forsaken. *Beauty can bring you back home.* Beauty tells your body it can be safe. Beauty is one of the surest ways back to the table with Christ, remembering and rising with the truth that our whole lives are still seen by God's face and followed by his grace. You need glimmers of goodness to feel safe in God's care, and noticing beauty will take you there.

In 1982 the Japanese government coined the term *shinrin yoku*, forest bathing, and in the decades since, reconnecting citizens to the beauty of forests has become standard preventive medicine there.[16] Researchers like Yoshifumi Miyazaki and Qing Li have

---

15. Ibid., 68.
16. Williams, *Nature Fix*, 19.

found that time spent in the forest effectively relieves stress states[17] and boosts natural killer (NK) cells, which fight infections and even cancer.[18]

Our stress was made to be soothed by the rhythms, scents, and sights of nature. Like Psalm 23's ring composition, this world's beauty encompasses our stress, needs, and longings in God's care.

Each evening revelation dances across the sky in colors we can't expect. Pale peach turns to neon pink, and the unfolding, soft sway of sunset into night whispers a sermon for those willing to watch and listen: you were made to rest and then rise.

Nearly every cell in your body was built to pay attention to the pattern of rest followed by rising. From your muscles to your hair cells, trillions of circadian clocks throughout your body take cues from your eyes to know when to rest, rise, and even repair DNA.[19]

The striated shades of the rising and setting sun speak through our eyes to tell our bodies how to live well. As Andrew Huberman has found, taking just ten to fifteen minutes to view a sunrise or sunset teaches your body—on a cellular level—to tell the time in order to thrive.[20]

What we see determines how we will live.

And you were made to behold.

God's kindness follows us all the days of our lives, and we will

17. Juyoung Lee et al., "Effect of Forest Bathing on Physiological and Psychological Responses in Young Japanese Male Subjects," *Public Health* 125, no. 2 (February 2011): 93–100, https://doi.org/10.1016/j.puhe.2010.09.005.

18. Qing Li, "Effect of Forest Bathing Trips on Human Immune Function," *Environmental Health and Preventive Medicine* 15, no. 1 (January 2010): 9–17, https://doi .org/10.1007/s12199-008-0068-3.

19. Signe Dean, "Every Single Cell in Your Body Is Controlled by Its Own Circadian Clock," Science Alert, October 2, 2015, www.sciencealert.com/your-body-has-trillions-of -clocks-in-its-cells; Veronique Greenwood, "How the Body's Trillions of Clocks Keep Time," *Quanta*, September 15, 2015, www.quantamagazine.org/20150915-circadian-clocks/.

20. Alyssa M. Rivera and Andrew D. Huberman, "Neuroscience: A Chromatic Retinal Circuit Encodes Sunrise and Sunset for the Brain," *Current Biology* 30, no. 7 (April 6, 2020): PR316–R318, https://doi.org/10.1016/j.cub.2020.02.090.

dwell secure in the divine presence as we look for glimmers of goodness in our ordinary days. Prayer is just paying attention.

So, Father in heaven, this we pray:

Hallowed—in everything—be your name. Give us this day our daily glimpse. Restore us from stress with our senses—from the scent of pine to the rhythm of the sun setting across the sky. Raise us from fear like the stars, shining brilliant up high. Forgive us for treating your world like something to use up before it burns. Forgive us for forgetting your face hidden in the holy but small—the bees, the hummingbirds, the seeds, the leaves as they fall. They all yearn, along with waterfalls and creeks, to communicate your call. Deliver us from evil's schemes to blind us to the goodness of every living human and thing. For yours is the kingdom and the power and the glory, we sing.

So make our triggers a place to find you again. And make our lives a daily amen.

31. WILL FOLLOW ME

WHEN I WAS WRITING MY FIRST BOOK, I felt harassed by the harm that had happened to us. Anxiety was my closest companion. She woke me up every day, whispered scary stories in my ear as I wrote, and wrestled sleep away from me at night.

I couldn't get past the possibility that God had allowed such harm to happen to us in the church. For months, I tried to lock my fears in a closet, pushing myself to put words on the page. But what really happened is that I ended up slinging my angst at my husband instead. I remember hours spent at our dining table, with pages spread out in front of us, with arrows from idea to idea, demanding Ryan's help to make sense of the story that was sitting like a mess in my head.

Eventually, I found my way and finished that book. But when it came time to write another book, *this book*, Ryan was adamant I couldn't do it the same way. He was firm but kind, letting me know that he wasn't good with being a receptacle for my dread. I needed and wanted to replace anxiety with trust. But I didn't know how.

At the same time, the treatment I had been on for years for my autoimmune disease failed. It was a hidden consequence of leaving dysfunction—the result of a lapse in care in losing our work insurance and getting a plan where I needed new doctors. My body rejected the new arrangement, making antibodies to my medicine in the month and a half I was off it.

When I resumed treatment, it never fully worked again. This meant my disease was now uncontrolled, and in the words of my rheumatologist, "one of the hardest cases of ankylosing spondylitis" he has ever treated. I was dependent on high doses of steroids to keep me moving and out of bed while we sought a treatment that could reduce the inflammation and pain that were becoming more widespread throughout my body.

Here I was, with a new book contract and a commitment to show up with more courage and more trust, in a body that couldn't guarantee my capacity to finish it. Even though I was commending my work to the care of God, I was struggling to sense a shift in *how* I could show up as though God's care was more sure than my suffering. Old trauma and pains were still hounding me and new ones were present, like the strange pain in my left eye and the ache on that side of my head.

"Follow" in Psalm 23 is a soft word for a stronger reality. *Radaph* is the Hebrew word here, and it means to pursue, chase, and perse-cute.[1] The goodness and love of God do not follow us like my dogs do, shadowing me as I hike up the hill behind my parents' house. No, the goodness and love of God *hound us*.

Remember how David spared Saul's life a second time after Abigail spoke him back into mercy? Right in that passage, in 1 Samuel 26, David says to Saul, "Now do not let my blood fall to the ground far from the presence of the LORD. The king of Israel

---

1. F. Brown, S. Driver, and C. Briggs, *The Brown-Driver-Briggs Hebrew and English Lexicon: With an Appendix Containing the Biblical Aramaic; Coded with the Numbering System from Strong's Exhaustive Concordance of the Bible* (Peabody, MA: Hendrickson, 2014), 922.

has come out to look for a flea—as one *hunts* a partridge in the mountains."[2] David is naming how Saul hunted him, using the verb *radaph*.

Radaph is most often used negatively. David employs *radaph* to describe being pursued and hunted by enemies in several of his songs. In Psalm 7 he prays, "Lᴏʀᴅ my God, I take refuge in you; save and deliver me from all who *pursue* me."[3] He cries out in Psalm 109 that his enemy "never thought of doing a kindness, but *hounded* to death the poor and the needy and the brokenhearted."[4] David almost exclusively utters this word in the context of hostility and harassment.

Of the 144 times *radaph* is used in the Bible, only here in Psalm 23 are God's goodness and love the nouns carrying out the action of pursuit. My friend Sam, who studies Hebrew *for fun*, said that by choosing this verb to describe God's activity, "David is flipping the script on persecution."[5] The same man who was chased down and hunted by Saul is saying that God's goodness and love hunt him down—even more than his enemies do.

We are not merely followed by mercy. We are hunted by it. We are haunted by beauty. Every day of our lives we are being chased down by grace.

Your whole life is not about finding God. It is about being found.

As I embarked on writing this book, I realized that I needed a way to root myself in *this reality*. I needed reminders to turn my attention

---

2. 1 Sam. 26:20, emphasis added.
3. Ps. 7:1, emphasis added.
4. Ps. 109:16, emphasis added.
5. Yes, I surround myself with nerds.

from all the harm that hounds me to the God who hounds me more. I needed rituals, prompts, and rest to return (*shuv*, be brought back, repent) to this reality every single day:

God's pursuit is not dependent on my performance.

"Without conscious rituals of loss and renewal," Romanian phenomenologist Mircea Eliade warns, "individuals and societies lose the capacity to experience the sorrows and joy that are essential for feeling fully human."[6] I was struggling to make the shift between the listlessness and losses I felt when writing my first book and the renewal and repentance with which I wanted to write this one. Between my disease and a raging pandemic that made it unsafe for me to be in public, I felt stuck. In sharing this with Mish, she offered to give me some of the space I had given her when we did her marriage funeral.

So as the aspens turned from green to gold, we drove to a lake flanked by mountains and sat down to make truth more tangible. I wanted to name the hurt I experienced and doled out while writing and releasing *This Too Shall Last*. I wanted to confess it, consciously releasing it so that my truest self, the self who is always pursued and embraced by God's goodness and love, could continue to emerge. I invited Mish to be my witness, a witness of the life of Christ filling mine.

With shining water stretching out in front of me and the sun overhead, I inked my insecurities into the light on a blank white canvas on my lap. "To confess," poet David Whyte writes, "is to declare oneself ready for a more courageous road, one in which a previously defended identity might not only be shorn away, but be seen to be irrelevant, a distraction, a working delusion that kept us busy over the years and held us unaccountable to the real question."[7]

6. Mircea Eliade, *Rites and Symbols of Initiation: The Mysteries of Birth and Rebirth* (Thompson, CT: Spring Publications, 2017), 10.
7. David Whyte, *Consolations: The Solace, Nourishment and Underlying Meaning of Everyday Words*, rev. ed. (Langley, WA: Many Rivers Press, 2014), 33.

I wrote down every way I fell and failed—from the way I used my husband as a trash can for my triggers, to the way I made my mentor feel commodified, to how I sometimes treated my friends like inconveniences or irritants.

With every sentence, I felt both pain and possibility. How I had hurt others was not who I had to become. And when the canvas was filled, I read each line aloud to Mish, because there is freedom in having nothing to hide. Honesty—heard and held—is where hope starts to rise.

Then Mish challenged me that I had more to confess—not just my sin but my courage. Confession is naming the truth of what we have lived and who we are becoming, and I needed to confess how God had already pursued and strengthened me as I showed up in the pages of my first book. I tilted the canvas one hundred eighty degrees and scrawled out all the courage I could name, intersecting my cowardice like a cross. Then I read it all aloud.

I brought a copy of my first book with me that day, not exactly sure how I would incorporate it into the ritual, but instinctively knowing it needed to be included. Suddenly, I knew: I wanted to tear it to shreds.

I wanted to physically embody the truth that I do not have to be so precious with the finished product of my words. I can rip it all up, and *I will remain.* Before I am a writer or a therapist, I am a human, and my humanness is what will endure at the end of the day. I tore the book in half, and then together Mish and I laughed as we ripped every last page into strips. My whole body felt a release, like I was the one being ripped open and freed.

Like grace envelops guilt and grief, I took glue and adhered the torn pieces over almost every inch of the canvas and my confessions. I decided to leave a long rectangle of my confessions visible, because like the scars on Christ's hands, the scars of my sorrow will become beautiful evidence of communion that in the new heavens and earth will still stand. Then I took aqua, persimmon, and crimson acrylics and painted newness on top—unplanned. Colors of my new courage, shades in shapes of the movement into which I sensed I would need to rise. I looped the crimson into concentric rings ascending to the top of the canvas.

When I got home, I hung the painting next to my desk, a visual reminder that every day I live and write, Christ's courage is there, coming for me with an outstretched hand.

I spent many of the weeks afterwards moving from my desk to my bed, as the next treatment I tried didn't help quiet my disease much at all. In the first months of starting this book, my body pressed me to practice what I preach, to rest myself into remembering that Goodness and Love reach me even when I cannot work, walk, or run. I started this book from a place of rest and chose rest every time hurt and harm nagged me to believe I was no longer one whom God blessed.

Every time I felt my old angst rise while writing, I looked up at the painting by my side. It beckoned me into the blessing that Julian of Norwich heard long before me: "Jesus gave me all that I needed. 'Sin is inevitable,'" she writes, "yet all will be well and all will be well and every kind of thing shall be well."[8]

Over the years, I've learned to see that my discouragement is often more about dysregulation than about anything being profoundly wrong with me. *Usually* when I'm sad, I'm mostly just tired. In traumatic family systems, many of us had to strive hard to be seen—exceptionally amazing, exceptionally good, exceptionally quiet, exceptionally un-needy. Our sense of worthiness was tethered

---

8. Julian of Norwich, *The Showings of Julian of Norwich: A New Translation*, trans. Mirabai Starr (Charlottesville, VA: Hampton Roads Publishing, 2013), 27.

to striving. Now we get the beautiful gift of cutting those entangling, exhausting cords by recognizing sadness or overwhelm as a prompt to rest.

Week by week, chapter by chapter, I have come to see that resting is not quitting. It's remembering and rooting ourselves in the story where we do not have to strive to be sought. Every time I put my work away for at least a whole day, I am learning to trust in the tender compassion of a God who doesn't bless based on effort or withhold based on weariness. It's common courage—the courage of communion.

Rest isn't the risk I once believed it was. The bigger risk is letting restlessness rule me.

In all our rushing and running, we forget who we are. Most of us need to discover that we will not begin to live more wholly until we practice the courage to do less and prove less. When we have spent our whole lives hounded by Satan's temptations to have more, hurt less, and rule faster, nothing is more difficult nor more necessary than to relinquish our reaching and just be still. Sometimes rest is the most courageous work of all. We often must be still in order to realize we are vessels God will always fill.

May *you* learn to honor your discouragement as a prompt to rest instead of proof that you will fail. May even your weariness remind you of your worthiness.

Radaph. The Shepherd is hounding us, hunting us, harassing us with kindness, grace, and love. No matter what we do or don't do, God pursues us. In rituals and rest, we can live from a place of realizing we are already being followed by the love we thought we had to earn.

32. ALL THE DAYS OF MY LIFE,

AT EUGENE PETERSON'S FUNERAL, his son Leif shared in a poem that even though his dad wrote dozens of books, he truly just had one message his whole life, words Eugene would whisper over him as he slept safe in bed at night: "God loves you. God is on your side. God is coming after you. He's relentless."[1]

Every single day, these words are true. Goodness and Love do not just follow us sometimes. They follow us on our days of doubt as well as delight. Just as the lyrics of Psalm 23 form a circle, beginning and ending with the Lord's presence, *all the days of our lives begin and end with God*. In the eleventh century, Saint Hildegard of Bingen put it like this:

> God hugs you.
> You are encircled by the arms
> of the mystery of God.[2]

---

1. Leif Peterson quoted in Stoyan Zaimov, "Eugene Peterson's Son Reveals His Father 'Fooled' Everyone, Had Only One Real Sermon for the World," *Christian Post*, November 5, 2018, www.christianpost.com/news/eugene-petersons-son-reveals-his-father-fooled-everyone-had-only-one-real-sermon-for-the-world.html.

2. Hildegard of Bingen, *Meditations with Hildegard of Bingen* (Rochester, VT: Bear and Company, 1983), 90.

My therapist once prayed over me that where there has been cursing, God would bring a new blessing.[3] After the curse that came with abuse, we needed to find our way back to the blessing of belonging with the people of God. While I no longer believe we *have to* worship with a local, institutional church in order to be part of the body of Christ, Ryan and I still longed to receive that communion. So after a year of belonging at our new church, we decided to be confirmed. Though we knew that with some of our own values and beliefs, the Anglican Church may not be our home forever, we decided to let *this* particular church be a place we could reaffirm that we still belong in the body of Christ.

Confirmation is just that—a *confirmation* of one's baptism and a new filling of the Spirit to live out one's unique vocation in the world. The entire previous year had been moving toward this, a reintegration and renewal of our vocations after the vulnerability and void of leaving abuse. We wanted to allow our church to share in that pilgrimage—the beauty of our blessedness, of becoming that which we already are—children of God and heirs with Christ.

In preparing to write this book, the concept of our baptismal identity captured my imagination. I was realizing and relishing the wonder that within Christ's baptism we have been given a name we could never earn nor can ever fully comprehend, one which changes everything about how we now live. I was realizing my whole life was encircled by the blessing I received as a fourteen-day-old baby in my pastor's hands.

So as I stepped farther into my vocation as one who writes of the wonder of belonging with God, I wanted more than ever to remember my baptism and be renamed within its blessing. I wanted the joy of what I had painted by that mountain lake to not just be outside but to be *inside*—both my soul and the church.

---

3. Yes, therapists have therapists—or at least, we all *should*.

Funny enough, during this season, I couldn't go inside almost any building other than our nine hundred square foot apartment. Because of both my disease and strong immunosuppressant treatments, my doctors had determined it wasn't safe for me to be in public until there was a covid vaccine. At the time, that felt like a distant dream, but as both someone who is sometimes disabled and homebound for weeks and months at a time and—let's be honest—an introvert, I felt like I had been training for this my entire adult life. But as the pandemic powered through season after season, when fall came, I was craving connection more than ever.

And so, the only day I stepped foot inside our church building from the beginning of the pandemic until two weeks after I was eventually vaccinated was to be confirmed by our bishop alongside my spouse. Part of the power of fasting is in the feast that comes. In abstaining from physical communion indoors for months, getting to step inside our church to be confirmed in the blessing of my baptism was the greatest taste I have ever had of the feast that is to come. Episcopal priest, author, and chef Robert Farrar Capon says, "The real secret of fasting is not that it is a simple way to keep one's weight down, but that it is a mysterious way of lifting creation into the Supper of the Lamb. It is . . . a major entrance into the fasting, the agony, the passion by which the Incarnate Word restores all things to the goodness God finds in them."[4] He goes on to say that one way or another God will give us back feasts for all that we have fasted. In this, I hear echoes of the prophet Joel, who said God would repay his people for the years the locusts had eaten.[5] For all

4. Robert Farrar Capon, *The Supper of the Lamb: A Culinary Reflection* (New York: Modern Library, 2002), 115.
5. Joel 2:25.

my time spent in bed, for all the wages lost to weakness and then abuse, for all the friendships that ended in betrayal or cowardice, there will be a feast.

We stepped through falling snow into the sanctuary when it came time for the liturgy for our confirmation. It was our compromise, to come inside only for the smallest window of time. And so, with masks and winter jackets on, we made our way to the front, where many times before we had received the Eucharist with tears and joy. The bishop had only met us briefly the day before and had read short written testimonies of our stories of faith, but if you heard the words he spoke over us, you would have thought he was our close friend. Jordan stood by his side, with a shepherd's staff in one hand and the other outstretched in benediction as Ken placed his hands on my head in blessing. I had not been touched by someone outside of my own family for seven months, and it felt like coming home. *I was still named into the hands that hold the whole world.*

"Your joy has been under assault for a long time," Ken said. I looked up and nodded in recognition. *How did he know?* It was as though he saw into both my history and heart. "Joy is your gift," he continued. "Your joy will be a gift through which God blesses many." My jaw hung open in amazement.

I had written similar words in my journal months before, right after Ryan and I had that hard conversation about needing to write this book differently. As I poured out prayers for help on the page, it was as though a cloud had dispersed from over my soul, shining light to remember who I am at my core. My hand scrawled out the blessing I heard in the Silence: *Joy is who you are.*

I stepped back after receiving the bishop's blessing and listened as he uttered similar strangely personal words over Ryan about his vocation as a shepherd, a strong and spacious presence for others.

In the quiet of my heart I knew what was happening was not

conjured but created. Through others, God was filling us, following us, and renewing us all the way through.

Schmemann posits that "our whole life stemming from Baptism has been made into a 'passage'—the pilgrimage and the ascension toward the 'day without evening' of God's eternal Kingdom. And as we proceed and fight and work, the mysterious light of that Day already illumines our way, shines everywhere, transforms everything, makes everything life in God and the way to God."[6]

Confirmation was a moment when I could see the passage that had already come to be. It was no less true when contempt was spewed on us. It was no less real when we lost friends and finances along the way. It was as authentic in our abuse as in our awe. There was no part of life that was outside of the circle of God's embracing arms.

Sometimes I think there is a blessing only the broken can hear. Those who have been silenced or shamed sense in a fractal what Christ held in whole. Some Kabbalists teach that Psalm 23 has special significance to our livelihood because it contains 227 Hebrew letters, which is the numerical value of the word *barak*, blessing.[7]

The Broken One brought the blessing down to us who could never earn it ourselves. Patterned in his passage, there is now always this possibility: blessing comes in the breaking.

"God in Christ has taken into Himself the brokenness of the human condition," priest Martin Laird reminds us. "Hence, human woundedness, brokenness, death itself are transformed from dead

6. Alexander Schmemann, *Of Water and the Spirit: A Liturgical Study of Baptism* (Crestwood, NY: St. Vladimir's Seminary Press, 1974), 129.

7. Shlomo Chaim Kesselman, "Psalm 23: L-rd Is My Shepherd," Chabad.org, accessed November 2021, www.chabad.org/library/article_cdo/aid/3832324/jewish/Psalm-23-L-rd-Is-My-Shepherd.htm.

ends to doorways into Life. In the divinizing humanity of Christ, bruises become balm."[8] In the shadow and shelter of the cross, Jesus' broken body still speaks through groans and scars that it is among the broken that God's blessing resides.

God chases us down with this blessing—whether in the doors of a church, on the couch of a therapist, or in the silent sobs we share alone or with friends—baptizing us into belovedness everywhere we go. He's on our side. He loves us. He's relentless—*all the days of our lives.*

---

8. Martin Laird, *Into the Silent Land: A Guide to the Christian Practice of Contemplation* (New York: Oxford Univ. Press, 2006), 119.

33. AND I WILL DWELL

THE FIRST THING WE RECEIVE when we enter the world is breath. The moment we leave our mothers' wombs, we must open our lungs and mouths to make our way. Our first cries clear our airways of fluid, allowing our diaphragms to contract and relax into the rhythm of expansion and release.[1]

As the vagus nerve signals to the brainstem that our lungs are expanding to regulate our bodies with oxygen, we experience our first moment of separation from our mothers and our connection to this world at the same time. "When we take in our first breath," America's poet laureate Joy Harjo says, "it is a promise to take on this human story, a story that has dimension in time and place. Breath is our entrance into story-making—it is a promise. It is a constant ritual we all share."[2] Our first breaths are the moment we receive the birthright of the rhythm of regulation as *ours*.

---

1. Navaz Habib, *Activate Your Vagus Nerve: Unleash Your Body's Natural Ability to Heal* (Berkeley, CA: Ulysses Press, 2019), 65.

2. Joy Harjo, "The Field of Stories," interview by Laura Da', *Poets and Writers*, September/October 2021, 59.

When God made the world, Breath made you. When the earth was formless and shapeless, as Hebrew scholar Wil Gafney translates Genesis 1:2, "She, the Spirit of God pulsed over the face of the waters."[3] Like a mother gives her energy and oxygen to the baby in her womb, God kneeled to dirt of this world and breathed you into being with the same Spirit who fluttered over the waters.[4] The Breath of God, the *Ruach* of God, is our beginning and our becoming.

When stress sinks us down the autonomic ladder, breath is one of the first things to go. When we sense too many cues of danger, our vagal brake is released, charging the body with the energy of the sympathetic nervous system to ready us for fight or flight. Our heart rate soars and our shoulders rise up to our ears as our breath becomes shallow and rapid to fill our bodies with oxygen from head to toe.

Trauma tends to disrupt our body's path of return to the rhythm of rest. Even when the real danger has stopped, our nervous systems become acclimated to assessing risk. We get stuck in hypervigilance, subconsciously scanning everyone and everywhere for threats through our body's function of neuroception. Our breath gets stuck there too.

Take a moment to find your breath. Place one hand over your belly and the other over your chest. Now close your eyes and breathe as you would normally. Really. I really want you to do this. You can set down the book and pick it right back up. Breathe.

What did you notice? Did your shoulders rise as you breathed or did your belly expand the most?

Many of us have adapted to living most of our lives in a sympathetic state to survive stress and trauma, which teaches our bodies to breathe using our accessory muscles rather than our diaphragms.

---

3. Wilda C. Gafney, *Womanist Midrash: A Reintroduction to the Women of the Torah and the Throne* (Louisville: Westminster John Knox, 2017), 19, Kindle.
4. Gen. 2:7.

We become bound to shallow breathing, overusing the same muscles that are most involved in responding to stress—the muscles of the neck, shoulders, anterior chest, and back—to control our inner, unacknowledged sense of chaos.[5] Instead of the deep belly breathing of the diaphragm that we were made for, we get stuck in the shallows.

As the common refrain in neuroscience goes, neurons that fire together wire together.[6] What gets repeated gets strengthened. And when we are repeatedly having to scan all the time for danger (under the surface of our awareness), searching for cues like judgment or annoyance or volatility in others that might threaten our survival, our bodies learn to wire into pathways of self-protection. This includes our shallow breathing. In a real sense, we can't catch our breath.

The prophet Ezekiel knew the way that false shepherds could shatter the goodness of their sheep's lives. His words were a riot of rebellion against the false shepherds of Israel who ruled the people "harshly and brutally" just like the domineering pastors of today.[7] If you are still struggling to see how grievous these dynamics are, one listen to the popular podcast by Christianity Today, *The Rise and Fall of Mars Hill*, can give you a window into what stories like mine look like from the inside of church systems that are ordered around dominance, celebrity, and control.[8]

5. Habib, *Activate Your Vagus Nerve*, 67.

6. While psychologist Donald Hebb was probably the first to propose this concept, the phrase appears to be first used by Carla Shatz in 1992. See Donald Hebb, *The Organization of Behavior: A Neuropsychological Theory* (New York: Wiley, 1949). See also Carla J. Shatz, "The Developing Brain," *Scientific American* 267, no. 3 (September 1992): 60–67, https://doi.org/10.1038/scientificamerican0992-60.

7. Ezek. 34:4.

8. Mike Cosper, *The Rise and Fall of Mars Hill* (podcast), Christianity Today, 2021, www.christianitytoday.com/ct/podcasts/rise-and-fall-of-mars-hill.

Ezekiel knew the way that bullies can leave us breathless. And just a few chapters after his stark judgment against the shepherds of Israel, he describes a vision God gave him where the life that is stolen is returned.

Ezekiel is standing in the middle of a valley, and everywhere he turns, there are dry bones. Everywhere I look, I too see bones. I receive hundreds—actual hundreds—of emails from readers telling me their stories of spiritual abuse. Not one week goes by without receiving another message or email from someone who has found my writing or my husband's writing and is desperate to have the breath that was stolen from them acknowledged and believed and restored. God asked Ezekiel, "Son of man, can these bones live?"[9] As a therapist, I stand daily in the middle of a dark valley full of bones and like Ezekiel, I reply, "Sovereign LORD, you alone know."[10]

If the church has stolen your sense of joy, hear these words. If life has left you breathless—for any other reason—listen closely.

What God said to Ezekiel, I say to you. God will bend down to your dead bones and breathe you back to life.[11]

To all that has been slain in you, let there come Breath. To all that has been dried out by the darkness of what seems bright, let there be life.

Like the people of Israel, I have cried out that my very life is withered and my hope is gone, that I have been cut off from the community of those I called family.[12] And I have heard so many others who sigh with the same cry.

God says, *I will open up the graves of grandiosity that swallowed you whole. I will raise you from the ruins that crumbled your soul. I will*

9. Ezek. 37:3a.
10. Ezek. 37:3b.
11. The Hebrew word Ezekiel uses in this passage for breath is *ruach*.
12. Ezek. 37:11.

put my own Breath, my own Spirit, in you—the Breath who will make you new.[13]

I will give you a Shepherd who will dwell in the place you feared you were disowned. I will give you back the land and life that were overthrown. This Shepherd will make your body his home. And the whole world will know I am good because I will never leave you alone.[14]

The ritual of breath can be your rhythm of resilience. Like Thomas Merton once prayed, "My God, I pray better to you by breathing. I pray better to you by walking than talking."[15]

Any moment that stress starts to sink you down the autonomic ladder, you can remember that the Breath who formed this world breathes within you. The ancient practice of breath prayer that began in the lives of the Desert Fathers and Mothers can help you rise. This is how we embody Scripture's call to "pray without ceasing."[16]

When I silently turn my attention to the most basic function of living—breathing—I can acknowledge my need for the Shepherd to help me rise.[17] In and out. *Lord* [inhale], *have mercy* [exhale]. Lengthening my exhalation signals to my body that I am more safe than it seems. I am remembering the co-regulating presence of Christ.

"This magnificent refuge is inside you," Saint Teresa of Avila says. "Enter. Shatter the darkness that shrouds the doorway . . . Ask

---

13. I am referencing Ezek. 37:12–14 here.

14. I am referencing Ezek. 37:24–28 here.

15. Thomas Merton, *Dialogues with Silence: Prayers and Drawings* (New York: HarperOne, 2004), 57.

16. 1 Thess. 5:17 ESV.

17. Portions of this originally appeared in *Relevant* in 2018: Katie Jo Ramsey, "Why Learning to Breathe May Be the Best Way to Pray," *Relevant*, May 24, 2021, www .relevantmagazine.com/faith/why-learning-to-breathe-may-be-the-best-way-to-pray/.

no permission from the authorities. Slip away. Close your eyes and follow your breath to the still place that leads to the invisible path that leads you home."[18]

In the last twenty years, psychology and neuroscience researchers have demonstrated the potency of mindfulness on well-being. Mindfulness training has been shown to increase life satisfaction,[19] positive emotions, self-compassion,[20] and immune function. It has even been found to increase levels of the enzyme responsible for maintaining and repairing the ends of chromosomes that shorten as we age, lengthening our life span.[21]

Breath prayer is essentially an embodied mindfulness practice, because it offers us singular focus, present-moment awareness, and a nonjudgmental posture toward our feelings, sensations, and thoughts.[22] Studies have shown that contemplative prayer like breath prayer can help us manage stress, perceive our stressors differently, and increase our spiritual awareness.[23] Research has shown that, breath by breath, contemplative prayer builds a life with less worry, depression, anxiety, and stress.[24] Breathing in and out, we

18. Teresa of Avila, *Saint Teresa of Avila: Devotions, Prayers, and Living Wisdom*, ed. Mirabai Starr (Boulder, CO: Sounds True, Inc., 2007), 53.

19. Julie Anne Irving, Patricia L. Dobkin, Jeeseon Park, "Cultivating Mindfulness in Health Care Professionals: A Review of Empirical Studies of Mindfulness-Based Stress Reduction (MBSR)," *Complementary Therapies in Clinical Practice* 15, no. 2 (May 2009): 61–66, www.sciencedirect.com/science/article/abs/pii/S174438810900005X.

20. Shauna Shapiro et al., "Mindfulness-Based Stress Reduction for Health Care Professionals: Results from a Randomized Trial," *International Journal of Stress Management* 12, no. 2 (2005): 164–76, www.upaya.org/uploads/pdfs/shapiro.study.pdf.

21. Tonya L. Jacobs et al., "Intensive Meditation Training, Immune Cell Telomerase Activity, and Psychological Mediators, *Psychoneuroendocrinology* 36, no. 5 (June 2011): 664–81, www.sciencedirect.com/science/article/abs/pii/S030645301000243X.

22. Joshua J. Knabb and Veola E. Vazquez, "A Randomized Controlled Trial of a Two-Week Internet-Based Contemplative Prayer Program for Christians with Daily Stress," *Spirituality in Clinical Practice* 5, no. 1 (2018): 37–53, https://psycnet.apa.org/record/2018 -03412-001.

23. Ibid.

24. Joshua J. Knabb, Thomas V. Frederick, and George Cumming III, "Surrendering to God's Providence: A Three-Part Study on Providence-Focused Therapy for Recurrent

learn the regulating rhythm of rising out of our self-protection and self-contempt. Research has even shown our capacity to cope with conflict improves as we practice breath prayer.[25]

Breath prayer brings us back to the wordless place where we first learned to trust we could make our way in the world. Whether we pair our breath with simple words like the shortened version of the Jesus Prayer I use throughout the day, it is our breath that can bridge us back to remembrance of the God who is with us.

The very function of living that you cannot survive without, which occurs so automatically most of us forget it is happening, is a force that when acknowledged can remind your whole body you are already united to God.

When abuse left me breathless, breath prayer returned my awareness to a better Shepherd. Any moment of any day, if I can remember my breath, I can remember I still dwell with God.

Worry (PFT-RW)," *Psychology of Religion and Spirituality* 9, no. 2 (2017): 180–96, https://psycnet.apa.org/record/2016-24578-001.

25. Marta Rubinart, Tim Moynihan, and Joan Deus, "Using the Collaborative Inquiry Method to Explore the Jesus Prayer," *Spirituality in Clinical Practice* 3, no. 2 (June 2016): 139–51, https://psycnet.apa.org/buy/2016-22460-001.

34. IN THE HOUSE
OF THE LORD

WHEN I WAS LITTLE, I dressed up for church because I thought I was dressing up to go visit God. Of course, I thought that because I was told some version of it. My mom made me and my younger sister wear dresses every Sunday out of respect for "God's house." Sometimes I would twirl and twirl after the service while the adults drank coffee and talked, feeling special, like wearing a dress had somehow made God smile.

It's strange how damaging it can be to believe God lives only in a house as small as sanctuary. Or that God needs a house at all.

Scholars don't know for sure when David wrote Psalm 23, but I like to think that he wrote it at least a while after he was king. I like to imagine that he sang this song with rich memories of rescue from Saul and his own ambition to do something grand that God didn't want or need. I love that David ends this song in God's house, because wanting to build God a house was a pivotal moment in David's life, and, as Brueggemann writes, "the dramatic and theological center of the entire Samuel corpus."[1]

---

1. Walter Brueggemann, *First and Second Samuel: Interpretation: A Bible Commentary for Teaching and Preaching* (Louisville: John Knox, 1990), 253.

After David was anointed king by the elders of the twelve tribes of Israel, he was becoming more and more powerful because "the LORD God Almighty was with him."[2] David wasn't hiding in caves and scrounging for food anymore. Even neighboring kingdoms were recognizing his rule. One king even sent cedar logs for David to use to build a grand palace.

It took David twenty or so years from Samuel's first anointing of him to finally being crowned as king, and now that he had a home and a kingdom, he wanted to make a home for God too. David brought the idea to his pastor, Nathan. "Here I am," he said to Nathan, "living in a house of cedar, while the ark of God remains in a tent."[3] At first, Nathan thought whatever David had in mind was a great idea. Until later that night, when God spoke to Nathan with a clear no.

God corrected David through Nathan, saying, "Go and tell my servant David, 'This is what the LORD says: Are you the one to build me a house to dwell in? I have not dwelt in a house from the day I brought the Israelites up out of Egypt to this day. I have been moving from place to place with a tent as my dwelling."[4]

God is making it clear: God does not need a house.

If David had filled Jerusalem with the sights and sounds of construction, the people would have been caught up in what he was doing, not what God was doing. How often do we dream up dazzling things to do for God, when God is wanting to do something *within* us?

God then reminds David where he came from, who he is, and whose he is. "I took you from the pasture, from tending the flock, and appointed you ruler over my people Israel. I have been with you wherever you have gone, and I have cut off all your enemies from

---

2. 2 Sam. 5:10.
3. 2 Sam. 7:2.
4. 2 Sam. 7:5–6.

before you."[5] God reminds David through Nathan that it is *God's activity* that is at the center of this story, not anything David needs to do for God.

And then God says that the Lord himself will establish a house for David, that God will give David a descendant of his own flesh and blood to establish a kingdom. This descendant will be the one to build a house for God's name, with a throne from which he will rule *forever.* "I will be his father, and he will be my son," God says.[6] And "my love will never be taken away from him, as I took it away from Saul."[7]

Brueggemann says this is "the most crucial theological statement in the Old Testament."[8] Through David's descendant, our relationship with God will always be grounded not in our performance but in God's promise.

Nathan tells David all of this, and then David sits before the Lord. Peterson says that he believes this was the moment in David's life when he was "about to cross over a line from being full of God to being full of himself."[9] But intercepted by Nathan through God's word, David is humbled before God. And it is while *sitting with God* that David shifts from talking about God as an impersonal object (wanting to build a house for God's ark) to talking with God as a person who is present.

The focus of the conversation moves from what David wants to do for God to what God has already done for David *and* all of Israel. He wraps his own story back into the story of God saving Israel from Egypt. How often we forget that God has been doing

---

5. 2 Sam. 7:8–9a.

6. 2 Sam. 7:14.

7. 2 Sam. 7:15.

8. Brueggemann, *First and Second Samuel*, 258–59.

9. Eugene Peterson, *Leap over a Wall: Earthy Spirituality for Everyday Christians* (New York: HarperOne, 1998), 161.

the work of saving from the beginning of time and that our grand plans to build a kingdom are but mist in the wind.

David wanted to build a house for God, but *God wanted to build David into a house instead.*

When David realizes this, he says that it gives him *courage.* He acknowledges all that God has done, and instead of needing to do anything amazing, he sits there amazed. Of this exchange, Peterson says that "there are times when our grand human plans to do something for God are seen, after a night of prayer, to be a huge human distraction from what God is doing for us."[10]

How much of my life has been spent trying to build a kingdom for God that God has already been building with me?

It takes courage to relinquish building something for God to instead be built up, in long and often invisible ways, by God into a house that God will dwell in forever. It takes courage to quit doing things for God to commune with God. And it's not that we never take action, but like David, we can choose to act after we sit with God, carrying out our labor from a place of communion instead of conceit or control.

In 1 Corinthians 6, Paul writes, "Do you not know that your bodies are temples of the Holy Spirit?"[11]

I first learned that verse from the scolding mouths of my Christian school teachers.[12] It strangely was directed mostly at female students, as though our bodies had a unique power to desecrate everyone else's. My independent fundamentalist Baptist school

---

10. Ibid., 160.

11. 1 Cor. 6:19.

12. A version of this story first appeared in *Fathom* magazine: K.J. Ramsey, "Too Holy to Hide: Finding That My Body Is Already Loved by God," *Fathom*, November 23, 2020, www.fathommag.com/stories/too-holy-to-hide.

required that I hide the body I already felt awkward about behind shapeless skirts and shirts. The school had somehow squeezed a law of female frumpiness out of the King James Version Bibles they revered like little leather-bound idols. I attempted to marginally improve the dress code by wearing a long denim skirt from the coolest store I knew, Old Navy, paired with the coolest shoes I could find, Adidas Superstar tennis shoes (it was the early 2000s!), as though anything could make being forced into a long denim skirt fashionable. I'm cringing even picturing it.

The only days girls were allowed to wear jeans to school were "Bucks for Bibles" days. One dollar bill bought me one day of freedom from the confines of a skirt and the marginal satisfaction of growing the school's fund to bind and box Bibles to send overseas. Somehow missionary efforts evoked a temporary day of jubilee, and our lady legs would get to slip into the devil's denim for the greater good of spreading God's Word to lands that supposedly didn't have it. On those days, my female classmates and I would report to the cafeteria instead of our homerooms, where we'd line up to hand a teacher a dollar and our dignity.

We stood single file like soldiers in front of Mrs. M. and her ruler. Since it was the era of low-rise jeans, the inspection began with bending over to see if any skin was showing. "Turn around," she'd demand next, glaring over the glasses perched on the end of her nose at our butts below. We had to be able to pinch an inch of denim in order for our jeans to leave more room for the Holy Spirit than for the male imagination. Mrs. M. was the judge and jury, scrutinizing the outline of our rears to rule whether the tightness would tempt the boys down the hall. Sometimes I'd have to tie a sweatshirt around my waist to be allowed back in class—after pocketing a demerit—because though my hips don't lie, apparently my curves create sin. It was an education in cover-up Christianity, where skin-showing leads to sin-flowing and female bodies are above all to be subdued.

Under their watchful eye, I learned that hating my body was the main way to be holy. As a survivor of childhood sexual abuse, it was not difficult to make the logical leap that to hear God, I needed to silence my sensations and make myself as small as possible. It's not surprising that I couldn't hear the Spirit of God warning me of danger years later in our spiritually oppressive church, for I had long practiced silencing myself and my body. I thought spirituality was submission, but really I was just practicing suppression.

Both purity culture and power-broking pastors teach us to approach our bodies like commodities to control and use. The gnostic gospel of the American Dream has discipled us in disembodiment. The good news of capitalism has chained us to treating our bodies like machines to master to get and be more.

The gnostic gospel tells an alluring story. Control your body and you'll be like Christ. Just have faith and you'll conquer your fears. Believe harder and you'll do more for God.

But when you commodify yourself into some*thing* to be *used by God*, you end up chopping off any part of yourself that would make you go slow or get low. You risk making yourself into a machine for more until there is no *you* left.

Your body isn't a tool to build someone's temple or kingdom. Cover-up Christianity teaches us to subdue our bodies for God, but faith in the real, risen, and reigning Jesus shows us that a body is what brings us God's love.

What I wasn't taught in school or church is that Paul's designation of our bodies as temples is revolutionary. The Greek word he used for temple is *naos*, and it is the word used to describe *the place where God personally resides.*[13] And *Thayer's Greek Lexicon* notes that *naos* describes not just the temple but the holy of holies.[14]

King David wanted to build God a temple. Instead, God promised a King whose body makes *ours* into living temples.

I never needed to dress up to go visit God's house. I was already God's house. I never needed to conquer my body. Christ already dwelled inside her. I never needed to build up someone else's church to feel like I was pleasing God. The holiest place was already within me.

Your body isn't a barrier to courage. It is the very place you can most hear God's voice, because *you* are where God's love resides.

13. See https://biblehub.com/greek/3485.htm.
14. Ibid.

35. FOREVER.

WE WILL DWELL in the house of the Lord forever, because God has already made a home within us.

Jesus is the promised descendant of David, and in his incarnation, our union with God was accomplished.[1] When the moment comes that we think we must do something for God to honor or even protect God, we must sit like David in the strange mystery that God has already secured a home within us. It's from the seated place that we can best see: *God is already within me.* There is nothing we can do and nowhere we can go where God's love will be removed from us. Like David, this is how God gives us courage and becomes our courage.

The most regulating thing for our nervous systems at any point of any day is co-regulation. Experiencing the presence of someone else with us who is kind emboldens us to face our fears with trust. This is what we have in Christ. There is never a moment that God is not in us and with us, carrying our fears and hopes into a future kingdom of love.

Courage is not something we have to muster up or manufacture for God. *Courage is choosing to commune with someone who has already*

---

1. Thomas F. Torrance, *The Mediation of Christ: Evangelical Theology and Scientific Culture* (Colorado Springs: Helmers and Howard, 1992), 64–66.

chosen to be with us. As psychiatrist Curt Thompson says, "Courage is not just about me having something that no one else has. Courage is about me having somebody else within me that enables me to do hard things that I otherwise wouldn't do on my own."[2]

The Lord is our courage.

This Lord, our Christ, showed himself to us as our true Good Shepherd who is already united to us and present with us everywhere we go. Because the Good Shepherd gave his life for the sheep, for us, we have been made one with God in Christ. This is the atonement, our at-one-ment with God, and our whole lives will be a discovery of just how united to God we are.

Theologian T. F. Torrance reminds us that this oneness, the atonement, is not an act done by Christ but rather the incarnate person of Christ himself embodying our redemption.[3] In him we now live and breathe and have our being.[4] As Saint John of the Cross reminds us, we now "breathe in God with the same aspiration of love which the Father breathes with the Son, and the Son with the Father, which is the Holy Ghost Himself."[5] The apostle Paul puts it this way: "God sent the Spirit of his Son into our hearts, the Spirit who calls out, '*Abba*, Father.'"[6]

There is a gap of a thousand years between David's shepherd

2. Curt Thompson, "With All Your Mind," *The Arthur Brooks Show* (podcast), March 21, 2019, https://podcasts.apple.com/us/podcast/with-all-your-mind/id1405001555?i=1000432691820.

3. Torrance draws from the tradition of Karl Barth, integrating Christology and soteriology as one whole. Thomas F. Torrance, *The Trinitarian Faith: The Evangelical Theology of the Ancient Catholic Church* (Edinburgh: T&T Clark, 1988), 159; Torrance, *Mediation of Christ*, 66.

4. Acts 17:28.

5. Saint John of the Cross, *A Spiritual Canticle*, trans. David Lewis (New York: Benziger Brothers, 1909), 292.

6. Gal. 4:6.

song and Christ's revelation as its realization. A thousand years of longing and loss, suffering and scattering, exile and hard emotions. And all throughout, God's people kept telling the shepherd story, finding space within it to situate their own stories in the hope of one coming with strength and love. Today, courage rises in us, in our willingness to do the same by the Spirit whom the Shepherd has given us as an ever-present help.

In Mark 6 Jesus consciously enacted Psalm 23, showing us once and for all that he is the long-awaited shepherd who is determined to seek and care for lost sheep. For the first time in history, the shepherd is not a metaphor but a man, standing in time and space to enfold the scattered into the story of union with God.

Jesus' cousin John the Baptist had just been assassinated by Herod—an anxious, irrational ruler who would do anything, it seems, to maintain adoration and power. John's murder would have been a deep personal loss to Jesus, and it would have brought great fear to the disciples questioning how to proceed in their mission. The people following Jesus likely felt a growing hopelessness, for in John they saw a true prophet of God and the potential for freedom from oppressive Roman rule.

As Jesus went away to pray and consider how best to lead them, he found himself followed by a massive crowd. In the shame-honor culture of his day, there would have been an expectation for John's family members to respond dramatically to his murder, perhaps even violently.[7] Bailey reminds us that an "eye for an eye and tooth for a tooth" would have been the law and custom of the day.[8] And Herod would have sent spies to see how Jesus responded and report back to him,[9] fearful of an uprising of the common people.

7. Kenneth E. Bailey, *The Good Shepherd: A Thousand-Year Journey from Psalm 23 to the New Testament* (Downers Grove, IL: IVP Academic, 2014), 161.

8. Ibid., 167.

9. Ibid., 164.

Kings in Israel were seen as shepherds of the flock, and Herod had just shown himself to be a bad shepherd.[10] Jesus, seeing the growing crowd, "had compassion on them, because they were like sheep without a shepherd."[11] He decided then and there to show his true identity as the shepherd God had promised.

Jesus taught as the day stretched toward night, and the disciples wanted to send the crowd away to go feed themselves dinner. Bailey describes what the disciples must have been murmuring to themselves about the crowd. "*We did not invite them. They totally disrupted our plans and we are not responsible for them. They must take care of themselves.*"[12]

At the banquet where John was beheaded, powerful people would have been in attendance, ready to spread news in their villages about Herod's feast of death. "Jesus decided to give the poor from those same towns and villages a *different kind of banquet* to talk about," Bailey underscores.[13]

Jesus made the crowd's hunger his responsibility and revealed himself as the Good Shepherd by reenacting Psalm 23 for all to see. The only food they were able to find was a small offering from the crowd—five loaves and two fish. In John's account of the same story, we're told this offering was from a boy who probably was fairly poor, because the barley loaves he gave Jesus were the bread most commonly eaten by the poor.[14]

Instead of exacting revenge or calling for an uprising, Jesus gathered up these sheep without a shepherd (which, remember, was probably a crowd of upwards of fifteen thousand people) and had them *lie down in green pastures*.[15] He then took the small offering

10. Ibid., 166.
11. Mark 6:34.
12. Bailey, *Good Shepherd*, 167.
13. Ibid.
14. John 6:8–9.
15. Mark 6:39.

of food, blessed it, broke the bread, and gave it to the disciples to distribute to the crowd, *feeding them* until they were more than satisfied. There was so much food left over that it filled twelve baskets after everyone was done eating.

A small offering, blessed, broken, and given from Christ's hands became more than enough for everyone that day.

The kingdom of darkness makes us doubt we'll have enough or be enough, so most of us double down two tight fists around our time, our space, our money, and our privilege—just in case anyone tries to take them.

But the kingdom of God walks into our world like a defenseless boy, handing Jesus his loaves of bread and fish on a hillside, just because people are hungry and he had something that could help. Even just a little.

The kingdom of God comes like loaves from open hands, given to the one who receives our small offering and blesses it as brave. And with our hands still empty, we watch as God takes our little bit, breaks it, and makes it more than enough to feed thousands.

The Christian life, the courageous life, is an invitation to show up every single day like that kid to watch Jesus bless your smallness as sacred, make breaking part of the blessing, and give more than enough for more than just you.

We who have been scattered, whose lives have been shattered and who wonder if we ever mattered to God, are being sought by this Shepherd right in the places that sting, where our stomachs rumble and souls quake. This Good Shepherd still looks out over the crowd of sheep without a shepherd and feels so much compassion he is compelled to act. As we sit on the hillsides where it seems hope might be lost, we are positioned exactly where small offerings over-shadow scarcity to soothe and strengthen us into seeing—even just for a day—the kingdom of God is in our midst.

Just as Psalm 23 and the passage in Mark are ring compositions, *courage is a circle of communion*. It is a place we return to, season after season, and a practice we choose again and again. And fed with our daily bread, the circle grows in meaning, scope, and strength.

One day this past spring, a couple reached out to Ryan and me, people we knew in college but had fallen out of touch with over the years. The husband is a pastor and the wife is a therapist. Just like us. Colby and Kat knew from what we have both written that we would be safe people for them to share that they were being spiritually abused in their church by their senior pastor, and that unless a miracle happened, they would have to resign.

The miracle didn't happen. Their pain was not heard.

I called up Mish, who also went to college with all of us and whose new home has a private apartment. I wanted to give Colby and Kat a space to be heard in a way we wished we could have been years before. Mish instantly said yes.

They came the following week, just days after resigning. We didn't have much to give—just our ears and our empathy—but we knew that their trauma could be lessened by experiencing that *they were not alone in their story*.

On their last night in Denver, as Ryan and I drove home from Mish's house, we looked at each other in amazement. This week, with this couple, in the moment of their greatest pain, we got to see something we had never dreamed. We realized that it had been three years since we drove to Montana in the wake of our own resignation and saw that spacious land spreading out before us. Three years since our life had fallen apart and eaten up all the courage we had, just to escape abuse. We didn't know it at the time, but God wasn't just bringing us to a spacious place. *God was making us a spacious place.*

I know that one day Colby and Kat will do the same for someone else, and the circle will grow. Because that is how courage works. Christ never stops chasing us into communion, especially where pain pierces us through. Courage is simply the choice to be found. And once you are found, you must free others. You must help the next person find their way through the shadows.

It is in hearing the fear in our own hearts and in others' hearts that we are healed to hear the Voice of Love again.

In the circle of courage, with a Shepherd this good and a story this spacious, we become people who see the small and vulnerable among us—including within our own selves—as holding precious loaves and fish. We watch for the miracle not among the mighty but on the margins.

Courage is a communion in which the God who blessed, broke, and gave more than enough food for his scattered sheep will always keep doing a miracle in our midst among the people and in the places the powerful usually reject.

In every moment we don't feel courageous, there is communion. *The Good Shepherd gives his life for the sheep.* So much of the Christian life is realizing that God has been so generous with us that we truly can be generous with each other. You have been made one with God in Christ. There is a presence within us that we are only beginning to sense and share.

> In the presence of the Giving God,
> we can't help but give.
> Grief where there was greed.
> Dignity where there was doubt.

272

The small offering of empathy, time, resources,
 and kindness that we have.
The kingdom of God is too present to keep
 self-protecting.
The miracle is too good to stay tightfisted.
The feast is too fantastic to withhold.[16]

---

16. Including from yourself.

ACKNOWLEDGMENTS

T HE TRUTH IS, courage is not an individual possession but a gift we hold in common. Courage belongs not to the brave but to those whose desire for love outweighs their wish to avoid being wounded. We are courageous because of and for communion.

It is within the gaze of those tender enough to see each other as sacred that we grow into people who can rise up in fierceness to demand wholeness as our truest collective story and inheritance.

When a community cut me apart, it was community that put me back together. I better hold and extend the gift of courage today because the following people have conferred their own courage on me through their kindness.

Ryan, my love, your courage to confront spiritual abuse at great personal cost is one of the most stunning glimpses of Christ I have ever witnessed. You valued integrity more than influence and Christ more than anything. I grieve to watch you continue to pay the cost of being courageous, but year after year I rejoice even more to see you shepherding others who bear scars like ours.

Josh, I am beyond proud to call you friend. You left with your integrity, and no one can ever take it from you. You are why I wrote this book. I know courage has cost you almost everything, and these pages are my prayer that courage will also give you more than you ever lost. Rachel, to walk alongside you through this dark valley of abuse and trauma has been one of the greatest honors of my life. Your presence, your prayers, your fierceness to fight for truth and wholeness for yourself, Josh and your family, us, and the church—you are the heart of how I know courage is a collective gift, for you have given us so much of yours. Friends, you have been my pastors. You are so much of why I can still trust Jesus today.

Mish, you've known me since I was a judgmental seventeen-year-old freshman in college, and somehow you still love me. In the constancy of your love and levity, I get to see some of God's smile. Watching you welcome your life—your whole life, including its grief—has shown me how to welcome mine.

Kat and Colby, thank you for entrusting your pain to us. Your integrity is beautiful.

Pat and Sarah, thank you for the gift of your belief. Your hospitality and laughter have made us feel like we have a people with whom we still belong.

Jordan Kologe, thank you for being a tender pastoral presence in our lives when our trust in pastors was shattered. To my GF Ladies, Sara Bartley, Kendis Paris, and Brenda Wright, time with you is sacred and strengthening. Church of the Advent, thank you for giving us a safe place to heal.

Kelly Kapic, thank you for always praying for me and Ryan, encouraging me in writing and life, and being accessible when I need wisdom.

Lore Wilbert, you were my companion from afar through so many of the moments and mysteries held in this book. And when this book was just a contract and an idea, you were the one whose curiosity led me to let Psalm 23 hold these stories and truths.

I believe with all my heart that scarcity is a myth and that courage happens as we choose abundance in relationships with one another. There is nowhere I love practicing that more than in friendship with other writers. Rachel Kang, Krispin Mayfield, Meredith McDaniel, Summer Gross, Jennifer Dukes Lee, Thelma Nienhuis, Shannan Martin, Bethany Rydmark, Liz Grant, Sarah Southern, Tabitha Panariso, J. S. Park, Phylicia Masonheimer, Ann Voskamp, Leslie Trovato, Nicole Zasowski, Chuck DeGroat, Adam Young, and many others: thank you for extending such generosity toward me. You show me again and again that joy is the fruit of gratitude and generosity.

To my publishing team, your tenderness in helping me share these painful stories has been a balm. Ryan Pazdur, thank you for believing these are healing words and for pushing me to make them even more potent. Alexis de Weese, I never dreamed I would get to publish books with a dear friend, let alone one who embraces being a weirdo just as much as I do. You make this work incredibly fun, but more so, I feel strengthened to keep showing up because you always remind me why it is worth it. Amy Bigler, thank you for your warmth and support in getting the word out about this message. Brian Phipps, thank you for sharpening this book with such kindness. Mike Bzozowski, thank you for protecting my vulnerability in sharing these words and showing me why they matter. To my agent, Alex Field, thank you for showing me that I deserve to be believed and supported all the way.

And to every reader who has ever shown me a glimpse of their story of harm or pain:

I believe you.

APPENDIX

ABUSE IS A CIRCLE TOO.

THE COURAGE OF CHRIST is a circle in which there is no circumference, only a wholeness that enlarges the stories and lives within its expansive embrace. But abuse is a circle too. Abuse happens in the circle of a closed system, just like what family-systems theorists call a closed family system, where change is resisted, harm is concealed or minimized, and everyone is limited in how whole they can become.[1]

As I mentioned earlier, this book was never meant to be a primer on spiritual abuse or religious trauma, but rather it was intended to be a long walk into the wilderness where we learn to be courageous. The landscape of spiritual abuse and religious trauma has simply been the ground where I've most learned to walk in the practice of receiving the courage of Christ. When shepherds cursed me and my family,

---

1. D. M. Wirick and L. A. Teufel-Prida, "Closed Systems in Family Systems Theory," in *Encyclopedia of Couple and Family Therapy*, ed. J. Lebow, A. Chambers, D. Breunlin (Springer, 2019), https://doi.org/10.1007/978-3-319-15877-8_249-1.

THE LORD IS MY COURAGE

the Good Shepherd was still seeking us. Learning about the following dynamics of how abuse coils around our lives helped us better distinguish the Good Shepherd from those who, in the words of the prophet Ezekiel, rule harshly and brutally, slaughter, and plunder.[2]

In an allegorical retelling of the story of David, Gene Edwards reminds us that "authority from God is not afraid of challengers, makes no defense, and cares not one whit if it be dethroned."[3] All too often, Christian leaders choose to dismiss victims' allegations and defend themselves and their peers in circles of leadership, demonstrating that they care more about holding on to authority and protecting their precious institutions from collapse than they do about making sure the vulnerable are protected.

Time and space cannot afford the record of all the abuses that have been minimized, mishandled, and hidden by leaders even in this year alone.[4] It often seems that those who hold institutional power spend most of their time and energy trying to maintain it. When we who have been wronged speak up to expose the truth and help our communities become healthier, we often experience what researchers call "institutional betrayal" or "betrayal trauma."[5] Institutional betrayal describes the deep wound individuals experience when harmed in the context of an institution they are dependent on, but the institution fails to prevent the harm or to provide adequate support to heal from it.

---

2. Ezek. 34:3–8.

3. Gene Edwards, *A Tale of Three Kings: A Study in Brokenness* (Carol Stream, IL: Tyndale, 1992), 17.

4. The following article describes some of the abuse cases where power was protected more than people, from the Presbyterian Church in America, to my own current denomination of the Anglican Church in North America, to the Southern Baptist Convention and beyond. Rick Pidcock, "The Weakness of Complementarian Theology on Display in Duggar Trial," *Baptist News Global*, December 9, 2021, https://baptistnews.com/article/the-weakness-of-complementarian-theology-on-display-in-duggar-trial/#.YcT9SBPMI-Q.

5. Carly Parnitzke Smith and Jennifer J. Freyd, "Institutional Betrayal," *American Psychologist* 69, no. 6 (September 2014): 575–87, https://doi.org/10.1037/a0037564.

280

Every client I have ever worked with who has experienced religious trauma, especially from spiritual abuse, has experienced being gaslighted. Gaslighting is one way a person dodges the dissonance of owning that their behavior doesn't match their idealized self-concept. When someone deflects responsibility for their actions and diminishes the credibility or character of the person confronting them, they are gaslighting. When someone makes you question whether your reality is real, they are gaslighting.

In *The Gaslight Effect*, licensed psychoanalyst Robin Stern says that this dynamic "results from a relationship between two people: a gaslighter, who needs to be right in order to preserve his own sense of self and his sense of having power in the world; and a gaslightee, who allows the gaslighter to define her sense of reality because she idealizes him and seeks his approval."[6]

Researchers have shown that perpetrators of abuse often silence concerns and confrontations from victims by wielding the sword of a gaslighting strategy called DARVO: deny, attack, and reverse victim and offender.[7] We experienced this firsthand. Sitting with the reality of DARVO as a tactic of abuse and abusive systems can help demystify the confusion of what you (or people you love) have experienced.

- *Deny.* The person's experience is denied as false. Their sense of reality is denied or downplayed.

---

6. Robin Stern, *The Gaslight Effect: How to Spot and Survive the Hidden Manipulation Others Use to Control Your Life* (New York: Harmony Books, 2018), 4.

7. DARVO was first introduced in a 1997 article by Jennifer Freyd exploring betrayal trauma theory. The concept was further defined in a 1999 paper by Freyd and C. B. Veldhuis. Jennifer J. Freyd, "II. Violations of Power, Adaptive Blindness and Betrayal Trauma Theory," *Feminism and Psychology* 7, no. 1 (1997): 22–32, https://doi.org/10.1177/0959353597071004. C. B. Veldhuis and J. J. Freyd, "Groomed for Silence, Groomed for Betrayal," in *Fragment by Fragment: Feminist Perspectives on Memory and Child Sexual Abuse*, ed. M. Rivera (Charlottetown, Canada: Gynergy Books, 1999), 53–282.

- *Attack.* The person speaking up is attacked. Their character is maligned. Things shared in confidence or vulnerability are used against them.
- *Reverse Victim and Offender.* The script quickly gets flipped, and the dissident voices, victims, or whistleblowers are painted as the actual offenders and treated as such.[8]

Observers of abuse often subconsciously play into DARVO by conferring an assumption of integrity on people in positions of power and authority rather than those below. In an experiment exploring the potency of DARVO, researchers at the University of California Santa Cruz and the University of Oregon found that people who were exposed to DARVO tactics perceived the victim of abuse as less believable, more responsible for the fallout, and more abusive than the person who was actually behaving abusively.[9]

And that's certainly what happened with us. Scot McKnight and Laura Barringer describe how this dynamic often gets deployed in church systems, writing, "Elders, leaders, or other voices of authority at the church may explain how accusers are 'not behaving biblically' or are refusing to engage in relationship restoration."[10]

Wade Mullen is an expert in abuse dynamics in religious systems who has done extensive research on the image-maintenance tactics deployed by the system in the wake of a crisis. He says,

---

8. So much more can and should be said about DARVO. Chapter 4 of Scot McKnight and Laura Barringer's book, *A Church Called Tov*, has a helpful description of related tactics and narratives deployed to downplay and silence victims' voices. Scot McKnight and Laura Barringer, *A Church Called Tov: Forming a Goodness Culture That Resists Abuses of Power and Promotes Healing* (Carol Stream, IL: Tyndale Momentum, 2020), 55–80.

9. Interestingly, in the same study, researchers found that when observers were educated about the tactics of DARVO, they were able to more accurately see the real victims of abuse and feel empathy for them. Sarah J. Harsey, Eileen L. Zurbriggen, and Jennifer J. Freyd, "Perpetrator Responses to Victim Confrontation: DARVO and Victim Self-Blame," *Journal of Aggression, Maltreatment and Trauma* 26, no. 6 (2017): 644–63, https://doi.org/10.1080/10926771.2017.1320777.

10. McKnight and Barringer, *A Church Called Tov*, 65.

"When faced with an image-threatening event, the tribe [of the system's leaders] is more likely to cover up wrong in order to protect their own—to circle the wagons, as it were. They often choose to defend their image rather than confront the leader or protect the vulnerable."[11] When we expressed the way we and others were being crushed in our church, our vulnerability was met with verbal violence. We know scores of others whose stories are the same.

No one wants to grapple with the image of their beloved pastor bullying a church member or staff member. Barely anyone has the courage to deal with the financial and relational consequences of a pastor's or church's or family system's pristine image crumbling. It's easier to, as McKnight and Barringer describe, assume the worst of the more vulnerable (and less powerful) person, discredit and eventually demonize them, spin the story, gaslight anyone who says otherwise, defend the anointed and cherished leader as the real victim, and do whatever it takes to ignore, silence, and suppress the truth, including issuing a fake apology if need be.[12]

"Church is one of the least safe places to acknowledge abuse because the way it is counseled is, more often than not, damaging to the victim," lawyer, former Team USA gymnast, and abuse advocate Rachael Denhollander states.[13] In my work as a therapist, I have heard a sobering number of stories from victims whose abuse was dismissed or diminished by pastors and leaders whose responses ranged from covering up instances of abuse they were legally mandated to report, counseling them to "forgive" their abuser, and, often,

11. Wade Mullen, *Something's Not Right: Decoding the Hidden Tactics of Abuse and Freeing Yourself from Its Power* (Carol Stream, IL: Tyndale Momentum, 2020), 29.

12. McKnight and Barringer's chapter "False Narratives" helpfully names many of the ways blame is shifted in religious systems. McKnight and Barringer, *A Church Called Tov*, 55–80.

13. Rachael Denhollander, "My Larry Nassar Testimony Went Viral. But There's More to the Gospel Than Forgiveness," interview by Morgan Lee, *Christianity Today*, January 31, 2018, www.christianitytoday.com/ct/2018/january-web-only/rachael-den hollander-larry-nassar-forgiveness-gospel.html.

blaming the victim for either causing the abuse or not responding to it as "biblically" as they deemed worthy of respect. From sexual abuse to spiritual abuse, from emotional abuse in marriages to the religious trauma of patriarchy and purity culture, I cannot tell you how many people have been courageous to seek help in the church or among Christians for how they are being harmed, only to be further harmed instead.

Part of the reason is because spiritual abuse often follows the same cycle as domestic violence.[14] After tensions build and an explosion of violence (such as a verbal incident followed by a resignation) releases the pressure from the relational system, there's a honeymoon phase where overtures are made that make the system seem safe and good. Those who stay, recommit. The honeymoon phase is like amnesia, where everyone seems to forget how bad things just were. The pain of betrayal of our reality by people who seem to have fallen asleep is searing and trust-shattering. The horror of being harmed, only to have others seem to go about life as though nothing has happened, cuts against your capacity to hope.

Trauma happens and harms us. But I often wonder if the worst trauma is the second wave—when your story is disbelieved, mistrusted, and maligned.

If Jesus said the church is so strong that the gates of hell cannot prevail against her, I think she can handle her abuses being brought into the light.[15] Abuse is a circle in which the whole truth of our stories must be caged, controlled, and concealed. It is a circle that rolls and rolls and rolls, crushing many lives in its path while benefitting a select few, *until* we choose to let the Voice of Love be the loudest.

Abuse in one church is every Christian's problem. We can't call

---

14. Crystal Raypole, "Understanding the Cycle of Abuse," *Healthline*, November 29, 2020, www.healthline.com/health/relationships/cycle-of-abuse. The Religious Trauma Institute has excellent resources showing how the cycle of abuse manifests in religious systems: www.religioustraumainstitute.com/workshops.

15. Matt. 16:18.

ourselves a body and then refuse to stop the bleeding in another's limb, just because our arm seems to be working fine. We belong to each other. Until the whole church chooses to listen to the voices of the crushed, the body of Christ will not be healthy or whole.

If you have experienced abuse or trauma of any kind, may your story find safe harbor in the presence of people who will honor both your vulnerability and resilience. May you be surrounded by people courageous enough to let there be light.

The courage to choose wholeness and to listen to those languishing from its lack—this is the circle of listening that can envelop all of the circles of harm that have caged us, lifting us all into more real and abundant life.

This Too Shall Last

Encounter the Grace
That Enters the Middle
of Our Stories

K.J. Ramsey

This Too Shall Last offers an antidote to
our cultural idolatry of effort and ease.
Through personal story and insights
from neuroscience and theology, Ramsey invites us to let our tears
become lenses of the wonder that before God ever rescues us, he
stands in solidarity with us.

Follow along with KJ's writing on her website, through her email list, and in conversation on social media:

Site: KJRamsey.com

Newsletter: KJRamseyWrites.substack.com

Social Media: KJRamseyWrites (Instagram, Twitter, Facebook)